Forgotten Fields
Looking for Manchester's Old Burial Grounds

John Marsden

Bright Pen

A Bright Pen Book

British Library Cataloguing in Publication Data.
A catalogue record for this book is available from the
British Library.

ISBN 978 0 7552 1622 2

Authors OnLine Ltd
19 The Cinques
Gamlingay, Sandy
Bedfordshire SG19 3NU
England

To become lost in the grave is a hard, though common fate, but when the grave itself has thus perished the poor obliterated dust seems doubly abandoned.

Richard Wright Procter

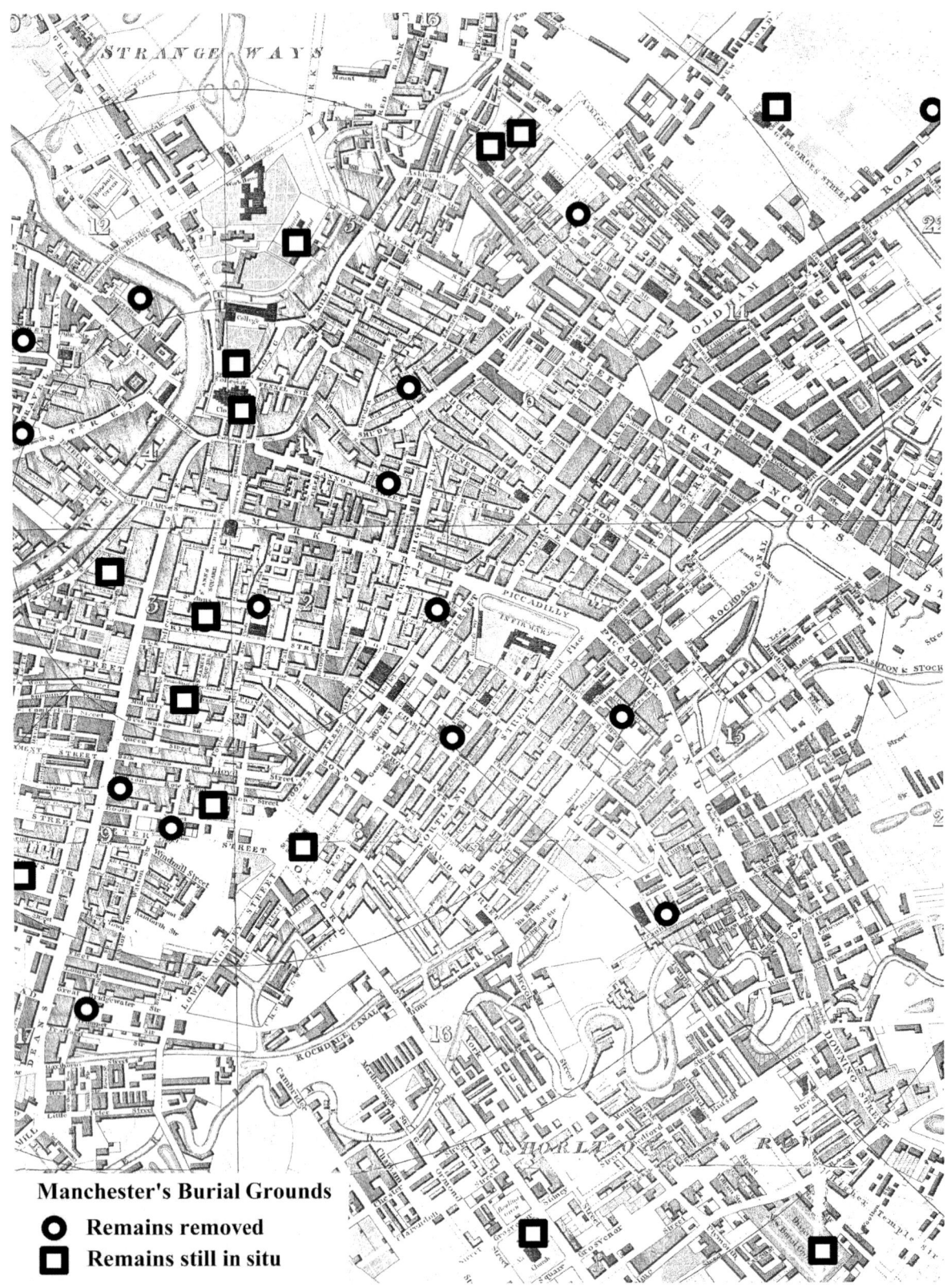

Manchester's Burial Grounds

○ Remains removed

□ Remains still in situ

Contents

Preface

The history of Manchester's burial grounds has received little attention from the city's local historians. Fragments of the story appear in many books and articles but these seldom amount to more than isolated references within the discussion of some broader topic. Nowhere is there a picture of the subject as a whole. How many burial grounds were there? Why were they established and by whom? Where were they? Who patronised them? What became of them and the people buried there?

One possible reason for this omission is that until recently it has been difficult to access sufficient material to assemble a coherent account. The full story, if a history can ever be fully reconstructed, lies in material deposited in Manchester's archives and particularly in the wealth of material which has long been hidden away in local newspaper articles. Newspapers, although a rich source, have until recently been difficult to access. Few were indexed at all and such indexes as existed were concerned more with the main story than with the passing reference. This has changed in recent years with the digitisation and online publication of increasing numbers of old newspapers. This is helpful but the game changer is that the complete text can now be searched for key words and phrases.

The first newspapers to appear on line were national titles such as the (Manchester) Guardian and the Times. These are useful, but inevitably limited in their coverage of local events. The more recent appearance of local titles such as the Manchester Times and Manchester Courier on the British Newspaper Archive web site has opened up a treasure chest of material. This is arguably one of the most exciting developments for local historians since the internet began.

In recent years there have been some impressive books on the subject of death and burial. Two essential and very readable texts are 'The Victorian Celebration of Death' by James Stevens Curl and 'The English Way of Death' by Julian Litten. These both, though, offer a quite broad brush picture. There have been some more focused studies. Catherine Arnold's 'Necropolis' is an excellent history of burial in London and Brian Parsons's 'Committed to the Cleansing Flame' provides an outstanding history of the beginnings of cremation in England. There have also been some excellent histories of individual cemeteries such as Ronnie Scott's 'Death By Design', which offers a very detailed history of the Glasgow Necropolis. Closer to home is Chris Makepeace's concise but informative 'Manchester Crematorium 1890-1990'. There are, however, few studies of the progress of urban burial outside the capital. I hope that this book will provide that missing picture.

The problem of disposing of the dead is an important aspect of the development of industrial cities in the 19th century. The rapid growth of the factory system drew people into the industrial centres at an unparalleled rate. Successive maps of Manchester from the late eighteenth century onwards show green fields rapidly disappearing under factories, warehouses and housing for the workers. Such rapid growth brought a host of problems in its wake. How do you feed this new population? How do you provide them with clean drinking water? How do you dispose of their wastes? No less a problem was how to dispose of their dead.

Not only did people flood into the cities from the surrounding countryside but once they had arrived, they frequently lived in conditions which shortened their lives. Children were particularly vulnerable, with a distressingly high percentage not living to see their first birthday. The closely packed houses, streets and factories encouraged the rapid spread of infectious and potentially fatal diseases such as measles. The combination of poor sanitation and drinking water drawn from wells was instrumental in the spread of cholera.

The industrial revolution also brought with it new ways to meet with an untimely death. If a miner was not killed in an accident, he was likely to die prematurely from lung disease. Chemical processes exposed workers to hazardous materials such as lead and mercury. Even those in less immediately hazardous occupations were exposed daily to the smoke and fumes from nearby factories.

The expanding cities were ill-prepared to deal with the consequent increase in the number of deaths. Burial facilities were still substantially centred upon the parish churchyard and there was little if any understanding of the health and environmental implications of shallow burial and the overcrowding of graveyards. The resulting problems and how they were addressed are an important aspect of the invention of urban living.

There are fascinating, sometimes shocking, and occasionally amusing stories to be told: a child's body clandestinely dismembered for medical research which finds a later parallel in the Alder Hey Hospital scandal; the impasse between the Canons and Churchwardens of the Cathedral over the purchase of a new burial ground following the closure of the last parish graveyard; the Corporation's purchase of the Ardwick private cemetery which ended with the Town Clerk suing the Daily Mail for libel; the regular conflicts between James Scholefield of Every Street Chapel and the law, which show a man of strong social ideals fighting to improve the lives of his community. If this book entertains as well as informs then so much the better.

A comprehensive history taking in all of the burial grounds in the extensive ancient parish of Manchester is beyond the scope of a single book, so I have generally limited my attention to burial grounds in the old Manchester township – graveyards where those living in the town would usually have been buried. This self-imposed boundary means that, with a couple of excep-tions, Salford, Chorlton-on-Medlock and the more distant townships of the parish have been omitted. Nevertheless, several graveyards outside the township's boundary drew much of their business from within it and so their inclusion is appropriate. This is particularly the case with the private, and subsequently the municipal, cemeteries.

This book started out as a small collection of historical notes which I contributed to Geoff Edge's invaluable 'Guide to the Burial Grounds of Manchester and Salford' published by Manchester and Lancashire Family History Society. As these notes grew it became apparent that there was a much bigger story to be told, well beyond the scope of what was chiefly intended as a guide to locating burial registers and records.

Not only did a fascinating history emerge, but in the process one of my own preconceptions was thoroughly dispelled. I had read George William Walker's 'Gatherings from Grave Yards', an account published in 1839 describing the dreadful state of London's burial grounds and on occasion remarked that the situation in Manchester never reached such dreadful extremes. As I found more and more contemporary accounts I realised that Manchester could boast (if boast is the right word) graveyards in which conditions were not dissimilar to those which had appalled Walker. The same combination of ignorance, incompetence and venality which Walker discovered in London is much in evidence in early nineteenth century Manchester.

One of the more difficult aspects of compiling a history of burial grounds is the relative scarcity of photographic records. While today we have few qualms about taking photographs in a graveyard, we still feel uncomfortable photographing a funeral in progress. In the early days of photography burials and burial grounds seem to have been a subject which photographers either felt to be an inappropriate subject or one which they simply had little interest in recording. Consequently, such early images as exist of graveyards tend to appear as the background to engravings and photographs of churches and chapels. Unfortunately, by the time photographers did take an interest in the subject, many of the earlier graveyards had already disappeared or lost their original buildings and memorials.

Were it not for the Ordnance Survey it might even be difficult to locate some of the earlier burial grounds. When producing the 60 inch to the mile series of maps of Manchester in the 1840s, their surveyors were diligent in plotting the boundaries of burial grounds and in some cases even the precise location of some of the more prominent tombs. If we do not know what the old burial grounds looked like, at least we can have some idea of their size, shape, layout and location.

Fortunately, Manchester's graveyards did not go wholly unnoticed. Some local writers took note and provide valuable information. Joseph Aston published a number of guides to Manchester's institutions in the early nineteenth century and, when referring to churches, frequently commented on their vaults and burial grounds. In 1834 Samuel Hibbert (with others) published a 'History of the Foundation in Manchester of Christ's Church, Chetham's Hospital and the Free Grammar School' which included extensive and detailed descriptions of the memorials both inside and outside the Collegiate Church. Many of these had disappeared when thirty years later the antiquary John Owen recorded his own observations of the memorials there. Owen was a prolific recorder of local history and particularly of graveyard memorials. His large collection of notebooks contain details about many chapels which disappeared long ago.

While I believe I have identified and recorded all of the burial grounds in the old Manchester township, there remains much to learn and I will welcome any new information which readers might supply.

John Marsden
February 2014

Manchester Cathedral in the 1890s

Introduction

For much of the first and second millennia AD the Christian church held an effective monopoly over the burial of the dead in England. The Church of Rome and, after the reformation, the Church of England served as self-appointed gatekeepers to the afterlife. The only decent means of disposing of a Christian's mortal remains was for them to be buried in consecrated ground by a duly ordained priest. Since adherence to the Christian faith was a given, no alternative could be countenanced. Only those whom the church rejected could be excluded. Heretics, murderers, suicides and those who had died while excommunicated were denied burial in the churchyard leaving their friends or family to find a burial place in some unconsecrated field or garden.

The church, as it still does today, divided the country into parishes, each administered from its parish church. Each parish had its own graveyard or *'God's Acre'*, usually surrounding the church, and it was usual that this is where those who died in the parish would be buried. The parish was, indeed, under an obligation to bury deceased parishioners, an obligation which extended even to the poorest parishioners, whose families were unable to pay the burial fees.

The break with Rome under Henry VIII did not affect where people were buried. Despite the period of religious instability which followed Henry's death, the parishes endured and their churchyards continued to receive new generations of parish dead.

Henry's reformation was consolidated under Elizabeth I but the Church of England which emerged was not universally accepted. One faction clung to the old beliefs and sought the return of the Catholic Church. Another faction, the Puritans, looked to the Protestant reformation in Europe and felt that reform had not gone far enough. This group would become increasingly vociferous and would even briefly displace the established church during the Commonwealth period 1653-1660.

Following the restoration of Charles II to the throne Protestant dissent faced a period of suppression but this soon eased, particularly following the Toleration Act of 1688. Toleration encouraged many dissenting sects to establish their own chapels and also often to establish burial grounds, where deceased members might be buried according to their own preferred rites. Protestant dissent grew substantially in the eighteenth and nineteenth centuries and it was during this period that most dissenter burial grounds were opened.

Roman Catholicism had been vigorously suppressed during the reign of Elizabeth I, and Catholics would continue to be subject to some degree of persecution for another century and a half but by the end of the eighteenth century a more tolerant attitude prevailed. Toleration enabled Catholics to worship openly. Churches were built and churchyards consecrated for the burial of deceased Catholics.

By the end of the eighteenth century the *established* church no longer monopolised burial of the dead but burial nevertheless remained a wholly religious monopoly.

Seeds of change were sown in the 1820s. A number of dissenting ministers, unhappy at the lack of burial places for their congregations, formed associations to set up cemeteries in which Protestant dissenters could be buried without the reading of the Church of England burial service. Rusholme Road in Manchester (first burial in 1820), Rosary Road in Norwich (1821) and the Liverpool Necropolis (1825) were each founded on the initiative of dissenters.

These new foundations were financed using a joint stock model. Capital to purchase land and establish the buildings was raised by selling shares to investors. Running costs were to be met from the sale of graves and from fees charged for burials. Any surplus income would be distributed to the shareholders in the form of a dividend.

The new cemeteries proved popular and in the short term at least profitable, a factor which did not go unnoticed by investors on the look-out for a healthy return. There was no shortage of willing investors and numerous private cemetery companies were floated to establish cemeteries in and around the larger towns and cities particularly between 1825 and 1850. These ventures initially looked promising but they would find business more difficult in the second half of the nineteenth century when the laissez-faire attitude of the authorities finally came to an abrupt end.

A FREE FOR ALL

It is difficult to believe that up to the middle of the nineteenth century the burial of dead bodies was largely unregulated. There was no regulation dictating how deeply a body should be buried and no limit to how many bodies might be buried in a single grave. The owner of a badly managed graveyard might in theory be prosecuted for public nuisance but there is little evidence that significant action was ever taken.

The euphemism 'six feet under' describes a luxury enjoyed by only a privileged few. A new grave might indeed be six feet or more deep but with each successive interment the grave became shallower until the sexton concluded, according to his own arbitrary measure, that the grave was full. Sextons' views of what constituted a full grave varied greatly but few would meet today's legal requirements. A covering of less than three feet of earth over the last coffin in a grave was common, and in the worst cases a coffin might be covered by no more than a few inches of soil. As burial space became more and more limited, the sexton would often expose previously buried coffins and compact both coffin and occupant to make space for another burial.

Overcrowded graveyards were not a new problem. "Alas poor Yorick! " cries Hamlet when the gravedigger unearths the jester's skull. As the gravediggers open the grave to receive Ophelia's body, they unearth no fewer than three skulls. Hamlet shudders at the indignity:

'Why, e'en so: and now my Lady Worm's; chapless, and knocked about the mazzard with a sexton's spade: here's fine revolution, an we had the trick to see't. Did these bones cost no more the breeding, but to play at loggats with 'em? mine ache to think on't.'

It seems likely that Shakespeare was describing a sight which could have been seen in many London churchyards of his time.

Conditions in Victorian industrial cities were far worse. It was common practice to bury the poor in so called common graves. In reality, a common grave was a large pit, sufficiently broad and deep to hold fifty coffins or more. The pit remained open until it could accommodate no more occupants. This might take several weeks during which the bodies would decompose. When the pit was full the coffins would finally be covered with a few feet of earth. Another pit would then be dug and the process repeated until there was no room left to dig another pit.

Wealthier families could afford to purchase a family grave for their exclusive use and so were spared the indignity of burial in the common pit. Ownership of a family grave allowed the owner to decide who should be buried there. Unfortunately many family grave owners sought to get the most out of their investment and the lucrative fee for each extra burial encouraged the sexton to pack in as many bodies he could. Bodies previously interred would often be disturbed to make space for the next occupant. Even recently buried coffins might be uncovered, disturbed and sometimes damaged in the process.

REFORM

This state of affairs could not be allowed to continue, though it took Parliament over a decade to investigate and legislate on a matter which had reached a desperate state long before they began to give it serious consideration. Nevertheless, by the early 1850s, the agitation of social reformers such as Edwin Chadwick had brought about a sea change. After a decade of agitation, Parliament passed a series of Burial Acts. The first Acts first addressed the burial grounds in London but by 1854 further Acts extended similar provisions to the rest of the country.

The Burial Acts granted three important powers. Firstly, they gave the Secretary of State authority to order the closure of any burial ground where continued operation was considered a danger to public health. Secondly, they enabled the Secretary of State to impose minimum standards on new burial grounds and on those burial grounds which remained open, in order to maintain them in a sanitary condition. The third and perhaps most important element was that the Acts authorised municipal authorities to procure land and establish publicly owned burial grounds. This important power provided a sound foundation for the expansion of burial capacity in a manner which was sustainable over the longer term.

Municipal authorities were quick to take advantage of the new powers. The first municipal cemetery outside London opened at Carlisle in 1854. Municipal cemeteries operated in parallel, indeed in competition, with private cemeteries. Some municipal authorities actually chose to purchase their local private cemetery from its shareholders rather than establish a cemetery of their own from scratch.

The Burial Acts created a serious problem for private cemeteries. The restrictions which they imposed resulted in a considerable increase in operating costs while at the same time their municipal competitors had access to low-cost finance. Over the following century many of the private cemeteries went into steady decline and municipal cemeteries established the model for burial which has survived to the present day.

FROM BURIAL TO CREMATION

For well over a thousand years the only recognised way to dispose of a dead body was by burial. However, in 1885 the first 'official' cremation was carried out in England and cremation slowly began to gain social and religious acceptance as an alternative. As had been the case with private burial grounds, the first crematoria were established as private joint stock companies but within twenty years municipal authorities were given authority to establish crematoria and thereafter cremation developed as a wholly municipal undertaking. Despite an early struggle to gain acceptance, cremation became increasingly popular and numerically, cremations overtook burials in the 1960s. Today cremation accounts for around 70% of UK funerals.

THE MANCHESTER STORY

We can see this national story played out in Manchester. The historic parish of Manchester extended from the River Mersey in the south to Blackley in the north, taking in Salford and Stretford to the west and Denton to the east. In all the parish contained an area approaching sixty square miles. At the heart of the parish was the

Manchester Parish

Collegiate Church. This served the residents of the town, while chapels of ease in the surrounding townships met the spiritual needs of those who lived outside its boundaries.

The Old Churchyard, which still surrounds the Collegiate Church, though today grassed over and without trace of a tombstone, provided virtually all Manchester's burial space up to the middle of the eighteenth century. As the town grew, and the number of burials rose accordingly, this relatively small churchyard proved increasingly inadequate so at intervals of about thirty years additional burial grounds were established in an attempt to match supply to demand. The third and last of these 'overspill' burial grounds closed in 1848.

The expansion of the town also created new communities. These were at some distance from the Collegiate Church and from the 1750s onwards new churches were built to serve the new population centres. Most had a burial ground and these provided much-needed burial space taking some pressure off the parish burial ground. These new churchyards offered only private graves and so became the preferred burial places of the middle classes, who formed a large part of the new churches' congregations. The Collegiate Church burial ground became almost wholly a burial place for the increasing numbers of parish poor.

Like many industrial towns Manchester was fertile ground for religious dissent and most sects at some time had a presence. Many dissenting chapels were established and as often as not, these would have their own burial ground. Some saw only a handful of burials over their lifetime, others perhaps a few hundred, but a few operated on a considerably larger scale. Some of the larger ones even provided burial for those who did not share their particular beliefs.

As the suppression of Catholicism was eased towards the end of the eighteenth century, a number of Catholic churches were founded in Manchester. Irish immigrants provided a significant part of their congregations and their number

was considerably swelled following the potato famine of the 1840s. By the middle of the nineteenth century Roman Catholics had become the largest single denomination in the city after the Church of England. Most of the early Roman Catholic churches were surrounded by burial grounds and these saw large numbers of burials.

By the second decade of the nineteenth century Manchester's Protestant dissenters were becoming increasingly unhappy with the existing burial facilities available to them. They addressed the problem in a novel way by setting up a joint stock company to raise funds to establish a dissenter's cemetery. The company opened England's first private non-denominational cemetery at Rusholme Road in Chorlton-on-Medlock in 1820. Within fifteen years the Rusholme Road Cemetery was providing a spectacular return to its shareholders.

Such an apparently foolproof way to make money encouraged two new joint stock ventures. Both of these were purely commercial undertakings. Manchester General Cemetery opened in 1837 and Ardwick Cemetery the following year. Neither had any problem attracting investors but although both enjoyed modest commercial success for a time, neither produced more than a modest return for its shareholders.

The requirements of the Burial Acts and growing competition from municipal cemeteries seriously undermined the business of the private cemeteries. All three were in serious decline at the close of the nineteenth century and they were compulsorily purchased by Manchester Corporation in the 1950s. By this time only Manchester General Cemetery was still a going concern and it continued to operate into the second half of the twentieth century. Between them the private cemeteries had provided a last resting place for well over a quarter of a million Mancunians.

There is clear evidence that the state of Manchester's graveyards was becoming a serious problem in the early years of the nineteenth century. There are graphic accounts as early as 1817 which show that all was not as it should be and these continue at intervals for the next thirty years. While Manchester did not produce either the number or the extremes of the abuses documented in London by George Alfred Walker in 1839[1], there were, nevertheless, many cases of overcrowded graves and concern as to the effect of this on public health, especially where burial grounds operated cheek-by-jowl with residential properties.

There was little local initiative towards addressing these concerns. The Old Churchyard, which had been in continuous use for seven centuries, was closed to further burials in 1819 but this stands out as an exception. It was not until the implementation of the Burial Acts that decisive action was taken. Orders in Council issued under the 1854 Act mandated the immediate closure of no fewer than twenty-three of the city's graveyards. Restrictions were imposed upon a further twelve, mostly limiting future interments to existing family graves and requiring a minimum covering of earth over each coffin. This long-overdue action was far from universally welcomed. It met with both opposition and complaint from those with vested interests. Those who owned graveyards saw their income reduced or wiped out overnight while the middle classes, who had invested in family graves, were now told that they could not inter any more family members in them. However, this was a turning point and there would be no going back.

The closures and restrictions dramatically reduced the number of burial places but Manchester somehow muddled through. There was, indeed, a boost in business for those cemeteries which were still able to operate and this temporarily benefited Manchester General Cemetery, which lay well outside the city boundary. The opening of the Salford municipal cemetery at Weaste in 1857 provided further additional local capacity. Manchester did not open its own municipal cemetery for over a decade. The city's first cemetery at Philips Park finally opened in 1866 and this was followed by Southern Cemetery in Withington in 1877.

Manchester was much quicker off the mark when it came to adopting cremation. A cremation society was formed in 1888, just three years after the first legal cremation had been performed at Woking. The society raised the necessary funds and Manchester Crematorium opened in 1893, only the second crematorium in the country.

This book looks at over thirty burial grounds in and around the centre of Manchester. Some were fashionable burial places for Manchester's upper and middle classes but declined as their exclusive clientele moved further and further out of the city. Others catered for those of particular religious persuasions, Quakers, Independents, Roman Catholics and other denominations. There were those which catered for the labouring poor and those whose lives came to their end in the workhouse. Each has its own story to tell.

The story takes us from an ancient parish churchyard, now long forgotten, to Manchester's first crematorium, still going strong into its second century. Aside from the appearance of a few more crematoria around Manchester little has changed in the last hundred years. The model put in place during Victoria's reign has stood the test of time and looks set fair for the future. However, we must first return to an earlier Manchester to see how it all began.

Notes for Introduction

[1] Gatherings from Grave Yards, George Alfred Walker, Longman & Co. 1839. Walker's book was the driving force behind the movement to improve city burial grounds which culminated in the Burial Acts of the 1850s. Walker catalogues the worst abuses in graphic, at times stomach-turning, detail.

The Parish Burial Grounds

The First Parish Church

Manchester was already settled by the time of the Roman invasion but knowledge of the size, shape and history of this settlement is limited to say the least. The first inhabitants would have cremated their dead but when Christianity arrived earth burial became the only acceptable way to dispose of the dead.

A Christian church had been established in Manchester, possibly as early as the 7th century. This early church was said to have been burned down during a Viking invasion and rebuilt in 923AD, though whether on the same site or one nearby has not been established with any certainty. It is believed that it was located in an area which became known as 'Acres Field'.

The first map of Manchester was created circa 1650 and shows a small town built within the junction of the Rivers Irwell and Irk. Manchester was what we would today call a 'ribbon development' with houses and business premises built along Deansgate, Cateaton Street, Hanging Ditch and Toad Lane through to Long Mill Gate. With the exception of large houses either side of Market Street Lane, the remainder of today's city centre consisted chiefly of farms and smallholdings. The map shows Acres Field to the south of the junction of Deansgate and Market Street Lane, an area which is today covered by St. Ann's Square and its surrounding streets.

Domesday Book, which was compiled in 1086, records the existence of a church in

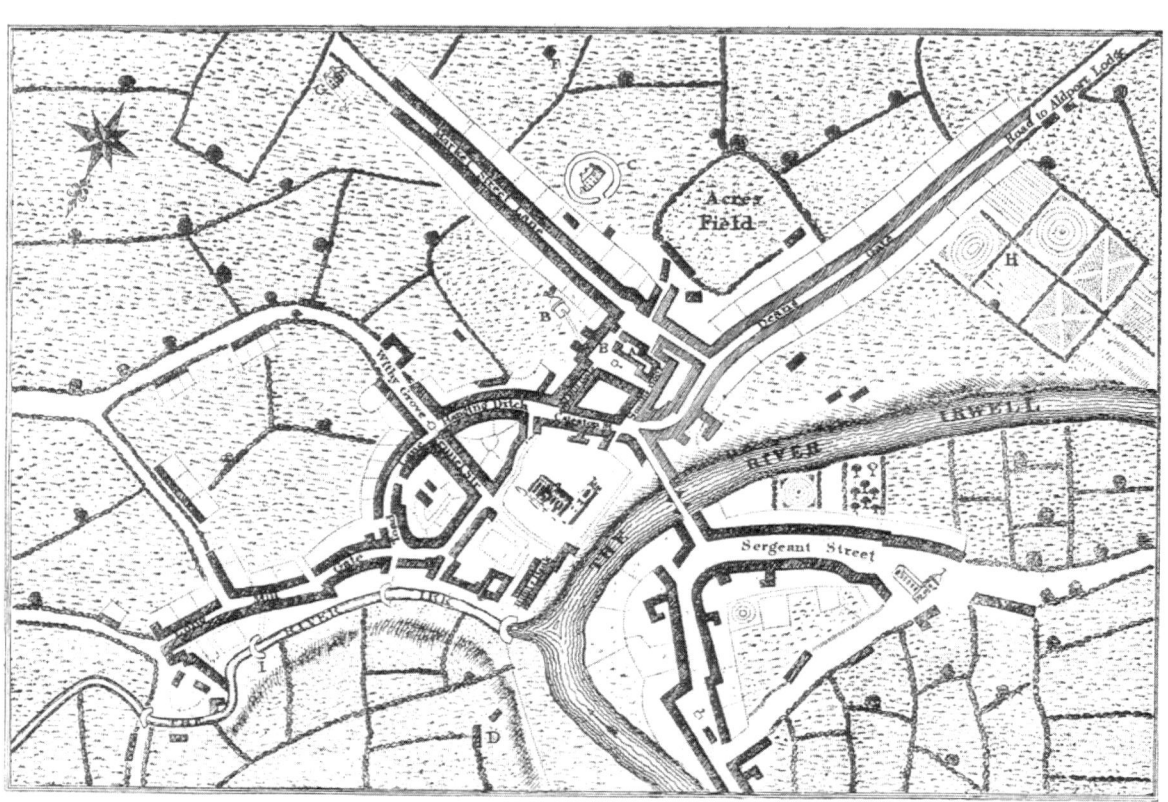

A map of Manchester circa 1650 showing the location of Acre's Field.
(Note the unusual orientation which places north towards the bottom of the map)

The Angel Stone

Manchester dedicated to St. Mary and it is believed that this refers to the old church in Acres Field. The church is remembered in the street name 'St. Mary's Gate' which once connected Acres Field with Deansgate, one of the oldest streets in Manchester. The church would have undoubtedly been surrounded by a parish burial ground and reports that human bones were unearthed when St. Ann's Church was built early in the eighteenth century provide some evidence to support this.

In 1215 Robert Greslet (or Gresley) built a new church close to the River Irk on what is now the site of the Cathedral and the old church in Acres Field was abandoned and demolished. It seems possible that some materials from the old St. Mary's were recycled and used in the new building. One piece of evidence for this is the so-called 'Angel Stone', a stone with an angel simply carved in relief, which was found during restoration work in 1871 and which has been dated to Saxon times.

Acres Field reverted to nature. In 1227 Manchester was granted the right to hold an annual fair and Acres Field became the usual site where these fairs were held. As can be seen from the 1650 map, Acres Field remained undeveloped well into the seventeenth century. A century later all trace of it had disappeared under new buildings.

Within its gates I heard the sound
Of winds in cypress caverns caught
Of huddling trees that moaned and sought
To whisper what their roots had found
From A Dream of Fear, George Sterling (1869-1926)

Burial Inside the Collegiate Church

Manchester Cathedral c1834

If you were one of Manchester's more prominent citizens you could hope to find a last resting place within the walls of the Collegiate Church. This privilege was at first granted only to the clergy but was increasingly extended to others of rank or wealth. Interment in the Collegiate Church at first involved direct burial in the earth directly under the floor of the church. The graves were covered by large stone slabs bearing the names of those buried beneath and these effectively became the paving of the floor of the church.

Some of the earlier interments, which took place before the start of the burial registers in 1573, can be identified from memorials. For example, James Stanley, a former Canon of the Collegiate Church and Bishop of Ely until his death in 1515 was buried in a tomb in the Ely chapel. Both tomb and chapel were destroyed in the blitz in 1940 but the inscription, which recorded Stanley's death on 3 March 1515, had been transcribed many years previous to its destruction. Similarly, a surviving memorial brass tells us that John Huntingdon, the Warden from 1422 until his death in 1458, was buried in the choir of the church.

The burial registers seldom differentiate those buried within the church from those buried in the churchyard and positively identify only nineteen burials as having been inside the church. The actual number was considerably greater. Thirteen of these fall between 1802 and 1810 which perhaps suggests unusual diligence on the part of the minister of the time. A better picture of the number of burials and the names of those interred can be obtained from records of the gravestones inside the church taken before the stones were removed during later restorations. Many were transcribed by Samuel Hibbert in the early 1830s and further records were made by the antiquary John Owen around thirty years later. A plan of gravestones which Owen recorded in the Jesus Chapel (undated but probably made around 1859) shows that barely an inch of available space remained unused for burials. Such a density of burials was probably the case in other parts of the Cathedral.

The practice of earth burial inside churches frequently gave rise to nuisances and this was very much the case at the Cathedral. At a meeting in 1856, two years after such interments had been prohibited, Thomas Clegg, a former churchwarden, described the problems which had arisen:

'In our Cathedral there was a general settling of the flooring, flagging and pewing and of the various things erected upon the floor, causing openings in the earth and

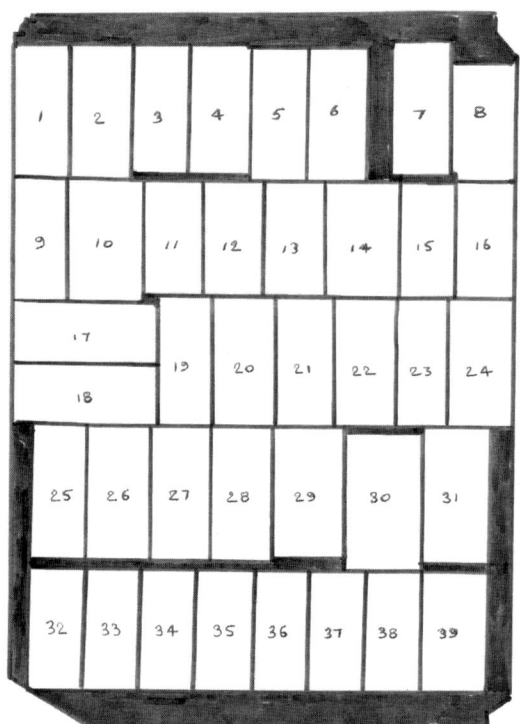

Gravestones in the Jesus Chapel of Manchester Cathedral (After a sketch by John Owen)

crevices through which there emanated most serious and alarmingly bad smells'.

He recounted the story of a workman who had been engaged to point the gaps between the gravestones with cement so as to seal the crevices. The workman's son had been forced to retire home, so foul were the smells emanating from between the slabs, and the workman himself only finished his work with difficulty. Clegg also said that he had been told by an older churchwarden that one of *his* predecessors had told him of a former sexton who had crammed the space beneath the floor *'...as full of bones as it could possibly hold'*[1]. The flooring was permanently made good during the major restoration of 1882-3.

THE BURIAL OF MALIBRAN

One of the best documented burials took place in 1836. The classical singer Maria de Beriot, known professionally as 'Malibran', the surname of her first husband, had come to Manchester to sing in the musical festival. After a particularly demanding performance at the Collegiate Church she collapsed after leaving the stage. It was popularly claimed that she had died as a result of the passion she put into her performance but the reality was less romantic. Maria had sustained serious injuries in a riding accident some weeks earlier and was still far from recovered. She had clearly been unfit either to travel or to perform. Despite receiving the best medical attention available she died within the week.

It was surprising, given that Maria was a devout Roman Catholic, that the Canons agreed to her body being buried inside the Collegiate Church in a grave in the south aisle of the chancel. Their religious toleration did not, however, extend to the performance of Catholic rites and so a Catholic burial service was held at St. Augustine's Roman Catholic Church in Granby Row on the first of October followed by a committal service at the Collegiate Church conducted by the Anglican priest, Cecil Wray.

Soon after the burial, however, events took an unexpected turn. Malibran's husband, Charles de Beriot, had left Manchester and returned to Belgium soon after her death and had not been present at his wife's funeral. This had, to say the least, caused some raised eyebrows, though it was said that it was not unusual in Belgium for the husband not to attend. Charles now was back in Manchester and stated that he wished his wife's body to be buried in his native Belgium and submitted an application for the body to be exhumed. His application was greeted with immediate opposition from the Canons and the issue escalated to involve first the Bishop of Chester (within whose diocese Manchester lay at this time) and then the Home Office. The Home Office clearly did not wish to get involved and declared it a matter for the church. While the Bishop was prepared to agree to an exhumation, the Wardens of the Collegiate Church argued in the Consistory Court that diocesan authority did not extend to the chancel, in which she was buried. The impasse was only broken when Malibran's mother made a personal appeal to those who opposed the application. A compromise was reached by which a new application for exhumation would be made in the mother's name and by which she agreed that the family would pay all of the legal costs which had accrued. Malibran's body was exhumed at 5am on the morning of Tuesday 20 December and quickly removed from Manchester where public feelings were running high. The total cost to Charles de Beriot of the exhumation, including legal costs, was reported to have been £40.

Mosley Memorial Brass

The Mosley family were lords of the manor of Manchester from 1596 until the manorial rights were finally sold to Manchester Corporation in 1846. Many members of the Mosley family were buried in the Collegiate Church where two fine commemorative brasses can still be seen.

THE IMPERMANENCE OF MEMORIALS

The exhumation of Malibran's remains was exceptional, though possibly not unprecedented but most of those buried within the church still remain there to the present day. Their memorials, however, were less secure. Writing in 1834 Samuel Hibbert reported:

'We have lately discovered a grave stone which forms part of the floor of a pig stye in the back yard of the Flying Horse public house at the top of Hunts Bank which we strongly suspect to have some time ago been removed from the inside of the church, it bearing the inscription "Here lyeth the body of Roger, son of Alexander Nowell who departed this life April ye 16, 1731"'.

It seems that such unauthorised removal of memorials was a common practice. Hibbert goes on to mention another memorial, that of Maria Chadwick, who had been buried inside the church in 1668, but whose memorial stone was found to have been removed to the churchyard in 1834:

'Here then is a clear instance of that notorious system, which formerly prevailed of removing monumental memorials from the interior of the church, under the vile pretence that the descendants of their former inmates were extinct, and replacing them with new stones over families of inferior consequence.'[2]

THE COLLEGIATE CHURCH VAULTS

In addition to earth burials, both family and communal vaults were created under the nave and the choir. The vault under the nave appears to have been the earlier and was well used. In 1912 Andrew Boutflower described looking into this vault during one of the renovations. He commented:

'It was possible to see into the vaults which were, so far as could be seen, piled up to the top with coffins. They were left undisturbed and are now permanently sealed up.'[3].

The vault under the choir, sometimes called the 'Wardens' Vault', was of relatively recent construction and was accessed by lifting a stone iin the floor of the sacristy which exposed a flight of stone steps leading into the vault. It is described in Hibbert's account written in 1834.

'The vaults are a modern erection, and occupy the space beneath the choir, from the end of the stalls, to the partition behind the communion table. They consist of an arched avenue, immediately below the space between the iron gates, and in length the width of the choir; having three arched vaults on the west, and three on the east side, the ends of which open into the avenue; but those on the east side, in length, are again divided into two by a cross partition, two of which are partially filled up with brick-work, and the one in the north east corner is entirely closed; the others are all open to the avenue; and here the spectator may behold the relics of mortality, released from the cares of this world, resting peaceably by the side of each other. These mansions of the dead are constructed with brick-work, and were completed about the middle of the last century, as appears from a memorandum in the registers: 'Buried April 24th 1755, Mrs Margaret Downes, in the middle vault under altar, the first that was buried in the new vaults.'

The grave-stones which covered the remains of those who had been interred in the east end of the choir, previous to excavating the vaults, were taken below and laid, we presume, over the places where their former inmates were re-deposited. Near the centre of the avenue lies the stone which covered Huntingdon, the first warden.'[4]

Hibbert's account suggests that the choir had already been used for burials before the vault was constructed and the expedient of re-interring these earlier burials beneath the floor of the new vault shows some creativity in maximising the burial space available. Hibbert describes a further eleven memorials relating to sixteen burials dating between 1667 and 1829. Within the vault ten coffins are described with coffin plates showing names and dates of interment between 1755 (the above named Margaret Downes) and 1807 (Charles Lawson, for 58 years master of the Free Grammar School).

One of the most prominent families to have a family vault in the Collegiate Church were the de Traffords. They had endowed the St. Nicholas Chapel as a chantry in the fifteenth century and had a vault constructed beneath the chapel into which the coffins of many members of the family

The Huntingdon Brass

had been placed. In 1809 the family substantially renovated the chapel and had a new vault constructed, the old one being at the same time bricked up. The new vault extended under about half of the chapel, the old one apparently occupying the other half. Between 1824 and 1852 eight members of the family were laid to rest in the vault, the last being Laura Ann, wife of Sir Thomas Joseph de Trafford, who died 22 October 1852. Her triple coffin (wooden shell, lead inner and wooden outer covered in black silk velvet) was the last to be interred. Further interments were prohibited two years later under the Burial Act.[5]

The de Trafford vault was not the only family vault within the Cathedral. There were also vaults owned by the Mynshull and Browne families. Visiting the Cathedral on 20 January 1859, John Owen describes the discovery of a family vault under the Strangeways Chapel, the presence of which seems to have been forgotten, though Owen concludes that it must have been constructed no earlier than 1681.[6]

The vaults were permanently closed and sealed up during the restorations of the 1880s but the de Trafford vault appears to have been briefly exposed in 1974 when paving was removed during installation of the memorial to Bishop Greer in the chapel above.

The Victorian renovations took away most of the evidence of the considerable number of graves and vaults which lay beneath the floors and it is only owing to the diligence of nineteenth century antiquaries that we have so much information about who was buried there.

The Gravediggers
Henry Liverseege

The Pauper's Drive

There's a grim one-horse hearse in a jolly round trot;
To the churchyard a pauper is going, I wot;
The road it is rough, and the hearse has no springs,
And hark to the dirge that the sad driver sings:
Rattle his bones over the stones!
He's only a pauper, whom nobody owns!

Oh, where are the mourners? Alas! there are none;
He has left not a gap in the world now he's gone;
Not a tear in the eye of child, woman, or man,
To the grave with his carcase as fast as you can.
Rattle his bones over the stones ;
He's only a pauper, whom nobody owns!

What a jolting and creaking, and splashing and din!
The whip how it cracks! and the wheels how they spin!
How the dirt, right and left, o'er the hedges is hurled!
The pauper at length makes a noise in the world.
Rattle his bones over the stones;
He's only a pauper, whom nobody owns !

Poor pauper defunct! he has made some approach
To gentility, now that he's stretched in a coach;
He's taking a drive in his carriage at last,
But it will not be long if he goes on so fast.
Rattle his bones over the stones ;
He's only a pauper, whom nobody owns!

You bumpkin, who stare at your brother conveyed,
Behold what respect to a cloddy is paid,
And be joyful to think, when by Death you're laid low,
You've a chance to the grave like a gemman to go.
Rattle his bones over the stones;
He's only a pauper, whom nobody owns!

But a truce to this strain, for my soul it is sad,
To think that a heart in humanity clad
Should make, like the brutes, such a desolate end,
And depart from the light without leaving a friend.
Bear softly his bones over the stones;
Though a pauper, he's one whom his Maker yet owns!

Thomas. Noel (1799-1861)

The Old Churchyard

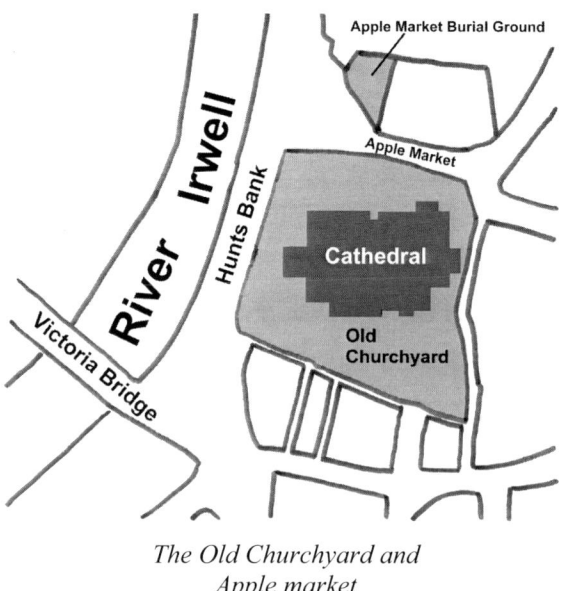

The Old Churchyard and Apple market

Manchester's elite might have been buried inside the Collegiate Church but for most of the population their last resting place would be in the churchyard surrounding the church. It is probable that burials commenced immediately the new church was built in 1215, though there would not be a register to record the names of those interred until well into the sixteenth century. Even the number of people buried there can only be guessed. There is little evidence concerning these early burials but a copper coffin plate bearing the date 1430 was apparently discovered during nineteenth century excavations for road-widening[7]. The plate was unfortunately lost and so this date cannot be confirmed.

Manchester's first burial register begins in 1573 and so we do not have a documentary record of any burial in the churchyard before the burial of Robert Fyssher on 1 August of that year. However, from this date onwards, we have a full set of registers taking us up to the final burial some three centuries later. The first register shows around three or four burials taking place

each week and, with notable exceptions due to outbreaks of plague in 1605 and 1645, continuing at fewer than 200 per annum up almost to 1700.

By the 17th century, it is clear that finding space for new graves was already becoming something of a problem. The churchyard of the Collegiate Church is not large and burials had been taking place there continuously for over four centuries. In the 1670s the sextons Robert and Philip Burnell kept manuscript records of burials and entries are frequently annotated *'a very throng place'* [i.e. very filled with bodies].

The Burnells' notes also suggest that specific parts of the Churchyard were, at least at one time, set aside for the use of the individual townships within the parish. A number of burials are annotated 'Stretford Hill', 'Droylsden Hill' and similar. Whether this was still observed in the Burnells' day or whether it was simply a convenient way for them to identify the location of a grave is unclear.

As the seventeenth century gave way to the eighteenth the number of burials began to rise steadily until by the middle of the century it had reached around ten burials a week and accommodating these in the Old Churchyard was becoming an impossibility. The burial registers from 1573 up to 1766 record in excess of 60,000 burials. How many more had taken place in the 358 years before the registers began is speculative, but even if it had averaged as few as 100 burials a year, this would bring the total number of burials by 1766 to approaching 100,000. This is an astonishing total in such a small area of ground. It is probable that attempts to open new graves would have frequently resulted in disturbance to older, but possibly also quite recent, graves.

In 1768 the parish purchased a plot of land adjacent to the Apple Market to use as an extension. Despite the undoubted congestion in the Old Churchyard, this did not mean the end of burials there. While the new plot was given over primarily to public graves for the poor, many families still claimed ownership of graves in the Churchyard and insisted upon their rights of burial. These burials were not small in number. Although the number of burials in the Apple Market over the 22 years from 1766 to 1788 was over six thousand, the number of burials recorded in the registers for the same period exceeds eleven thousand. Space for the other five thousand had somehow been found in the Old Churchyard.

A vivid description of the Old Churchyard appears in Richard Wright Procter's *'Recollections of Manchester 1808-1830'*[8]

'Previous to the churchyard being surrounded by the present iron palisading there were several entrances into it by wooden gates, one of which was opposite the Rev. N. Germon's house, and the stumps of this gate were only removed last summer, when the road of the old Apple Market was widened by taking into it a portion of the churchyard. Another of these gates was in Half Street, near Cateaton Street; it was called 'Clap Gate,' being made of strong oak, and so hung, that if left open it would close by its own weight, "clapping" heavily. There was then no entry to what is now called Church Gates, at the upper end of Old Millgate, where there is now the principal entrance. A range of shops on that side of the yard covered the site of the present south entrance; the great entrance on that side (prior to the churchyard being enclosed) being by a gate from Hanging Bridge. At that time the whole of the churchyard, from being surrounded only by a low wall, with decayed wooden gates, was quite open, and a great thoroughfare. Our correspondent once saw a man on horseback, like a farmer, enter the churchyard from Long Millgate, and ride through it. Nor was it uncommon (as may be seen from the old Court Leet entries), in days when swine roamed the streets at large, to see a pig or two routing in the churchyard. But at length anyone finding pigs there, and driving them to the Pinfold (which was near the site of the present Rising Sun Inn, at the top of Shudehill) received one shilling, which the owner was compelled to pay on claiming the stray animal.

Our correspondent describes the range of buildings on the west side of the churchyard next the river; they were built on the rock. Opposite the steeple was the Ring o' Bells public house; then north of it a few cottages; next to them The Black a Moor's Head public house; beyond it Some more houses; a third public house, The Flying Horse; followed by another range of houses and cottages, terminating in the soapery and chandlery house of Messrs. Fogg, Birch, and Hampson.'

By 1787 the Apple Market burial ground was full to capacity and a second, much larger, 'overflow' burial ground was opened at Angel Meadow. Conditions in the Old Churchyard had clearly become unacceptable and a parish meeting on 5 February 1787 determined:

'That the churchyard belonging to the Collegiate Church shall be immediately levelled and in future kept in good order … No graves shall be opened in the said churchyard, except for those persons who have gravestones, without the consent of the churchwardens'.

However, this restriction does not mean that an acceptable state of affairs was maintained in the Old Churchyard. The family graves were clearly just as full as the others and some questionable ways of making space for new burials were adopted. Procter's recollections continue:

From the building adjoining the Ring o' Bells was an unsightly piece of waste ground, shelving down from the yard to the river. This was called Tin Brow; it was a favourite place down which to shoot rubbish, and even human bones from the adjacent churchyard. About 1811, in consequence of the graves being over-filled, and there being much demand for space for interments, the sexton of that day was accustomed to excavate graves that had been long undisturbed, and throw the osseous remains of their departed tenants, with the fragments of half decayed coffins, down Tin Brow into the river, especially in seasons of flood, which speedily washed these relics away. At length, however, public decency was outraged by this practice, and by the swinish visits to the churchyard, and it was determined that it should be set apart and environed by palisades, as it now is.'

(The location of Tin Brow is believed to have been on the south bank of the River Irwell almost opposite to the Cathedral front door).

These conditions continued and worsened. Writing to the Manchester Mercury in 1817, a correspondent using the pen name 'Spero' complained loudly and at length about the site of the Old Churchyard. He described being subjected to a *'nauseous and powerful'* smell while standing some distance from a freshly opened grave. He warned of the danger to public health citing the (perhaps unlikely) case of a young boy who having approached the gravedigger who had opened a *'remarkably offensive'* grave contracted a *'putrid fever of a malignant kind'*. He objected to the way in which 'the dead are mangled and shifted about in order to make way for fresh corpses'. He concluded by demanding complete closure and the treatment of the soil with quicklime[9].

'JOTTY' BROOKES

A great deal of colour was added to services at the Collegiate Church by the Reverend Joshua Brookes (1754-1821), chaplain at the Collegiate Church from 1790 until his death and well-known for his eccentricity and irritability.

Reverend Joshua Brookes

A (possibly apocryphal) story tells how 'Jotty', as he was known, was frequently annoyed by the practice of young boys running along the top of the churchyard wall. On one occasion, while reading the funeral service, he spotted a young chimney sweep on the wall. Without breaking his funeral oration, he inserted a command to the beadle *'...and I heard a voice from Heaven saying 'Knock that rascal off the wall!''*. Another of Jotty's reputed eccentricities was to leave a graveside mid-service and wander off to buy sweets from the nearby shop run by a Mrs. Clowes. His sweet-tooth satisfied, he would then return to conclude the service.

Another story of Jotty's eccentricity concerns an encounter with Nathan Wood, a patten maker, who lived close to the church:

> 'Having occasion to use a barrow, he (Nathan) went to borrow one belonging to the church. Taking a near cut on his return, over the gravestones, instead of keeping to the path, he received a smart blow from behind given by the eccentric Joshua Brookes, and accompanied by the words, "How dare you wheel this barrow over consecrated ground?" Nat answered, "I thought the barrow was consecrated and all, as I borrowed it from the sexton!"'[10]

This was perhaps one of the few times when someone got the better of Jotty.

CLOSED AT LAST!

In 1819 the churchyard was at long last closed to new burials. The closure was supposed to be for a period of 31 years at the end of which time it was assumed that the remains of those buried there would have sufficiently decomposed to permit new graves to be dug. In the same year as the churchyard was closed, it was enclosed by a low wall surmounted by iron railings.

To commemorate the decision to close the Old Churchyard, Joseph Aston penned the following lines:

> A faculty asked for it long had been wanted –
> A thirty years fallow the Bishop has granted
> To enclose the Old Churchyard – no grave to be broke
> Till time has for thirty years worn winter's cloak
> Till that time is over adieu to infections!
> Till that time is over adieu resurrections
> Till that time is over no more will "Tin Brow"
> Sights shocking humanity bring to our view

> Till then will no bodies be dragg'd from their graves
> And, to make room for others, be thrown to the waves
> No more will the fish of the Irwell be fed
> With the wreck of the grave, with the flesh of the dead.[11]

Although the closure period expired in 1850 and re-opening was considered at that time, the churchyard was never to reopen for general use.

The final burial register includes a note written by the officiating minister, Cecil Wray, alongside the burial of William, the nine year old son of Thomas Prean. Wray records that William's was '...the last corpse interred in the Old Churchyard'. Wray was however, not quite correct. In an ironic twist, there was to be one more burial nearly fifty years later. This final burial took place on 3 May 1866 and, because the Churchyard was now officially closed, required special permission. The person buried was none other than 88 year old Cecil Daniel Wray himself. Wray had become related to the Lloyd family through his second marriage and the family owned a grave in the Old Churchyard. Though it had not been opened for nearly a century, this was to be Wray's final resting place.[12]

While the closure of the Old Churchyard put an end to the nuisances arising from burials in already overflowing graves, it did little to improve the appearance of what was essentially a utilitarian space, paved throughout with ledger stones, relieved only by the occasional chest tomb. Richard Wright Procter commented in 1874 'In our city graveyard Gray could never have composed his famous elegy'.[13]

Not long after Procter's remark and as part of a wider restoration of the Cathedral, the gravestones were removed and the whole area grassed over. Not one memorial remains.

The Apple Market

On Tuesday the 25th of November 1766 an announcement appeared in the Manchester Mercury and Harrop's General Advertiser:

> *'Notice is hereby given, that there will be a Towns-Meeting held on Thursday the twenty-seventh Day of November Instant, at three of the Clock in the Afternoon at the House of Mr. Joseph Budworth, the sign of the Bull's Head, in Manchester aforesaid, (pursuant to publick Notice given the Twenty-third Day of November Instant, in the Collegiate and Parish Church of Manchester, by Order of the Church Wardens of the said Town) to consult about purchasing a Plot of Land for a Burial Ground, for the Use of the said Town, at which Time and Place the Land-Owners and principal Inhabitants are desired to attend'.*

Two weeks later the paper reported that the meeting had agreed that:

> *'a burial ground was wanted adjoining the Collegiate and Parish Church for the sake of common decency and as a probable means of preserving the health of this great and opulent town'.*

Two plots had been discussed at the meeting, one of somewhat over 700 square yards and owned by. Walter Wilson, the other of 180 square yards owned by William Higginbotham. It was resolved that both plots should be purchased and that a public subscription be established to raise the necessary funds as quickly as possible.

Raising the necessary funds took something over a year but on 3 May 1768 Walter Wilson, an ironmonger, sold a plot of land *'at Hunts Bank, to the north side of the street'* to the churchwardens for the not inconsiderable sum of £535 2s 6d.[14] This was a particularly convenient location, just across the road to the north of the Collegiate Church. It allowed the funeral service to be read in the Church and the coffin to be either carried or transported on a wheeled bier across the Old Churchyard and over the road to the burial place. The Churchwardens do not appear to have proceeded the purchase of William Higginbotham's smaller plot.

The land having been purchased, matters now moved quickly and the new burial ground, on the north side of the street called the Apple Market, was opened on the 17th of June. There are few contemporary descriptions of the new burial ground but a newspaper article printed in 1878, almost a century after it had closed, tells us that *'It was enclosed in front of the street by an old brick wall which was replaced by the present wall of the college'.*[15]

The need for a new burial ground reflects the increasing difficulty of creating new graves in the Old Churchyard. By 1766 the number of burials at the Collegiate Church had risen to between six and eight hundred a year, between two and three times the number recorded fifty years earlier and the numbers were still rising. The specific reason for providing this new burial ground is spelled out in the ManchesterMercury:

> *'The design of this ground is for a public cemetery for the poor people of this parish who cannot possibly be provided for in the parish church yard nor yet afford to purchase graves in any other public burying ground'.*

Given the number of burials and the upward trend one might have expected the church to seek a substantial expansion in capacity but the plot purchased was remarkably small. Annual statistics for births, marriages and deaths were published in the Manchester Mercury and these show that approximately half of the burials recorded in the Collegiate Church registers relate to burials in the Apple Market graveyard; for the remainder space was somehow found in the Old Churchyard. I have been unable to find a contemporary account of how these burials were conducted but later accounts of burials at Angel Meadow suggest that the burials would have been in deep pits, each accommodating a large number of coffins.

Over the twenty-two years during which the Apple Market ground was used, no fewer than 6,383 bodies were interred there. The density of burials in this remarkably small space is more than double that which would be seen in any of the later parish graveyards. Even allowing for the density with which the coffins were packed into the available space, it is difficult to see how this number of burials could have been achieved without the kind of disturbance to earlier graves which was common in the Old Churchyard.

By 1788 it had become clear that further burials could not be accommodated and the deci-

sion was taken to close the Apple Market burial ground. The closure was to last for 30 years and the assumption was that it would then re-open, the remains of the previous burials having sufficiently dissolved to permit further burials. In the event, it was never to re-open. At a later date the ground was levelled and grassed over. It was remarked that during this work very few human remains were turned up or exposed.

The former Apple Market burial ground is now an open space which has been incorporated into the grounds of Chetham's College. The only clue that it was ever a graveyard is a noticeable elevation of the ground level within the walls above the level of the street outside. There are also fragments of what had clearly once been gravestones in an inner retaining wall, though these might possibly have come from the Old Churchyard when this was cleared.

The Apple Market Burial Ground
(Imagery © 2012 GeoEye, Infosystema Ltd. & Bluesky. The Geoinformation Group)

Angel Meadow: The New Burial Ground

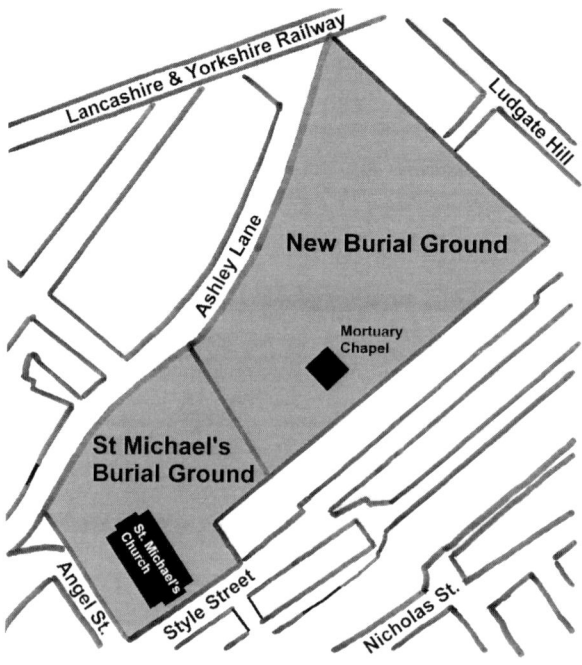

The New Burial Ground
Angel Meadow

As one door closes, another opens. At the same time as the Apple Market burial ground was reaching the limit of its capacity, Humphrey Owen was planning to build a new church on a plot of land which he owned some distance from the Collegiate Church in an area called Angel Meadow. Angel Meadow was literally a green field site and in the 1760s still very much on the outskirts of the town. Owen's new church, which would be dedicated to St. Michael, was planned to stand at the south western end of the site, which is the higher and more level part. From here the ground falls away quite steeply towards the River Irk to the northwest.

It was always planned that St. Michael's would have its own churchyard (see page 60) but the land on which the church was to be built was considerably larger than was necessary for this purpose. The parish vestry therefore decided to purchase more than half of the site for use as a new parish burial ground.

The original proposal, agreed by the vestry at a meeting on 22 March 1786, was to purchase some 10,483 square yards of land but this was subsequently reduced to 8,000 square yards (about 1.65 acres). The £416 13s 4d which it cost to purchase the land from Humphrey Owen together with the cost of erecting a 9 foot high boundary wall around it was raised, as had been the case with the Apple Market, by a public subscription. The parish's latest burial ground was consecrated by the Bishop of Chester and opened for burials on the 24th of July 1789. It became known as *'The New Burial Ground'* or sometimes *'The New Burying Ground'*

Although the New Burial Ground was effectively an extension of the Old Churchyard, it was some distance from the Collegiate Church. It would have been inconvenient to conduct the burial service at the Collegiate Church and then transport the coffin, accompanied by the mourners, to Angel Meadow for interment. A small mortuary chapel was therefore built on the site within which the burial service could be performed. Access to the burial ground was from Back Style Street, providing convenient access to the mortuary chapel. Burial services were not conducted by the Collegiate Church priests but by the minister of St. Michael's Church, who presumably received a fee for his services.

CHOLERA BURIALS

It has been suggested in a number of articles that the New Burial Ground was used for the burial of cholera victims. This idea seems first to have appeared in a newspaper article in 1848, which stated that the New Burial Ground had last been used in 1832 as *'the main burial place of those who died of the cholera'*[16]. The claim is simply incorrect.

Asiatic cholera did not visit England until 1832 and by this time the New Burial Ground had been closed for many years. Although the disease did not arrive in Manchester until June of that year, in April a meeting at the Town Hall was told that £1,000 had been allocated towards the costs of dealing with an expected outbreak and that 'a burial ground had also been provided'.

A Special Board of Health met frequently from 1831 to 1833 to manage the epidemic. Burial arrangements were discussed and Walkers Croft is specifically identified in the Board's minutes as the only burial ground in which the burial of victims was to be permitted. There is no mention in the Board's minutes of any burial taking place in the New Burial Ground or, with some specific exceptions, of burials anywhere other than at Walkers Croft.[17] There would seem to have been no need for an alternative burial ground for cholera victims. Walkers Croft still had sufficient space to accommodate the victims whereas the New Burial Ground was full and digging new graves there would have necessitated substantial disturbance to earlier burials.

PAUPER BURIALS

Another common misconception is that Angel Meadow is frequently referred to as a pauper burial ground. This is, however, not strictly true. The substantial majority of those who were buried at Angel Meadow were certainly poor, but were not paupers. A pauper was a person whose circumstances were so straitened that neither they nor their friends or family could afford to pay the burial fee and so was buried at the parish's expense.

Paupers would often, though not always, be those who died in the workhouse but even this is an over-simplification. To die in the workhouse did not automatically mean that the deceased would receive a pauper burial. Family members who had been unable to support the deceased while they were alive might still have been able to find or borrow the money to pay for a 'decent' burial. Some workhouse inmates might during their lives have contributed a burial club which on their death would have paid out sufficient for a basic funeral. In many cases such societies would have paid sufficient to pay for a private grave.

However, whether the deceased's family paid for the most basic of burials or whether the deceased was buried as a pauper, the difference was largely semantic. Both would have been interred in the same common grave.

Angel Meadow was predominantly, if not exclusively, used to provide common graves. Burial in a common grave was the cheapest form of burial and one which the parish was under an obligation to provide for any parishioner.

BURIAL IN COMMON GRAVES

The rules set out by the parish vestry for the New Burial Ground required the sexton to maintain two open graves at all times, one for the interment of adults and the other for children. The vestry also stipulated that these graves should be nine feet deep and, when the last body had been interred, that it should be covered with two feet of earth. This minimum covering of earth, which the vestry considered necessary for a decent burial in 1789, would come to be regarded as scandalously inadequate less than a century later.

At Angel Meadow, the use of common graves was developed into a near-industrial process. Joseph Aston observed:

'A very large grave or, more properly, a pit, for the reception of mortality is digged, and covered up (when not used for depositing the remains of the dead) with planks which are locked down in the night, until the whole is packed with coffins piled besides and upon each other. The cavern of death is then closed and covered up with earth, and another pit is prepared and filled in the same manner.'[18]

Aston's account was probably written based upon practices which he had observed shortly before the New Burial Ground was closed. As we shall see, the closure of the New Burial Ground did not mean the end of this method of mass burial. If anything, the graves became larger and the conditions grimmer.

The vestry was also quite specific concerning the times at which the poor were to be buried at the New Burial Ground. They required that the burials of poor persons should take place at 2pm from 29 September to 25 March and 6pm from 25 March to 22 September.

It is difficult to say whether there were any private graves in the New Burial Ground. Neither the burial registers nor the sexton's books are specific as to whether a burial took place in the Old Churchyard or the New Burial Ground. It is certain that by 1789 there were several alternative graveyards in which a private grave might be purchased. It is therefore reasonable to believe that the New Burial Ground catered only for a poor or pauper clientele. However, references many years after its closure to the removal of gravestones from the site suggests that there might have been some graves over which individual memorials had been erected. The common graves would have had no memorial.

CLOSURE AND NEGLECT

The demand for burial space continued to increase and by 1815, less than thirty years after it had opened, the New Burial Ground was declared full and closed to further burials. As was the case with the Apple Market burial ground, the closure was nominally for a thirty year period, but like its predecessor, Angel Meadow would never be used for burials again.

Following closure the New Burial Ground was neglected and fell into increasing disrepair. The mortuary chapel was demolished soon after the closure. It appears on Pigot's map of Manchester published in 1821 but not on Swire's map which appeared three years later. Given the time-lag from survey to printing, it is possible it had already even been removed by the time the Pigot map was published. In the early 1840s a small

part of the northernmost corner was traversed by a viaduct carrying the Manchester to Leeds (later Lancashire and Yorkshire) Railway. This did little to enhance the appearance and atmosphere of the graveyard but at least it did not involve any disturbance to the graves.

There is some confusion as to the number of burials which took place in the New Burial Ground. A figure of 40,000 is frequently quoted but this is closer to the total for both the parochial burial ground and the graveyard of the adjacent St. Michael's Church. This confusion of the two separate burial grounds is common. Between the consecration and closure of the New Burial Ground, a total in excess of 31,000 burials were recorded in the Collegiate Church registers. Some of these would have been burials in family graves in the Old Churchyard but the substantial majority were probably burials at Angel Meadow. The total for St. Michael (as discussed later) was about 3,800, so the 40,000 figure, even if it included St. Michael, seems to be somewhat over-estimated.

At the time the New Burial Ground opened, Angel Meadow was both a pleasant and respectable area but this was not to last long. By the early nineteenth century the area had declined considerably and the local population was increasingly being replaced by poor Irish immigrants. The journalist Angus Bethune Reach wrote at some length in 1849 of his observations of Angel Meadow. He described the area:

> 'The lowest, most filthy, most unhealthy, and most wicked locality in Manchester is called, singularly enough 'Angel Meadow'. It lies off the Oldham-road, is full of cellars, and inhabited by prostitutes, their bullies, thieves, cadgers, vagrants, tramps, and in the very worst sties of filth and darkness, by those unhappy wretches the 'low Irish'"[19]

The state of the burial ground deteriorated rapidly. A correspondent using the pseudonym 'A Citizen of Manchester' wrote to the Manchester

Guardian in 1865. His letter, published under the headline *'A Disgrace to Manchester'*, described how the boundary wall had been substantially dismantled to repair local pigsties and cottages and how the area facing Back Style Street was used as a dump for domestic refuse. He described how the graveyard was now a popular venue for fights which attracted hundreds of spectators and for gamblers to congregate on the Sabbath to play 'pitch and toss'. Perhaps worst of all, he described how gravestones have been removed and bones disinterred, a human skull being kicked around as a football.

The authorities appear to have paid little heed to the plea of *'Citizen'* that the graveyard be rescued from its degraded state and it was not until 1867 that any action was taken. Even then their response was not a local initiative but to an Order from the Home Office requiring that the graveyard should be surfaced and fenced[20]. In consequence of this, the graveyard was levelled and the whole area covered with flagstones, earning it the enduring name 'St. Michael's Flags'.

Little was done with the site for the next two decades. It was occasionally used as a convenient open space for political rallies, such as those supporting the Liberals Joseph Bright and John Slagg in the election campaign of 1880. Other public meetings held there included a meeting of around 300 unemployed workmen in 1886.

A New Future

In 1887 the chairman of the Corporation's Parks and Cemeteries Committee, Jabez Faulkner, who also happened to be the councillor for the St. Michael's Ward, announced a proposal to spend £1,500 to turn St. Michael's Flags into a children's playground. The plans included removing the flags, levelling the ground and providing play equipment. Faulkner expressed the hope that *'the change from a burial ground to a pleasant open playground with some little vegetation about it will make the mediaeval name Angel Meadow a little more appropriate than it is'*. Unfortunately Faulkner lost his seat at the election later that year and the proposal lost momentum.

It was not until 1890 that the proposal was revived and this time it was well supported by the councillors and voted through. The Corporation did not, of course, own the graveyard but negotiated to rent it from the vestry for a nominal sum. The necessary works were quickly started so that it was possible for the Manchester Courier of 13 May 1891 to offer the description:

*The disused steps from Irk Street
into Angel Meadow*

> *'St. Michael's Flags, Angel Meadow, which is now converted into something more than a bare playground, swings for boys and girls have been erected together with the provision of a large double ball court, and a sand bed for children and a drinking fountain'.*

30

It was possibly at this time that pedestrian access was provided from Ashley Lane (now Aspin Lane) and from Ludgate Hill (now Irk Street) by means of two flights of stone steps. The steps have until recently been unsafe and closed to public use.

The new open space continued to see improvement. Public toilets were installed and a bandstand erected (both long since having disappeared). Musical entertainments were a regular attraction with the Manchester Police Band appearing regularly. Not all was perfect; there were a number of altercations between the park attendant and *'drunks'* and *'roughs'* who seemed to be attracted to the swings and became violent when confronted. There appears, however, to be consensus that the park was a great improvement on what had gone before.

The playground was extended in 1894 when two rows of back-to-back housing, which occupied the space between Old Mount Street and the graveyard boundary, were demolished. The land was cleared and incorporated into the playground. The Angel Meadow playground was a favourite subject of the artist L. S. Lowry and featured in several of his paintings including *'The Steps, Irk Place'* (1928) and *'The Playground'* (1945).

DECLINE (AGAIN) - AND REBIRTH

Unfortunately, the playground fell into decline once more during the post war period. By the dawn of the new millennium there were reports that it had become a regular haunt of drug addicts and was littered with used syringes and other refuse.

The situation was, however, turned around when in 2004 an action group founded the Friends of Angel Meadow. The group agitated for the restoration of the site as a public park. As a result of their efforts, funds were raised, the site was cleared of refuse and the landscaping improved. Further improvements included the installation of lighting, two new entrance gateways and a number of information boards which tell the history of the park and the surrounding area.

The most recent development is the restoration of the steps on the Ashley Lane boundary of the park. In the process of restoration, which involved the dismantling and rebuilding of the steps, the remains of four burials were exposed beneath the foundation. These were left in place under the restored steps. Perhaps in time the second flight into Ludgate Hill will also be restored.

Today the park is one of the most pleasant open spaces close to Manchester city centre. It straddles a space between the modern developments in Style Street and Angel Street to the south west and the rather run-down industrial buildings of Ludgate Hill to the north east.

Angel Meadow has gone full-circle and once more lives up to its name.

The entrance to Angel Meadow Park

31

To the Dead in the Graveyard Underneath my Window

How can you lie so still? All day I watch
And never a blade of all the green sod moves
To show where restlessly you toss and turn,
And fling a desperate arm or draw up knees
Stiffened and aching from their long disuse;
I watch all night and not one ghost comes forth
To take its freedom of the midnight hour.
Oh, have you no rebellion in your bones?
The very worms must scorn you where you lie,
A pallid mouldering acquiescent folk,
Meek habitants of unresented graves.
Why are you there in your straight row on row
Where I must ever see you from my bed
That in your mere dumb presence iterate
The text so weary in my ears: "Lie still
And rest; be patient and lie still and rest."
I'll not be patient! I will not lie still!
There is a brown road runs between the pines,
And further on the purple woodlands lie,
And still beyond blue mountains lift and loom;
And I would walk the road and I would be
Deep in the wooded shade and I would reach
The windy mountain tops that touch the clouds.
My eyes may follow but my feet are held.
Recumbent as you others must I too
Submit? Be mimic of your movelessness
With pillow and counterpane for stone and sod?
And if the many sayings of the wise
Teach of submission I will not submit
But with a spirit all unreconciled
Flash an unquenched defiance to the stars.
Better it is to walk, to run, to dance,
Better it is to laugh and leap and sing,
To know the open skies of dawn and night,
To move untrammeled down the flaming noon,
And I will clamour it through weary days
Keeping the edge of deprivation sharp,
Nor with the pliant speaking on my lips
Of resignation, sister to defeat.

I'll not be patient. I will not lie still.
And in ironic quietude who is
The despot of our days and lord of dust
Needs but, scarce heeding, wait to drop
Grim casual comment on rebellion's end;
"Yes, yes . . Wilful and petulant but now
As dead and quiet as the others are."
And this each body and ghost of you hath heard
That in your graves do therefore lie so still.

Adelaide Crapsey (1878-1914)

Walkers Croft

The impending closure of the New Burial Ground presented the churchwardens with a problem. Where could they find a reasonably large, plot of land to serve as a replacement? By 1815, the expansion of the city to the south and east of the Cathedral had left few substantial areas of vacant land on which a burial ground might be created within something like a mile of the Collegiate Church. To the north, however, on the far side of the River Irk, there had been very little development. Situated between the river and the Manchester Workhouse was a very suitable plot of land called Walkers Croft which was owned by the Trustees of the Grammar School. Walkers Croft consisted of a large field, divided into a number of smallholdings, which amounted to an area of 7,700 square yards; similar in size to the Angel Meadow burial ground which it was to replace. The plot also included two gardens which were leased by Dr. Jeremiah Smith and Dr. Robinson Elsdale the head and second master respectively of the Grammar School.[21]

The churchwardens of the Collegiate Church purchased the freehold for £1,899 5s 6d and in 1817 they extended their holding by purchasing a further adjoining small plot to the north east from Lord Ducie. This extended the graveyard up to a new road which connected Miller's Lane to Cheetham Hill Road.[22] Presumably Drs. Smith and Elsdale were less than impressed with the idea of having a graveyard next to their properties since in 1818 both sold their leases to a Mrs. Clowes, who presumably had fewer qualms about having a graveyard for a neighbour.

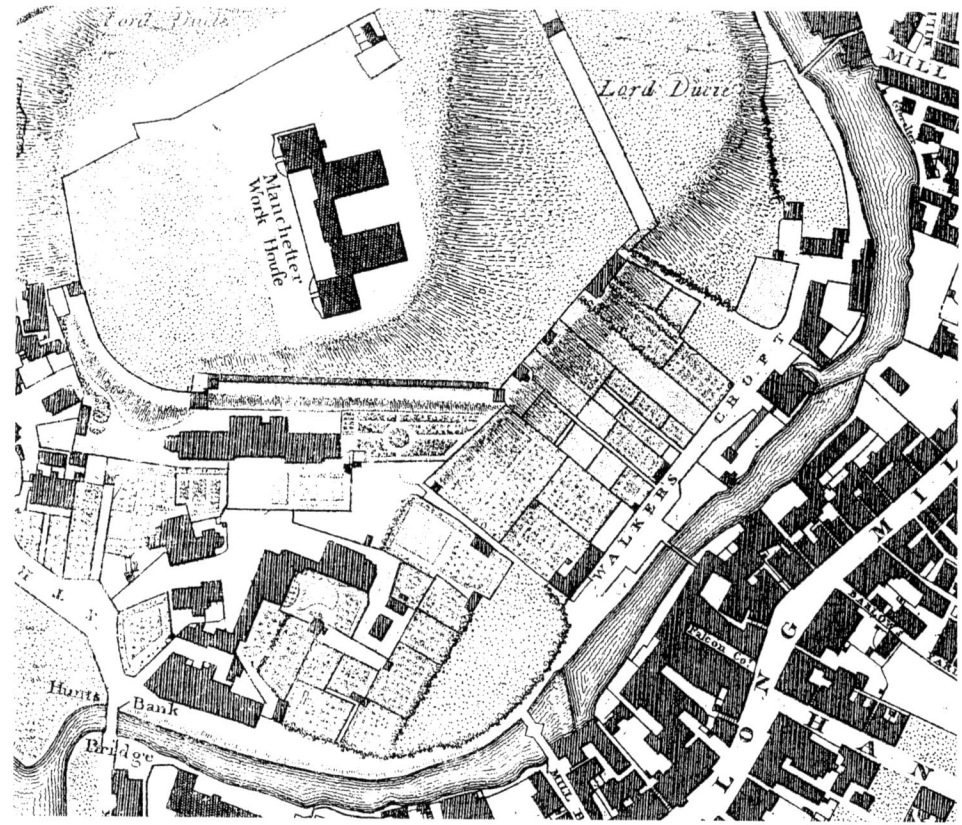

Walkers Croft in 1794

Walkers Croft Entrance
If the building to the right is the mortuary chapel, the drawing would appear to have
been made after the entrance was moved to the north side circa 1832.

The origin of the name Walkers Croft does not derive, as may first appear, from a former owner but from the earlier use of the field as the location of a cloth fulling works. The fulling process, before it was mechanised, involved workers walking on newly woven cloth immersed in a tub containing water, urine and a variety of other substances. The process served to clean, whiten and thicken the cloth. The surname 'Walker' (as did the surname 'Fuller') became associated with those engaged in this work. By the time the land was purchased for a burial ground, the cloth fulling activities were already history.

The churchwardens built a wall around the field and established a main entrance to the site on its southern boundary. From the entrance, the street (which also took the name Walkers Croft) ran alongside the River Irk to Hunts Bank Bridge, where it crossed the Irk and led onwards to Long Millgate and then to the Collegiate Church. They also erected a mortuary chapel at the centre of the burial ground so that, just as at Angel Meadow, burial services could be conducted on site. It appears that the ministers of the Collegiate Church once more resumed the reading of the burial service.

Burials commenced in 1815, following the consecration of the burial ground by the Bishop of Chester on 16 January of that year.

SUSPICIONS OF FOUL PLAY

Walkers Croft burial ground lay immediately adjacent to the Manchester Workhouse and there was a gate in the wall between them. This entrance provided a direct route into the burial ground from the workhouse so that the bodies of deceased pauper inmates, which would account for many of the burials, could be easily transported to the graveside. The existence of this entrance gave rise to rumours that inmates were being murdered and quietly disposed of. These rumours caused the Manchester Town Clerk to write to the Home Secretary in 1820 requesting that deaths in the workhouse should be made subject to coroners' inquests in order to rule out any suggestion of foul play. It is not known whether any action was taken as a result.[23]

Walkers Croft in 1832

COMMON GRAVES

The considerable majority, if not all of the burials at Walkers Croft were in common graves. The way in which common graves were managed was little different to that described at Angel Meadow by Joseph Aston in 1815 (see page 28). It appears, however, to have given rise to a greater number of complaints of nuisance.

A correspondent to the Manchester Guardian under the pseudonym *'An Eye Witness'* described in 1842 how he had seen an open grave with at least nine coffins exposed. Another correspondent identifying himself as *'One who has both eyes and nose'* writing in 1847, not long before the cemetery's closure, reported on what he had seen on a visit to the burial ground some years previously:

'...at that time the dead were interred in large graves, each of which would hold from 50 to 60 bodies. One of these monster graves was inspected on the outside, it being then covered up with a lid. The stench which came through the crevices of the boards was very bad, and about the orifices large numbers of blue bottle flies were collected. Upon opening the grave, a swarm of flies rushed out, accompanied by a stench which made the observers reel again. In this hole were some fifty decomposing bodies but the sexton stated that he could pack ten more into it. Some of the lids of the frail coffins were convex and appeared to be hard set to contain the decomposing bodies within, which foamed out at every orifice.'[24]

Given the average rates of mortality at this time it would have taken anything from two to four weeks, to accumulate the 50 to 60 bodies which our witness describes. The correspondent said that his visit had been in September. The appalling conditions which he describes would hardly be unexpected if bodies were left unburied for so long in summer temperatures.

'One who has both eyes and nose' also reported on a more recent visit to the cemetery, but had found things to be no better . He continued:

'Last week I was at the railway station, and saw a large grave open in which I counted seven coffins, piled one over another, and on the outside were two other

plain boarded coffins, which after remaining half an hour on the edge of the grave, were put into it without any burial service being read over them. A woman, who appeared to be drunk, after uttering some disgusting language, threw several heavy clods on the coffins, and then a man shovelled a dozen spadefulls of earth into the grave, which was then covered with a few boards and left ready for the next interment.'

Shocking as the idea of burying 50-60 coffins in a single pit may seem, things may in truth have been even worse than this. The Walkers Croft gravedigger, when giving evidence to a Parliamentary committee in 1839, explained that each of the pits would contain *'...about a hundred bodies'.*[25] This vast number is also suggested in comments made at a vestry meeting in 1832.

BODY SNATCHING

In 1820 there was a report that seven bodies had been stolen from the burial ground (by implication Walkers Croft)[26]. Leaving coffins in an open grave over a period of several days or weeks must have presented a great temptation to those who were prepared to carry out the grim crime of body snatching. This is not the only case recorded in Manchester and a number of incidents, including one specific to Walkers Croft, are discussed in Appendix 4.

THE CHOLERA RIOT

In 1832 an epidemic of Asiatic cholera swept the country and by by May the first case had been reported in Manchester. On Friday 31 August three year old John Brogan, whose Irish parents lived at 88 Silk Street, Oldham Road, was admitted to the temporary cholera hospital which had been opened in Swan Street. By the evening he was dead. His coffin was taken to Walkers Croft for burial the following Sunday.

For reasons which are unclear, but possibly relate to the child's name not being written on the coffin, the boy's grandfather, John Hayes, insisted on the coffin being opened. His suspicions were well-founded – although the coffin did contain the *body* of the child, the boy's head had been removed and a brick put in its place, presumably as a make-weight.

Hayes and the boy's parents left the graveyard and went to consult their priest, Father Hearne of St. Patrick's Catholic Church in Livesey Street, who agreed to make enquiries. In the family's absence, a rumour began to circulate that the boy had been murdered at the hospital. A mob gathered and seized the coffin, which they paraded through the streets. The mob rapidly grew to number an estimated three to four thousand and descended on the hospital, which they ransacked causing considerable damage. They also burned the van which was used as an ambulance. Through the timely arrival of three troops of the 15th Hussars, order was restored. The town constables managed to arrest the ringleaders and Father Hearne, having returned from investigating the atrocity, calmed the crowd by explaining the reality of what had happened. The crowd dispersed and the body was taken to the Town Hall.

Hearne had discovered that John Brogan's head had been removed from his body by Robert Oldham, one of the dispensers at the hospital. This he had seemingly done in connection with medical investigations which he had been undertaking on his own initiative. We are not privy to Oldham's personal explanation, since he had left town in some haste and was not seen in Manchester again. Fr. Hearne and Mr. Lynch, the resident surgeon at Swan Street, traced the head to a friend of Oldham's, recovered it and restored it to the body.

The following day, John Brogan was buried at St. Patrick's. His burial is recorded in the St. Patrick's burial register with the annotation

'This child whose corpse was mutilated in the Cholera Hospital by R. Oldham who was obliged to fly on this act to appease

the populace, the body after the head had been attached to it was re-interred in St Patrick's burial ground in a lead coffin'.[27]

John Brogan's burial at St. Patrick's shows a measure of compassion on the part of the Board of Health. The Board had imposed a requirement that the bodies of all cholera victims should be buried at Walkers Croft (We will see later that James Scholefield of Every Street Chapel found himself in court for ignoring this order) so this was a significant concession. Burying the body in a lead coffin probably addressed any health concerns and the authorities may have felt it wise not to risk a further riot by insisting that the child was buried at Walkers Croft. The lead coffin was paid for by the Board of Health[28].

A NEW LEASE OF LIFE

The cholera epidemic placed an unusually heavy demand upon Walkers Croft and burial space was apparently becoming limited. Had it not been for some creative thinking it might have been necessary for the churchwardens to look for yet another new graveyard.

A deceptively simple solution to the lack of space was announced at the annual vestry meeting in May of 1833. A significant expenditure of £134-14-8½, it was explained, was payment for the carting and spreading of a large quantity of soil. This had been used to cover the existing graves and raise the ground to such depth as *'...to effectively create a new burial ground'.*[29] The soil had come from the excavations involved in building new sewers. The equivalent value of the ground 'created' in this way was estimated by the churchwardens to be around £2,000 so both the depth of soil and the area covered must have been substantial.

SOLD TO THE RAILWAY

Thanks to the churchwardens' creative thinking, Walkers Croft continued to accommodate burials for another fifteen years. When it finally closed, it was not because it was full. It was simply sold for cash.

Manchester was at the forefront of railway development and in 1830, Britain's first passenger railway opened between Liverpool and Manchester, with the Manchester terminus located on Liverpool Road. By 1836 an Act of Parliament had been passed to authorise the construction of a new line between Manchester and Leeds. It was planned for the line to terminate at the northern end of the town and the new terminus to be built on land adjacent to the workhouse. However, to bring the railway into what was to become Victoria Station, it was necessary to procure a strip of land which spanned part of both the workhouse grounds and the Walkers Croft burial ground.

It is difficult today to conceive of a proposal to drive a railway line through a working cemetery being raised without a considerable public outcry. It is not without irony that the Manchester Times of 10 May 1839 had published a *'Diary from America',* written by Captain Marryat, in which he describes his surprise at finding himself on board a train which passed directly through a church yard *'...with tomb stones on both sides of us'.* Marryat comments *'...the sleepers of the railway are laid over the sleepers in death...'* and he asks *'would any engineer have ventured to propose*

All that remains of Walkers Croft today is a street name

such a line in England?'[30] The answer to Marryat's supposedly rhetorical question was that indeed they would.[31]

The proposal to sell this strip of land was agreed with surprisingly little difficulty. The Manchester churchwardens and overseers of the poor made vigorous representations against the proposed Bill but their acquiescence and Parliamentary approval was secured in large part because the railway company gave earnest assurances that the lines would be laid over the surface and that no bodies would be disturbed in the process. For this portion of the graveyard the railway company paid £3,125-1s-6d.

The company did not wish to offend its passengers with a similar sight to the one described by Captain Marryat, so they erected a ten foot high wall on either side of the line to conceal the graveyard on the one side and the workhouse on the other side from passengers' eyes. Despite the assurances that no bodies would be disturbed, to create a stable foundation for walls of this size, it would have been necessary to dig footings several feet deep and to fill these with rubble and concrete. It seems implausible that such a wall could be built without substantial interference to the graves along its line. The desecration was witnessed by Friedrich Engels:

'In Manchester, the pauper burial ground lies opposite to the Old Town, along the Irk: this, too, is a rough, desolate place. About two years ago a rail-road was carried through it. If it had been a respectable cemetery, how the bourgeoisie and the clergy would have shrieked over the desecration! But it was a pauper burial-ground, the resting-place of the outcast and superfluous, so no one concerned himself about the matter. It was not even thought worth while to convey the partially decayed bodies to the other side of the cemetery; they were heaped up just as it happened, and piles were driven into newly made graves, so that the water oozed out of the swampy ground, pregnant with putrefying matter, and filled the neighbourhood with the most revolting and injurious gases. The disgusting brutality which accompanied this work I cannot describe in further detail.[32]

The line was completed in 1844 but in the remaining portion of Walkers Croft business continued as usual, indeed the number of burials if anything increased. However, in 1846 the railway company announced its plans to extend Victoria Station as part of a scheme to provide a connection to Salford Station. Further legislation followed, which authorised the purchase of the remainder of the graveyard and in 1848 the churchwardens, following arbitration, were paid a further £9,874 for the remainder of the land. Once more assurances were given that the railway company's proposed use would not involve disturbance to the burials.

The promoters of the new bill claimed:

'We may state that the railway company want Walkers Croft for the enlargement of the station and probably to form an entrance from Ducie Street and there will be no excavation in the burial ground, but on the contrary, a large quantity of earth must be thrown down to raise it. Any distur-

This plaque marks the location of the former Walkers Croft Cemetery, which opened in 1815 and closed in 1832 in preparation for the coming of the railway. Remains recovered during rebuilding work in January 2010 have been removed and interred in Southern Cemetery Manchester.

The Victoria Station Plaque

bance of the remains is positively interdicted by the act giving the powers of purchase.'[33]

Again, the company went to great lengths to calm any fears of desecration. Again the company was to renege on its promises.

THE FINAL DISAPPEARANCE OF WALKERS CROFT BURIAL GROUND

The final burial at Walkers Croft took place on 25 February 1848 but having acquired the whole of the cemetery, the company found themselves in some financial difficulty and so it was not until 1855, when finances were more stable, that work commenced on the site. The first part of the work was to construct a further platform over the graveyard. This was completed in 1857.

Major development followed with the construction of a connection to Salford Station over the period 1861 to 1865. This was a major undertaking and involved, amongst other works, the construction of a culvert over the River Irk. It also involved establishing four more platforms and a large waiting room building on former graveyard land. The work paid scant attention to the assurances given in 1846.

No attempt was made to remove and re-bury the bodies in an appropriately respectful way. There are reports that coffins were broken up and the corpses moved across the site in wheelbarrows to be dumped in an excavation[34]. It should be remembered that some of the burials may have taken place only as little as fifteen years previously, so it is quite possible that some of the bodies which were disturbed would have been far from fully decomposed. There was a measure of outrage at this disgraceful treatment of the dead but no action was taken to censure the company or to require them to arrange for the proper reburial of remains which had been disturbed. By the time the work was completed, the western half of the burial ground had disappeared under the extended station.

BONES NEAR VICTORIA STATION.

WORKMEN'S STRANGE FIND.

During the last few days workmen engaged in the excavations which are being made in the Hunt's Bank approach to the Victoria Station, Manchester, came across a large number of human remains, together with a coffin. The bones are stated to be in an excellent state of preservation, one skull in particular, thought to be that of a woman, being still covered with long tresses. As the position of the coffin did not interfere with the work in hand it was left undisturbed. The bones have been re-interred at a greater depth.

The site is conjectured to be one that was used as the last resting-place for the victims of an epidemic of cholera which occurred in Manchester in the early part of the last century.

Manchester Courier and Lancashire General Advertiser 1 December 1906

WALKERS CROFT TODAY

While Walkers Croft burial ground is now out of sight and out of mind, it occasionally reminds us of its presence. Human remains are unearthed from time to time when it is necessary to excavate on the site. One of the more recent discoveries occurred during the construction of the Metrolink platforms, which lie directly over the former burial ground. Even up to the present day, bones may be discovered when it is necessary to excavate on the site[35].

There was, until very recently, no indication on the station that it stood on the site of a former burial ground. This is not, I suppose, something which the operators felt would enhance the station's appeal. Following the discovery of further remains in 2010, this time decently removed for reburial at Southern Cemetery, a small plaque was fixed to the railings at the end of platform 1. The plaque erroneously states that

'Walkers Croft Cemetery … opened in 1815 and closed in 1832 in preparation for the coming of the railway'.

The closure date given is premature by sixteen years and the wording rather sidesteps the reality of how the station developed.

At the time of writing, Network Rail are involved in a large scale project to improve Victoria Station. This will necessitate the probable disturbance and removal of remains from part of the site[36]. The work will not, however, involve a repeat of the appalling practices of the past. The work is overseen by archaeologists, who will record any remains uncovered. Any human remains recovered will be reburied at Southern Cemetery.

Should any deceased person's remains be identifiable and should any relatives wish to have them reinterred at an alternative place, this will be arranged. Since it is now nearly two centuries since the first burial at Walkers Croft and since most bodies would have been buried in unmarked common graves, this is a provision unlikely to be called upon.

Early excavations have so far brought to light only fragmentary remains and these appear to have been from previously disturbed burials, rather than from undisturbed graves. This tends to support the historical accounts of remains being casually uncovered and moved, but it is still too early to come to any sound conclusion on this matter.

During the three decades that Walkers Croft served as the parish burial ground, the Collegiate Church registers record approximately 40,000 burials, the substantial majority of which before, and all after 1819, would have been at Walkers Croft. Although burials continued right up to the time the land was sold, it seems likely that by 1848 it was nearing the end of its useful life. Had events not hastened its closure, it would, perhaps, have served for a few more years. In any event closure would almost certainly have been demanded in 1854 with the imposition of the Metropolitan Burial Acts.

About City Gravestones

The word 'graveyard' conjures up the image of a green field filled with rows of headstones, some large, some small, some plain, some ornate but each standing, or perhaps leaning at the head of a grave. This is unsurprising as it is what we see when we visit a country or suburban churchyard or when we visit a municipal cemetery (though the latter now increasingly discourage any show of individuality and insist on small, regular-sized headstones). This is not what you would have seen had you visited most of Manchester's city churchyards during the nineteenth century.

In city churchyards space was at a premium, and graves were packed in. The typical city graveyard was divided neatly into plots, each about six feet by three, arranged in tight rows with no space between plots, no pathways and no floral borders. Each grave was covered by a flat 'ledger' stone, which precisely covered the grave plot. Adjacent ledgers butted together so that the entire churchyard became one large paved area. Inscriptions were carved into these slabs to record the names and dates of those buried beneath. Ledgers also compensated to some degree for the sometimes very shallow depth at which some of the bodies would be buried. They both helped to suppress the smell of decomposition and to prevent remains from being exposed by animals.

In a few cases the ledger would be topped with a 'chest' (or 'box') tomb, a hollow stone box which might have inscriptions on the side panels as well as on the top. An alternative was the 'table' tomb, which as the name suggests was simply a second stone raised a couple of feet above the ledger on four or six stone pillars.

Some good examples of chest tombs can be seen outside St Ann's church and of ledgers, (possibly still in their original positions), on the site of the former St. Michael's churchyard.

The End of Parish Burial

The closure of Walkers Croft in 1848 left the parish without a burial ground but at least the churchwardens had the consolation of £13,000 in the bank. Surely it would not be difficult to find another suitable plot of land?

Despite the possibility of the sale having been apparent for best part of a decade, no plans had been made for a burial ground to replace Walkers Croft. The closure did not, of course, stop people dying and so some answer had to be found. Contemporary accounts suggest that for a period the burial ground of St. Michael's Church was used. However, this was said to have resulted in a large number of complaints owing to the very unsatisfactory nature of what was already a crowded cemetery. It is not clear from the registers whether any parish burials actually took place there.

The answer was found in an early public-private partnership. Manchester General Cemetery at Harpurhey had opened as a commercial venture in 1837 (see page 136). They had already made a strong pitch in their advertising to attract the 'economy' end of the market and so it was mutually beneficial that the cemetery should take on parish burials. If it was to become a parish burial ground this would only be possible if the ground was consecrated, a requirement which he General Cemetery did not meet. The consecration of a private cemetery was not a simple matter. It was necessary to obtain a private Act of Parliament for it to be permitted. This was duly obtained and a section of the cemetery consecrated for Church of England burials in 1848.

This arrangement did not, however, mean that the parish had given up the idea of replacing Walkers Croft. From the outset, the contract with Manchester General Cemetery was seen as a temporary measure pending the acquisition of a suitable site. The subject was discussed at length in parish meetings and concern at the lack of action was raised in several letters to the newspapers. In 1849 it then seemed that the matter was being taken seriously. An advertisement appeared in the Manchester newspapers inviting tenders to supply 'land for a burial ground'. It was desirable, the advertisement said 'that there should be convenient approaches to the land by road and railway'.[37] A large number of possible locations were proposed and were surveyed. However, despite a number seeming eminently suitable and affordable, no action was taken to proceed with a purchase.

At the heart of the problem seems to have been a disagreement between the Cathedral clergy and the churchwardens as to location. The clergy wanted a burial ground close to the Cathedral for their convenience in conducting services. The churchwardens were of the contrary view that sanitary considerations should prevail and to this end an 'out of town' location was to be preferred. To complicate the decision further, there was a faction which advocated purchasing all or part of the Ardwick private cemetery. Another faction suggested that it would make greater sense to establish as many as four smaller cemeteries distributed around the city, for the convenience of providing burial places closer to local communities. It was clearly not an easy matter to reconcile these diverse views and for five years there was little evident progress.

By 1853, however, the differences seem to have been resolved and the matter was moving ahead once more. The Earl of Derby owned a plot of land in a location described as 'behind the house of the late Mr. Gilbert Winter', near Peel Lane in Cheetham. Some six acres were available at a price of £4,750. When this particular site had first been discussed, there had been comments that the heavy clay soil would be unsuitable for it to be used as a burial ground.

Despite this objection the canons and church-wardens decided to proceed with the purchase. This was to prove a disastrous decision. The churchwardens' decision to sign the purchase contract appears at best ill-informed and at worst perverse. The Metropolitan Burial Act, which passed into law on 20 August 1853, made it clear that new graveyards would not be permitted within any town boundary. It is difficult to believe that the churchwardens would not have been aware that legislation was in the pipeline which was likely to impact on their decision.

Some legal difficulties had delayed the completion of the contract for several months and it was still not completed when the Order in Council which implemented the Act in Manchester was published on 21 March 1854. Consequently the land which the churchwardens were committed to purchase was useless for its intended purpose.

At the annual churchwarden's meeting held on the 18th of April 1854 the retiring church-warden, Malcolm Ross, reported that the convey-ance of the Cheetham land had been completed but the money had not yet been paid. He expressed a view that the Earl would not insist upon payment for land which was now useless for its intended purpose and that he would release the churchwardens from the contract.[38] Unfortunately, Mr. Ross's view proved consider-ably wide of the mark and the Earl, not unreason-ably, insisted that the contract be honoured. Clearly the Earl was not swayed by their entreaties since a notice published in the Manchester Courier the following November refers to land *'lately purchased from the Earl of Derby'*.[39] It is unclear what eventually happened to this land but it is assumed that it was resold.

This failed attempt to obtain a parish burial ground left the canons and churchwardens back where they had started. They had little alternative but to continue the 'temporary' arrangement with Manchester General Cemetery.

By the end of 1854 any serious idea of the canons and churchwardens acquiring a new burial ground seems to have been abandoned. There was a proposal that the money obtained from the sale of Walkers Croft should be used for the maintenance of the Cathedral (as the Colle-giate Church had become in 1847). This was, however, widely criticised and not pursued. In 1857 Manchester Corporation obtained an Act of parliament to transfer the fund to the Corporation. The explicit purpose of this action was to put the money towards establishing a municipal ceme-tery.

The Corporation's proposal raised a major objection from members of the Salford Council who argued that since Walkers Croft had been purchased by means of a rate levied on the entire parish, which included both Salford and Broughton, the proceeds should be similarly divided. When eventually, in 1866, funding was agreed for Manchester's first municipal cemetery at Philips Park, the proceeds *'less [the] Salford proportion'* were hypothecated against the costs of the consecrated section.

The money was not, however, spent on the municipal cemetery but invested. In 1893 £11,000 was invested in Manchester Corporation Stock. It is unclear what became of the other £2,000 – possibly this was the 'Salford portion'. This investment remained untouched until 1957 when the Corporation, in agreement with a Parliamentary committee, agreed to transfer the funds back to the Dean and Canons of the Cathe-dral for use in improving the Cathedral precincts. By this time, the stock was valued at £6,000, having lost nearly half of its cash value and nearly 90% of its purchasing power.

The Collegiate Church and its churchyard had been the only burial place of any significance in Manchester up to the early part of the eighteenth century. As the churchyard became filled, a succession of burial grounds had been estab-lished for the burial of the growing numbers of poor parishioners, beginning with the Apple

Market and followed in succession by Angel Meadow and Walkers Croft.

For the expanding middle classes, who expected to be buried in a private family grave, the solution to the lack of burial places came with a series of new Anglican churches which were established to serve the new communities which were beginning to appear at some distance from the Collegiate Church and to which the more prosperous families were beginning to migrate. Between 1712 and 1832, nine new churches were built and each had its own burial ground. The rise and decline of these new churches is the subject of the next section.

Notes for Parish Burial Grounds

1 Manchester Courier & Lancashire General Advertiser, Saturday 6 May 1856.

2 History of the Foundation in Manchester of Christ's Church, Chetham's Hospital and the Free Grammar School, Samuel Hibbert, John Palmer, William Robert Whatton & J. Greswell, 1834. This book provides an extremely comprehensive description of the Collegiate Church before the extensive Victorian restorations. It contains transcriptions of a considerable number of the memorials which were removed during these 'improvements'.

3 Personal Reminiscences of Manchester Cathedral, Andrew Boutflower, 1912.

4 History of the Foundation in Manchester of Christ's Church, Chetham's Hospital and the Free Grammar School, Samuel Hibbert, John Palmer, William Robert Whatton & J. Greswell, 1834.

5 Manchester Courier & Lancashire General Advertiser, Saturday 6 November 1852. The article provides a detailed description of the funeral and, more unusually, the interment.

6 Owen Manuscripts Vol. 23 Page 15. The Owen Manuscripts consist of 89 notebooks (each containing as many as 500 pages) and were compiled by the Manchester antiquary John Owen (born Bolton, 1815). They contain transcriptions of numerous memorial inscriptions and parish registers as well as a host of other historical material relating to north west England.

7 Personal Reminiscences of Manchester Cathedral, Andrew Boutflower, 1912.

8 Recollections of Manchester 1808-1830, Manchester Collectanea Vol. 2 , Chetham Society Vol. LXXII 1867.

9 Manchester Mercury, 11 November 1817

10 Memorials of Manchester Streets, Richard Wright Procter, 1874. The Reverend Joshua Brookes appears as a character in the novel 'A Manchester Man' by Mrs. Linnaeus Banks. Mrs. Banks would have known Joshua Brookes and the novel provides further insights into the character of this larger than life individual.

11 Metrical Records of Manchester, Joseph Aston, 1819. Metrical Records is a lengthy history of Manchester presented in the form of rhyming couplets.

12 Manchester Courier & Lancashire General Advertiser, 5 May 1866.

13 Memorials of Manchester Streets, Richard Wright Procter, 1874. Chapter 5. 'God's Acre', Procter discusses a number of the burials in the Old Churchyard.

14 Deed of bargain and sale Walter Wilson to Henry Fielden and others for land at Hunts Bank, Manchester Archives and Local Studies GB127/M3/2/102A

15 Unidentified newspaper in Manchester Archives and Local Studies Cuttings Collection (Box 74).

16 Manchester Courier & Lancashire General Advertiser, Wednesday 25 October 1848.

17 Minutes of the Board of Health 1831-3, Manchester Archives and Local Studies GB127/M9/36/1&2. The board met almost daily throughout the epidemic and decisions relating to issues such as burial arrangements were meticulously recorded.

18 A Picture of Manchester, Joseph Aston, 1816.

19 Manchester and the Textile Districts in 1849, Angus Bethune Reach, Ed. C. Aspin, 1849. The book is an edited compilation of reports by Reach (pronounced Re-ack) originally published in the Morning Chronicle in 1849.

20 London Gazette 21 May 1867.

21 Reports of the Commissioners of Charities in England and Wales 1827-8 (3rd Volume).

22 Manchester Mercury 8 July 1817.

23 Letter from John Thompson to the Home Office, 1820, The National Archives HO44/1 folio 5-5a.

24 Manchester Guardian 24 November 1847.

25 Manchester Guardian 11 May 1839. The gravedigger was giving evidence to the committee examining the proposal to enable the railway company to purchase part of Walkers Croft. While he is candid as to the number of coffins in each pit, he appears to have been under some pressure to downplay the number of such pits which would be affected by the proposal.

26 Letter from John Thompson to the Home Office, 1820, The National Archives HO44/1 folio 5-5a.

27 Manchester Times 8 September 1832.

28 Minutes of the Board of Health 1831-3, Manchester Archives and Local Studies GB127/M9/36/2.

29 Manchester Times, Saturday 25 May 1833.

30 Recounted in Gatherings from Grave Yards, George Alfred Walker, 1839.

31 Building a railway over a graveyard was, in fact, not unique. The Leeds end of the Leeds-Bradford Railway was carried on an embankment which was built over the graveyard of St. Peter's Church. This was completed in 1846.

32 The Condition of the Working Class in England, Friedrich Engels, 1844.

33 Manchester Courier & Lancashire General Advertiser, Wednesday 25 October 1848.

34 Manchester Victoria Station, Tom Wray, 2004. The abuses which Wray describes as attending the extension of the station do not appear to have raised any comment in the local newspapers.

35 Manchester Evening News, 22 January 2010. The report concerns the unearthing of several bones, believed to belong to a single skeleton. There is reference in the report to previous discoveries of remains in 1993 and 1995.

36 Manchester Evening News, 3 April 2013 (and subsequent issues).

37 Manchester Courier & Lancashire General Advertiser, Saturday 9 June 1849.

38 Manchester Courier & Lancashire General Advertiser, Saturday 22 April 1854.

39 Manchester Courier & Lancashire General Advertiser, Saturday 18 November 1854.

Other Church of England Burial Grounds

Other Church of England Burial Grounds

Manchester's spiritual needs had been adequately served by the Collegiate Church for some five centuries before any other Anglican place of worship was established. St. Ann's, the first new church in the town, was consecrated in 1712. Unlike the Anglican churches which would follow, St. Ann's was not built to cater for an expanding population but because of religious differences between its founder and the ministers of the Collegiate Church.

Fifty years later, however, the population was beginning to expand rapidly as Manchester's growth as a manufacturing and commercial centre drew thousands of people each year from the surrounding towns and villages as well as from further afield and new churches were needed to accommodate the numbers to serve the new population centres which developed.

As prosperity increased, the wealthier members of the population began to move away from the old town centre with its bustle, noise and smoke. New housing was built on what had previously been green fields on the southern side of the town. This southward expansion came about partly because the old town was bounded to the north and west by the Rivers Irk and Irwell and partly because the prevailing winds tended to carry the considerable quantity of smoke created by the factories off to the north and east and away from the new houses. Housing which was vacated in the old town centre was increasingly sub-divided and rented to low paid workers.

This process resulted in the creation of new population centres. These were predominantly the preserve of the middle classes and there was a demand for churches to serve their spiritual needs. Consequently, between 1756 and 1831, no fewer than eight new Anglican churches were built.

Although each new church served a defined area of the town, these areas were not true parishes carved out of the old parish but more properly 'districts' within the old parish. Each district functioned on a day-to-day basis much like a parish. It would have an incumbent minister who would lead daily services but it was not wholly independent.

A particular imposition concerned the payment of fees for baptism, marriage and burial services. Previous to the establishing of the new churches these fees were received by the ministers of the Collegiate Church who were not in any hurry to give up this lucrative source of income. To protect their interests and as a condition of their agreement to the building of a new church, they required the customary fees to be paid to the Collegiate Church for each baptism, marriage or burial service conducted at the new church in addition to any fee charged locally. In effect, if you wished to be married, baptise your child, or bury your parent at the new church, you were required to pay a double fee. A natural consequence was that many people who worshipped at the new churches chose to marry or baptise their children at the Collegiate Church, so as to avoid the unwelcome extra charge. This became more common in the nineteenth century as the populations surrounding these churches became increasingly working class and less able to afford the additional charge.

Each of the new churches was either surrounded by a churchyard or incorporated burial vaults beneath its floor. Some had both. These offered a much more attractive burial place for those who could afford it than the increasingly overcrowded parish burial ground and the only place where one could procure a private grave in consecrated ground after the Old Churchyard was closed in 1819. None of the new churches offered burial in common public graves. Burial of the poor was left to the parish church and has already been described at some length. The new churches had been established with a middle class clientele in mind and only private graves were provided. These could be purchased for a family's exclusive use with a further fee being payable to open the grave for each interment.

All of these new Anglican churches shared a similar life cycle. This would begin with the building of new houses attractive to the middle classes and more prosperous artisans. The church would enjoy strong financial support from its congregation and healthy fees for performing baptisms, marriages and burials. Over time, the wealthy population would drift away, particularly once the railway made commuting from the suburbs a practical proposition. The housing would either be taken over and sub-divided to provide working class accommodation or demol-ished to be replaced with office or warehouse buildings. The church would now be now left with either a much impoverished congregation and in some cases no congregation at all.

As the nineteenth century drew to a close, these once fashionable churches had almost all become redundant. In 1890 St, Mary's was the first to be close and over the next seventy years was followed by the others. Only St. Ann and St. Andrew's survived into the second half of the twentieth century. St. Ann's was spared, though even this historic building twice came close to demolition. Even though the other churches are now all long gone, in many cases their late parishioners sleep on undisturbed.

Church of England Churches
With their dates of their consecration and closure

Dedication	Consecrated	Closed
St. Ann	1712	Still open
St. Mary, Parsonage	1756	1890
St. John, Deansgate	1769	1928
St. James, George Street	1788	1928
St. Michael, Angel Meadow	1789	1930
St. Peter, Mosley Street	1795	1906
St. George, Oldham Street	1817 (note 1)	1874
St. Matthew, Campfield	1825	pre 1939
St. Andrew, Ancoats	1831	1958

Note 1: St .George's was built as a speculative venture and was home to a variety of different nonconformist groups until it was purchased by the Warden and Canons of the Collegiate Church and consecrated for Anglican worship by the Bishop of Chester. A new St. George's was built nearby after the demolition of the original church.

St. Ann

St. Ann's Church was built by Lady Ann Bland (1664-1734). Lady Ann, a member of the Mosley family, considered the rites at the Collegiate Church to be too 'high' and so she commissioned the building of a church to provide her with an alternative. The dedication to St. Ann (whether intentionally or otherwise) is ambiguous. Does it commemorate the saint, Queen Anne, who was monarch at the time, or Lady Ann herself?

The church, which was constructed of red sandstone, originally had a three tier cupola surmounting its tower as shown in the print above. This was removed in 1777 and replaced with a spire, which itself was removed around 1800, leaving the plain tower which we see today.

The land on which St Ann's was built formed part of Acres Field, as discussed earlier. This is believed to have been the site of the churchyard of the pre-Conquest Church of St. Mary and large quantities of human remains, believed to have come from the old churchyard, were discovered

at a depth of about six feet during the digging of the foundations of the new church.[1]

St. Ann's was consecrated by the Bishop of Chester on 17 June 1712 and immediately attracted a fashionable congregation who leaned towards the Whigs in their political affiliation. The church was surrounded by a modest, and in time well-filled, burial ground. Around 600 individual graves surrounded the church on all four sides, each grave covered by a flat ledger stone. A few of the graves were marked by more impressive chest tombs.

Fashionable it might have been, but a century after its founding the churchyard was in a poor state. Writing in 1816, Joseph Aston described the churchyard as '...filthy and disgraceful.'[2] Shortly after this, it was given a facelift:

> 'The gravestones were crumbling and the epitaphs fast becoming obliterated by the feet of passers-by. Rails were erected at an average distance of six feet from the

walls and the graves outside the boundary were covered with soil and flags. [3]

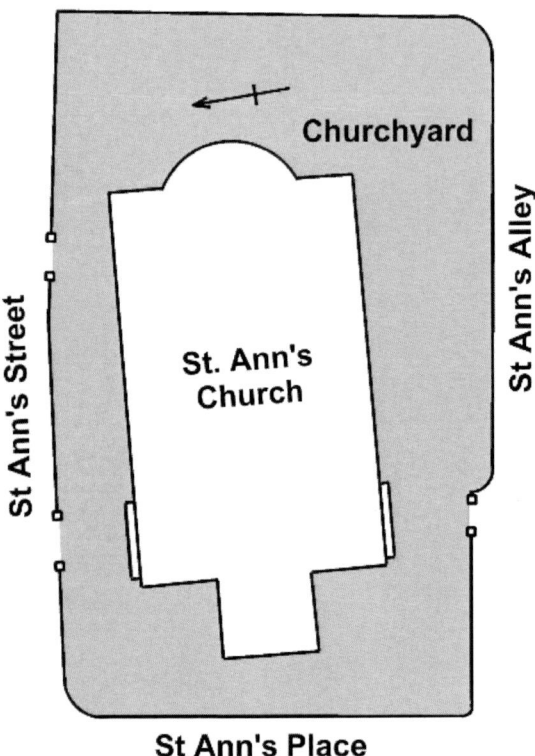

Churchyard

St Ann's Street

St Ann's Alley

St. Ann's Church

St Ann's Place

Judging by the graveyard plan, Aston's description places the considerable majority of the graves well outside the new railings. It is not clear whether the gravestones outside the railings were removed at this time.

In November 1842 a strip amounting to some 150 square yards in area was taken over by the Corporation to allow St. Ann's Street to be widened. The graves were left *in situ* and the churchyard remained otherwise little changed until 1892, when the railings were removed. At the same time the gravestones were lifted, lowered by about twelve inches, covered with soil and the whole churchyard area paved over to leave St Ann's Square looking much as it does

today. The graves themselves were not disturbed and occasionally bones are uncovered when it is necessary to install underground services.

St. Ann's is one of the few Manchester churchyards where any of the original gravestones have been preserved. Eleven of the old gravestones have been leaned up against the church wall and seven of the chest tombs have also been preserved, though they have almost certainly moved from their original locations.

Among these few surviving gravestones are those of the first two Rectors of St. Ann's and one which bears the names of members of the family of Thomas de Quincey. The '*Opium Eater*' himself is absent. He was buried in St. Cuthbert's Kirkyard in Edinburgh.

The graveyard remained open for burials until it was closed following the Burial Acts in 1854. In its early years burials in St. Ann's churchyard were recorded in the Collegiate Church registers and some, if not all of the burial register entries, are specifically identified as relating to burials which took place in St. Ann's churchyard. From 1737 onwards the church maintained its own registers and these record 6,335 burials. Given that this substantial number of burials was accommodated in only around 600 separate graves, it seems inevitable that the available space was somewhat overcrowded.

St. Ann is the only one of the Anglican churches in the city centre (aside from the Cathedral) which has survived to the present day. There was a serious proposal in the 1870s that this attractive and historic church should be demolished but wiser opinions prevailed and the idea thankfully did not proceed.[4] In 1890 its future was once more in question when the parish had to make a choice between demolishing either St. Ann's or St. Mary's.[5] Fortunately, they chose the latter – itself perhaps a sad loss, but historically and architecturally by far the less important of the two.

St Ann's Church. This illustration by H. E. Tidmarsh shows the church as it would have looked before the removal of the railings in 1892.

*Some of the Remaining Gravestones and Chest Tombs
Outside St. Ann's*

St. Mary, Parsonage

St. Mary's Church

A new church dedicated to St. Mary was consecrated 29 September 1756. It has been suggested that St. Mary's was founded specifically to attract the congregation away from St. Ann's and initially it *'...enjoyed the patronage of the gentry'*. St. Mary's was located between Deansgate and the River Irwell to the rear of the present House of Fraser (formerly Kendall's) department store. Joseph Aston described it as *'...a pattern of decorum and neatness...'*[6] and when Aston wrote this in 1816, it was probably a fair description. However, the middle class congregation drifted away and the area declined, leaving St. Mary's ministering to a considerably impoverished flock.

The burial ground surrounding the church consisted of regularly spaced graves, each covered with a large flat ledger stone. The churchyard was therefore effectively a large paved yard.

It may be that despite Aston's description, the problems were already beginning to show, since in 1818 the rector and churchwardens of St. Mary's found it necessary to place a notice in the Manchester Mercury addressed to grave owners. The churchwardens complained that the owners of several graves had failed to cover them with a gravestone and that if this was not carried out by 29 September, the graves would be forfeited and resold. The notice does not explain what might become of any bodies already buried in the grave in the event of such a forfeit.[7]

The illustration shows St. Mary's as it would have looked before 6 December 1822, when the ball and cross at the top of the spire were blown horizontal. They remained in this precarious state until they were removed the following May by the intrepid Francis Wootton of Nottingham and his son, who ascended the spire using a flight of eight ladders and lowered the ball and cross 230 feet to the ground.[8] The spire itself proved to be unstable and by 1854 had started to lean. It was removed down to the base of the lantern, giving the church, once described as *'universally admired for its elegance and fine proportions'* a very unbalanced look.[9]

St. Mary's closed on 4 October 1890 but remained empty and decaying for nearly forty years, until it was finally demolished in 1928. The memorials were cleared and the site levelled but the human remains were left in place. Today St. Mary's churchyard is a public garden. There is nothing there to inform the public about its former use but the noticeably raised ground level of the garden above the surrounding street provides a clue.

St. John, Deansgate

St. John, Deansgate

The Church of St. John was founded by Edward Byrom as a memorial to his father John. Edward obtained an Act of Parliament in 1768 to build a new church on land between Higher and Lower Byrom Streets off Quay Street to *'provide for the spiritual wants of the genteel residents who had migrated to the south sides of the town'*. The foundation stone was laid on 28 April that same year by the Bishop of Chester and the finished church was consecrated on 7 June 1769.[10] In 1815 St. John's was described glowingly:

'This church is very well attended and its congregation is comprised of persons of the first respectability in the town and neighbourhood.'[11]

Joseph Aston wrote in 1816 that :

'The church yard is very extensive and offering a strong lesson in mortality by being entirely covered in grave-stones, in so short a period as hath elapsed since it was opened for the reception of the first corpse'.

There were also several burial vaults beneath the church. These were owned by the Peel, Bazley and Byrom families amongst others.

St. John's was described as *'...the principal burying place of Manchester'* around the end of the eighteenth century. We may take it that the word *'principal'* relates more to its appeal to the middle classes than to the number of burials, which, although numerous, barely exceeded in any year one third the number at the Collegiate Church.

A Peterloo Veteran

The burials in St. John's churchyard include many locally notable names. Thomas Ashworth, who was buried on 20 August 1819, was sabred and trampled to death during the Peterloo massacre. He was the proprietor of the Bull's Head tavern on Market Street. Thirty-five year old Ashworth was serving as a special constable on the day and so was, nominally at least, on the same side of the law as the yeomanry who carried out the massacre.

The Founder of Owens College

John Owens (not to be confused with the anti-quary John Owen), a successful cotton merchant but also a modest and retiring man, died on 29 July 1846 and was buried at St. John's three days later. Owens, a bachelor, left £96,654 in his will for the founding of a college which would not place any religious requirement upon the admission of students (universities at this time required their students to adhere to the Anglican faith). Owens' College opened in 1851 and in 1880 received a royal charter to become Victoria University of Manchester. It merged with the University of Manchester Institute of Science and Technology (UMIST) in 2004 and the whole is now known simply as the University of Manchester.

THE MANCHESTER OPHELIA

Twenty year old Lavinia, the daughter of a wire-worker, William Robinson was engaged to a surgeon named Holroyd (or Oldroyd), a man-mid-wife at the Lying-in Hospital. On the night of 16 December 1813 Lavinia disappeared following a rumoured 'lover's tiff' with her fiancé. Despite extensive searches no trace of her could be found. A month later, she was still missing and rewards to the value of £100 were offered for information concerning her whereabouts but none was forthcoming.

The winter of 1813 was particularly severe. The River Irwell had frozen over and remained frozen until on 7 February the next year Lavinia's body was found by a Mr. Goodier of Eccles, who owned a mill near Mode Wheel. The frozen river had thawed and had revealed Lavinia's body, which had been perfectly preserved in the ice.

Because of the nature of her reappearance, Lavinia soon acquired the soubriquet 'The Manchester Ophelia'. She was buried in her family's grave at St. John's on 8 February 1814. Hundreds of people attended the funeral.[12]

Some of the witnesses at the subsequent inquest said that they had seen a couple, believed to be Holroyd and Lavinia, arguing violently. Some claimed to have seen the man strike the woman but there was insufficient evidence for the coroner to record anything other than an open verdict. While there were suspicions of foul play, there is a more plausible argument that Lavinia took her own life.

The family's advertisements offering the reward mention the discovery of a note in her handwriting '...from which' says the advertisement 'there is reason to fear she is not living'. The note strongly suggests that Lavinia committed suicide. It read: 'With my dying breath I attest myself innocent of the crime laid to my charge! Adieu! God bless you all! I cannot outlive his suspicion!'

There have been a number of interpretations of the 'crime' to which she refers but these gener-ally centre on rumours that she had been unfaithful to Holroyd. A somewhat dramatised account, which appears in 'The Dark River' by Cyril Bracegirdle, suggests that she had been accused by Holroyd of a continued association with a former boyfriend.

Although no charges were laid against Holroyd, there were many who thought him guilty either of her murder or of making unfounded allegations concerning her chastity, which had driven her to take her own life. Holroyd's house in Bridge Street was attacked by mobs on a number of occasions until the continuing demonstrations finally forced him to leave town. One newspaper account suggested that he had committed suicide at Wolverhampton some months later[13] but there were also reports that he had subsequently established a practice as a surgeon in his native village of Middlestown near Wakefield in Yorkshire.[14]

THE WILY FRENCHMAN

One final burial which is deserving of mention is that of sixty-seven year old Thomas Raspo of Withington, who was, buried at St. John's on 23 January 1824. Raspo (possibly an anglicisation of Raspeau) was a Frenchman of whom it was said, '... [he] was clever enough to keep a wife and a concubine in the same house'.[15] Unfortunately, I have been unable to discover any further details of his unusual domestic arrangements. His (presumably long-suffering) wife, Alice, joined him in his grave three years later. Raspo had clearly lived in Manchester for some time, since his name appears as a Juror in the Court Leet records for 1798.

FAILING FORTUNES

The fortunes of the area surrounding St. John's declined. The 'genteel' population gradually moved away to be replaced by one of a more working class character.

In 1827 a correspondent, who used the pen name 'Orthodox', wrote to the Manchester Courier to express concern about the state of the

The St. John's Memorial Cross

churchyard, which he said was *'desecrated by the rude and wanton sports of heedless children' and 'in the dark shadows of the night ... [was] the resort of vagabonds and idle dissolute persons'*.

Eventually, even the working class drifted away. The area became increasingly dominated by commercial premises and the church was left with a much reduced congregation.

AFTER THE BURIAL ACTS

St. John's was one of the few city burial grounds which were not closed under the Burial Acts in 1854. Restrictions were imposed on future interments but in the case of St. John's these were not particularly severe. Bodies could still be buried in existing family graves and it was permitted to open new graves, provided no more than a single body was buried in in each.

Since the orders issued under the Burial Acts had required most of the city burial grounds to discontinue burials completely, St. John's experienced an upsurge in popularity as a burial place. The number of burials doubled from just over one hundred in 1856 to over two hundred in 1857. Numbers exceeded three hundred in each of the next ten years, reaching a peak of five hundred in 1865. Following the opening of Philips Park municipal cemetery in 1867, numbers began to decline once again and after Southern Cemetery opened in 1879 they fell to well under ten a year. The fifty-two people buried in the last two decades were possibly the few surviving grave owners or their relatives. Very few of them had local addresses and some came from as far afield as Wilmslow and Oldham. One gave an address in Gloucestershire and another Boulogne in France.

The last person to be interred at St. John's was sixty-five year old Ellen Holt, who was buried on 10 March 1900. Shortly after Ellen's burial, the Secretary of State issued an Order in Council which prohibited any further burials. St. John's Church was by now little used and eventually, in 1928, the church was closed. The building was demolished in 1931 but the graves and vaults were left *in situ*. The site is now a public garden. At the centre of the garden is a memorial stone which commemorates the former church and bears the words *'...around lie the remains of more than 22,000 people.'* This number is somewhat shy of the mark since the burial registers record in excess of 24,000 burials.

It is unclear whether, when the gardens were created, the memorials were simply covered over with soil or whether they were removed entirely. Only the gravestone of John Owens remains visible in one corner of the former graveyard.

St. James, George Street

St. James's, George Street

Consecrated on 18 August 1788, the Church of St. James, a fairly plain building, stood on a site at the junction of George Street and Charlotte Street. The church was built by the Reverend Cornelius Bayley and funded by the sale of rents for the pews. At the time of building, the area was wholly residential with prosperous residents who *could afford the whim for an eloquent preacher in their midst.*[16]

St. James's was surrounded by a churchyard of which Aston said in 1816 *...in the space of sixteen years the yard was covered with gravestones....*[17]

THE VAULTS

Although the graveyard was small there were extensive vaults under the church. Aston gives us an evocative description:

'Underneath the church are vaults for the reception of the dead. They are separated by regular aisles, from which the coffins (which are all prudently lined with lead) are exposed to the eyes of visitors of this awful mansion. Many of the vaults are guarded by iron grates, which are locked; a measure which will probably be carried through the whole.[18]

The provision of burial vaults implies that St. James had a congregation possessing sufficient wealth to afford both the cost of the vault and of the expensive coffin in which to be interred. It was usual to use a lead-lined coffins for interment in vaults. This would consist of a relatively plain inner coffin enclosed in a lead casing and then, on the outside, a decorative shell either of finely finished hardwood or of plain timber covered with velvet. When the Duke of Wellington was buried at St. Paul's Cathedral in London in 1852, his body was encased in no fewer than four coffins. These consisted of an inner coffin of pine which was then cased in lead and placed in an oak coffin. The whole was then cased in an outer decorative coffin of Spanish mahogany[19]. Four layers is exceptional but a three layer coffin would have been the norm for the fashionable congregation which St. James's attracted in its heyday. We are told that:

'The coffins are of enormous size, owing to the then prevailing custom of burying in these [lead-lined] coffins. The largest of them contains the remains of Joseph Nadin, constable of Manchester at the time of Peterloo. A staff of office said to have belonged to this redoubtable man, is still preserved in the church. Many other men, prominent in the Manchester of the past, also lie within the vaults or churchyard of St. James's Church.'[20]

Nadin was six foot four inches tall and broad in proportion. His coffin was said to measure between seven and eight feet in length, 3 feet in width and two feet in height.

Another of those buried in the vaults was the founder of St. James's, the Reverend Cornelius Bayley himself, following his death on 2 April 1812. It is said that his widow would take her knitting and sit in the vault where her late husband was interred.[21]

Burials in the churchyard and interments in the vaults were completely prohibited in 1854 by the Orders in Council issued under the Burial Acts.

DECLINE

The fashionable congregation did not remain. As the wealthier citizens moved out of the city attendance declined and the church moved down market. In 1887, almost one hundred years after its founding, the financial state of the church was so parlous that the churchwardens were forced to make a public appeal for funds to re-build the wall around the churchyard, a part of which had recently collapsed and the remainder of which they described as *'in a rotten condition'*. The reason for the appeal is explicit: *'The parish is exceedingly poor ... it is utterly impossible for us to provide for an exceptional expenditure of £120 net.'*[22] In 1907 the parishioners were described as poor, though not paupers. An estimated 1,050 people inhabited just 98 houses. There were very few young people.[23]

CLOSURE AND CLEARANCE

The final service was held at St. James on 21 October 1928. The vaults were cleared in the late summer of 1930 and the coffins, numbering somewhere between 250 and 300, were taken at night over a period of several weeks to be reburied at Southern Cemetery.[24] The work was contracted to Thomas Maiden of Lime Kiln Works, Ardwick, who was to be paid £2-10-0 for the removal of each body in a suitable wooden case.[25] The church was demolished and despite public pressure to turn the churchyard into a

garden, a garage was built on the site of the church and the churchyard and its occupants concreted over. From 1939 it was used as a car park.

The site was subsequently acquired by the St. James's Club. The social club, which continues to the present day, was formed in 1962 through the amalgamation of the Union Club (which was founded in 1825) and the Clarendon Club (which was founded 1868 and was itself a descendant of the Union Club dating from 1837). The amalgamated clubs took their new name from the former church. The club built St. James's House where the church had once stood. The building opened in 1964 and the club occupied several floors of the building until finally moving out in 2001.[26]

The development of the site, which also involved widening of Charlotte Street, required the graveyard to be cleared. The remains were removed to Southern Cemetery as before. Contemporary newspaper accounts referred to clearance of the graves of *'more than three thousand people'*[27] but this would appear to be something of an over-statement since only 2,932 burials are recorded in the registers, including the 250-300 previously removed from the vaults.

A plaque was attached to the boundary wall to commemorate the church which previously stood on the site. This appears to have been removed during refurbishment in 2003 and has not been replaced.

The St. James House Plaque

St. Michael, Angel Meadow

Angel Meadow & St. Michael's Church circa 1894

St. Michael's Church was built by Humphrey Owen and consecrated on 23 July 1789. It possessed its own burial ground, separate to the parochial 'New Burial Ground' (see page 27) which it adjoined and which surrounded the church. This was initially a quite popular burial place with around one hundred burials taking place annually.

At the time St. Michael's was built, Angel Meadow lived up to its appealing name and the church attracted a prosperous congregation. However, the area declined rapidly and by the early 19th century it was being increasingly taken over by poor families, including an increasing number of Irish immigrants. This population grew significantly following the Irish potato famine. The journalist Angus Bethune Reach wrote in 1849:

> *'The lowest, most filthy, most unhealthy and most wicked locality in Manchester is called, singularly enough, 'Angel-meadow.' It is full of cellars and inhabited by prostitutes, their bullies, thieves, cadgers, vagrants, tramps and, in the very worst sties of filth and darkness, by those unhappy wretches the 'low Irish.'[28]*

The move down market was reflected in the burial register, which by 1836 shows that the number of burials each year had fallen to as few as ten. The local population were now too poor to

60

find the price of a private grave at St. Michael's and an increasing number of those who died locally would have been buried in common graves in the parochial burial ground.

Then from 1838 onwards, the number of burials suddenly increased once more. This did not signal any improvement in the area's fortunes. Far from it, the area continued to decline. The increase came about because the churchwardens had acknowledged reality. The explanation appeared in the Manchester Courier:

> *'St. Michael's Burying Ground. We see by an advertisement in our paper that the large burial ground attached to St. Michael's Church is now made free. We understand that the churchwardens, with the assent of the incumbent, have adopted this measure, in order to offer to the poor the means of procuring a decent burial place for their relatives at a very low charge, without compelling them to purchase a grave, which is generally beyond their means.'*[29]

The change was immediately effective in increasing the number of burials which rose from 33 in 1838 to 88 in 1847.

In the following year, 1848, these numbers more than doubled, but the source of the new business was far from local. On 1 March 1848 47 year old Mary Sharrocks was buried, her residence recorded as '*Salford Workhouse*'. Mary was the first of 186 Salford Workhouse inmates who would be buried at St. Michael's over the following eighteen months.

Salford, like Manchester was faced with the problem of where to bury its poor following the final closure of the Walkers Croft parochial burial ground in February 1848. While the Manchester Poor Law Guardians had established a contract with Manchester General Cemetery for the burial of their deceased inmates, this does not seem to have included those who died in the Salford Workhouse and it appears that the Salford Guardians established their own arrangement

with the churchwardens of St. Michael's. It was not only Salford's Workhouse inmates who benefited from the arrangement. A further 129 burials are recorded with Salford addresses, presumably either those who paid their own fees or those who were not inmates of the workhouse, but for whom fees were paid by the Salford Guardians.

The fee which St. Michael's charged the Salford Guardians was astonishingly low, between two shillings and sixpence and three shillings against the four shilling fee for burial at Manchester General Cemetery. Such a low fee suggests that not only were large common graves being used, but that corners were being cut. This is borne out in a memorandum which the Manchester churchwardens addressed to the General Board of Health at Westminster. The churchwardens referred to an arrangement:

> '...made by the officiating clergy of the parish church, with the incumbent of St. Michael's Church … for the interment, in the yard belonging to the said church, of all corpses application for the burial of which is made at the parish church.'

This suggests that the clergy had become aware of the attractive deal secured by Salford and wished to achieve some savings through a similar arrangement. The churchwardens went on to set out their objection to the proposal, primarily:

> 'That your memorialists having been informed that several burials have recently taken place in Saint Michael's Churchyard on or very near to the surface so that earth had to be brought to the place in order to cover the coffins, have caused an investigation to be made, the result of which is that they find their information was correct, and there are coffins now in the said churchyard covered with only about fourteen inches of soil on the top and less than six inches of soil at the sides; a state of affairs which your memorialists consider

as well indecent as fraught with serious and prejudicial consequences to the health of the neighbourhood.'30

The churchwardens conclude by requesting that the Board of Health investigate and also that they should exercise such powers as they are able towards hastening the procurement of a new parish burial ground. In subsequent correspondence exchanged between the churchwardens and Canon Clifton, it becomes clear that in addition to genuine concerns about public health, the memorandum is another shot in the running battle between the canons and churchwardens concerning the choice of location for a new parish burial ground.

The churchwardens' memorandum did, however, achieve some results. The first result was that the last burial from Salford Workhouse took place on 7 November. It appears from the register of Manchester General Cemetery that Salford Workhouse had transferred its business to their somewhat better managed, if more expensive, cemetery. The second result took a little longer. The first burials from Manchester Workhouse had

taken place about a week before the churchwardens had issued their memorandum and about a dozen in all were buried at St. Michael's. I have found no record of action by the Board of Health and it may simply be the case that the canons recognised the unsatisfactory state of the St. Michael's churchyard and ceased to commission burials there.

The final burial at St. Michael's was that of 79 year old Anne Williams of Manchester on 18 June 1854. Shortly afterwards further burials were prohibited by Order in Council issued under the Burial Acts. By the time of its closure, around 3,800 burials had been recorded in the registers.

The church remained open until 1930 but it was finally demolished in 1935. The site of the church, churchyard and the adjoining parochial burial ground has in recent years been merged with the adjoining Angel Meadow parish burial ground and landscaped as a public park (see page 27). The remains have been left in situ and a small number of gravestones have been retained as a feature to remind visitors that a church and churchyard once occupied the site.

A Pretended Sexton

The following article appeared in the Manchester Courier and Lancashire Weekly Advertiser on Saturday, 30 June 1827.

On Friday the 22d instant, the body of a new-born male infant was found in a box in Love Lane, Ancoats. On the following day an inquest took place before J. Milne Esq., When it appeared by the testimony of a midwife, that she had delivered a woman on the preceding Sunday, of a dead child, which was put into a box, and given to two women together with a certificate from the midwife, with directions to take it to the sexton of St. George's church and pay him a shilling for its interment. The women, however, to save time, took it to

Every Street chapel, close by Ancoats Hall, when a man at the gate having guessed their errand said "Give it to me, I will do the business." The women supposing him to be the sexton gave him the box, the note and the shilling, and then departed. On the following morning, a boy found the box in the place above-mentioned, and on enquiry it was ascertained that the man to whom the women gave the box had nothing to do with the chapel. The jury having heard these particulars, and the statement of Mr. Ollier, the surgeon who examined the body, found a verdict that the child was still-born.

St. Peter, Mosley Street

St. Peter's Church circa 1816

The Church of St. Peter was Manchester's only church in the classical style. It was designed by James Wyatt and built on what was at the time a field on the outskirts of the town. The foundation stone was laid on 11 December 1788 but the church was not consecrated until 6 September 1795. In 1818 a tower was added but this was somewhat out of sympathy with Wyatt's original design. As Manchester expanded, St. Peter's came to command an imposing position at the southern end of Mosley Street.

The compact site was almost entirely filled by the building itself and offered no space in which to create a burial ground so extensive burial vaults were created under the church. These became the last resting place for many of Manchester's gentry.

Only 213 burials are recorded in the registers and this small number is probably because the cost of purchasing a vault, together with the further cost of a lead-lined coffin, would have limited access to all but those from the more prosperous families.

HUGH HORNBY BIRLEY

Arguably the most famous (or infamous) of those interred at St. Peters was Hugh Hornby Birley (1778-1845). Birley was a member of the Royal Manchester Institution, which later became the Manchester Art Gallery, and a principal figure in the founding of Owens' College, later to become Manchester University. He is better known, however, as the man who led the charge of the Manchester and Salford Yeomanry at the Peterloo Massacre in 1819. His body was interred on 8 August 1845 in the family vault alongside his wife Cicely, who had died two years earlier, and three year old son Edward Hornby Birley, who died in 1839. There is some irony in his being interred close to the site of what many would consider the scene of his greatest crime.

CLOSURE AND DEMOLITION

Further interments in the vaults were prohibited by the Orders in Council published on 15 April 1854. Around this same time a rumour began to circulate that the Corporation was considering demolishing the church, which undoubtedly presented an obstruction to the increasing flow of traffic at the bottom of Mosley Street. The rumour provoked a flurry of letters to the Manchester Courier, all of which roundly condemned the proposal. Whether the rumour was unfounded or whether the Corporation recognised the scale of potential protest and backed away from the idea, there was no further discussion of demolition and St. Peter's survived for another half-century.

However, like so many of its contemporaries, St. Peter's fell victim to falling attendances in the second half of the nineteenth century and the church finally closed in 1906. The building and site were purchased by Manchester Corporation for the sum of £20,000. The Corporation planned, as had been rumoured half a century earlier, to demolish the church and to widen Mosley Street. They agreed that the site of the church would remain undeveloped and that it would be permanently preserved as a public open space. As a further condition of the purchase, the Corporation agreed not to disturb the remains of those who had been buried there over the preceding 120 years. One final stipulation was that the sum of £500 should be spent on the erection of a cross or other memorial to keep alive the memory of the former church.

The church was subsequently demolished. The memorials in the vaults were recorded and the vaults were sealed and concreted over. A cross was erected at the centre of the site bearing the inscription:

'This cross was erected AD 1908 to record the place where the Church of Saint Peter stood from AD 1794 to 1907'.

The cross remains in place to the present day.

St. Peter's Memorial Cross

THE CENOTAPH

Following the end of the Great War, the site was chosen as the location for Manchester's Cenotaph. This was designed by Sir Edwin Lutyens and erected in 1924 approximately over where the altar of the church would once have stood.

At the time of writing there are proposals to relocate the cenotaph as part of a major redevelopment of St. Peter's Square. The projected new layout will not require the vaults to be disturbed and the memorial cross will remain in place. The plans also involve the removal of the Metrolink platforms which lie along the old church boundary. Once this work has been completed, the memorial cross will be at the centre of a more open and pedestrian friendly St. Peter's Square.

St. George, Oldham Road

St. George's differs from Manchester's other eighteenth and nineteenth century Anglican churches in that it was not originally built for the Church of England. The church was apparently built as a speculative venture and remained uncompleted for several years. The foundation stone was laid on Wednesday 21 April 1790 by the Reverend Samuel Nugent.[31]

From 1798 it was used by the Countess of Huntingdon's Connexion, a group which had seceded from the Church of England in 1781. They did not, however, remain long and in 1817 the trustees put the church up for sale[32]. St. George's was sold by auction at the Bridgewater Arms on the 8th October for the price of £2,550. The purchasers were the Warden and Fellows of the Collegiate Church. It was consecrated for Anglican worship on 17 January 1818 by the Bishop of Chester[33], but operated as a 'Free' Church, outside diocesan or parish control. From the outset it was in a poor district.

TURBULENCE AND UPROAR

Joseph Aston wrote of St. George's Church in 1816: *'It has a burial place which has not yet been inclosed'*[34]. The absence of a boundary wall or railing was becoming the cause of some concern and the matter was raised in an article in the Manchester Courier in April 1827. The article described how *'carts and carriages of every description[are] daily driven over it'* and complained about the *'scenes of turbulence and uproar frequently enacted within its precincts particularly on the Sabbath'*. The people of the neighbourhood were described as *'too poor to do much themselves by way of inclosing it'*[35]. A meeting was convened in the vestry some weeks later at which it was resolved to remedy the situation. A public subscription was raised; the Bishop of Chester opening the list with a donation of £10.[36] The necessary funds were soon raised and the work was completed later that year.

Conditions in the churchyard were said to have shown *'a visible improvement'* the following year.[37]

THE REGISTERS

The registers tell us that burials commenced in 1798 and continued until the graveyard was closed by Order in Council of 15 March 1854. Up to the time of its adoption by the Church of England in 1818, some 989 burials had been recorded. A further 260 followed between 1818 and the time of its closure

St. George's attracted burials not only from its local area, but also from surprisingly far afield, with a number of the register entries showing residences at Salford, Chorlton, Miles Platting, Harpurhey and in one case Ashton-under-Lyne.

The entries are otherwise unremarkable, except perhaps for the burial of the unfortunate 28 year old Priscilla Sedgley on 15 September 1819, whose register entry is annotated *'killed by a fall from a window'*.

THE END OF ST. GEORGE'S

In the 1870s the church, which seems to have been becoming something of a maintenance liability, was sold to the Lancashire and Yorkshire Railway Company for £5,000. The proceeds were put towards the purchase of land nearby where a new St. George's was erected. This opened for worship in 1877[38].

Old St. George's was demolished and the railway company's goods yards laid out over the site. There is no record of the human remains being removed and it is assumed that the rails were laid directly over the graves, much as they had been at Walkers Croft. The area has since been redeveloped once more and the site of the graveyard is now under a car park and roadway area behind Royal Mail's Manchester Mail Centre. It is believed that the human remains still rest under the tarmac.

St. Matthew, Campfield

St. Matthew, Campfield

St. Matthew's Church was built between 1823 and 1825 on a site bounded by Liverpool Road and Tonman Street. It was designed by the architect Charles Barry, renowned for his later design for the present Houses of Parliament. The church was consecrated on 24 September 1825 by Dr. Blomfield, the Bishop of Chester[39].

THE BURIAL VAULTS

The churchyard was not used for burials but there were extensive vaults under the church which provided space for as many as a thousand coffins.[40] They saw little use. From the first interment in 1828 up to 15 April 1854, when the vaults were closed by an order under the Burial Acts, a mere thirty nine coffins had been deposited.

The churchwardens of St. Matthew petitioned the Home Office that exceptions should be made to the order so as to permit the burials of Thomas Mann, Robert Smith and the Reverend Canon Bently and their respective wives when the occasion arose. This dispensation was granted in 1863. Elizabeth Smith was subsequently interred in 1866 and her husband six years later. Thomas Mann and his wife appear to have been buried elsewhere.

Five of the interments relate to Thomas Rothwell Bently, who served as minister of St. Matthew from 1840 up to the time of his death and his family. The first of the family to be placed in their family vault under the chancel of the church was Elizabeth (nee Middleton), Bently's first wife whom he had married at the Collegiate Church in 1837. She died in November 1840 aged 42. She was followed in 1850 and 1854 respectively by Bently's four year old son and five month old daughter by his second wife, Elizabeth (nee Bently and possibly a cousin) whom he had married in 1851. Thomas himself died in 1884 aged 78 followed by Elizabeth in 1899 aged 83. Both were laid to rest in the vaults, Elizabeth being the last person to be interred at St. Matthews.

THE END OF ST. MATTHEWS

St. Matthew's Church closed before World War 2 but during the war was used as a factory for making barrage balloons. It was later used as a storage depot. The building became badly dilapidated and the decision was taken in 1950 that it should be demolished. There was some opposition to the loss of such a fine building and suggestions that Barry's impressive 186 foot spire should at least be preserved. These appeals were rejected and the church, including the spire, was demolished in April 1952[41]. Subsequently a depressingly banal office building has been erected on the site.

St. Andrew, Ancoats

St. Andrew, Ancoats circa 1894

St. Andrew's once stood on the south side of Travis Street in Ancoats It was built in 1830-31 on land which was once part of a large field owned by John and James Entwisle[42]. The site was at the edge of the town and largely surrounded by undeveloped green fields which extended south from the church to the banks of the River Medlock. St. Andrew's was built at a cost of £13,000 and was consecrated on 6 October 1831.

The new church was large, capable of seating some 2,000 worshippers. It opened with a relatively prosperous congregation, but this was not to last for long. Within twenty years the once green fields had disappeared under mills and terraced housing for those who worked in them.

St. Andrew's would soon serve one of Manchester's poorest communities.[43]

THE CHURCHYARD

The church was surrounded by a modest churchyard. A total of 1,080 burials were recorded in the burial registers between the first interment which took place, just a week after consecration, on 14 October 1831 and the final burial on 1 April 1855.

THE VAULTS

The first two entries in the burial register record the interments of James Kennedy and Sophia Kennedy. These register entries are unusual in that they are undated. The incumbent minister, Reverend Dugard, helpfully explains that the bodies had been removed from the burial ground at St. Luke's, Chorlton Row and reinterred at St. Andrews. A marginal note in the register tells us that they were interred *'in vault'*.

St. Luke's registers tell us that Sophia was the nineteen month old daughter of James and Jane Kennedy and that she had been buried at St. Luke's on 28 March 1829. Fifty-five year old James (titled *'Esquire'* in the register), the father of Sophia, had been buried a month after his daughter on 22 April. Both bodies were removed from St. Luke's on 12 October 1831 on the instructions of James Kennedy, the son of the deceased James.

The third register entry, dated 14 October 1831, refers to eleven year old Janet Anne Crichton Kennedy. Unusually for the interment of a child, her parents were not named, but she may have been the sister of Sophia and so another daughter of James and Jane. This register entry is also annotated as *'in vault'*. The timing suggests that it was Janet Kennedy's death which precipitated the decision to remove the bodies of Sophia and James from St. Luke's to St. Andrew's.

The Kennedy family in question appear to have been the owners of the Great Ancoats

Street cotton mill. St. Andrew's in 1831 probably appeared to James Kennedy to be the ideal place to establish a family vault, certainly sufficiently attractive to warrant going to the trouble of exhuming the bodies of his father and sister so that they could be interred there. The appeal of St. Andrew's did not last, for Janet was the last of the Kennedys to be buried there.

I have found nothing to indicate the extent of the vaults under St. Andrew's. Only three other register entries specifically mention the vaults, the interments of Mary Louisa Hall in 1836, Thomas Bainbridge in 1847 and Mary Ann Cameron of Liverpool the following year.

AN UNUSUAL BURIAL

On 29 October 1854 Mary Sullivan, aged 37 and from 2 Scholes Square, was buried at St. Andrew's. A note against the register entry says: *'Interred without service by the friends of the deceased as belonging to the communion of the Church of Rome'*. The date is significant. Most of the other Catholic burial grounds in the city had been closed or severely restricted some months earlier under the Burial Acts. There are no other such burials and the reason why Mary's burial was permitted is not known. It would have been somewhat irregular for a burial to be permitted in Anglican consecrated ground without reading of the burial service.

CLOSURE AND DEMOLITION

An Order in Council published on 15 April 1854 required the closure of the vaults and graveyard but an appeal delayed closure for a further year, when closure with effect from 1 June 1855 was demanded. The last burial took place on 1 April of that year. Over the next century the area continued to decline. Post-war slum clearance left the church without a congregation and so St. Andrew's was closed in 1958. The building was demolished in June 1961.

The workmen demolishing St. Andrew's received something of a surprise. After working on the building for about six weeks, Mike Gallagher, the foreman, was demolishing the altar when he unearthed the top of a six inch thick wall just below ground level. Knocking down part of the wall he discovered a fifteen foot deep vault under the floor of the church. Inside the vault were four well preserved lead coffins. One of these was identified by a plate as that of Mary Ann Cameron. The others were of Mary Louisa Hall who was buried in 1836 aged 26, Samuel Moor who died 1855 aged 79 and Louisa Moor who also died in 1855 aged 80[44].

The workmen do not appear to have found the coffins of the three Kennedys or that of Thomas Bainbridge and so possibly there was more than one vault. Only one vault seems to have been been discovered, however. The newspaper reports do not say what became of the coffins so possibly they were left in the vault.

All but one of those whose coffins were discovered appear in the burial register. The exception is Samuel Moor. Samuel's coffin plate gives a date of death of 25 September 1855 by which time no further interments were permitted. One must assume that the minister turned a blind eye so that Samuel could lie beside his late wife Louisa so wisely omitted the interment from his register.

The churchyard survived until 1967 when the memorials were removed.[45] The graves were not, however, disturbed and the graveyard was levelled and sealed under a concrete raft.

ST. ANDREW'S TODAY

The site where St. Andrew's Church once stood was marked with a stone standing cross, which was the memorial to parishioners killed in the Great War. The cross was still *in situ* in 2004, when it was photographed[46] but it has subsequently been removed. The site is currently somewhat unkempt and used as a car park. Some surviving parts of the old churchyard wall are all that remain, at least for the present. St. Andrew's Square, which surrounds the site, may provide a more lasting reminder of this once fashionable church.

Notes for Church of England Burial Grounds

1. History of the Foundations in Manchester of Christ's College, Volume 1, S. Hibbert and others, 1830.
2. A Picture of Manchester, Joseph Aston, 1816.
3. The Story of St. Ann's Church, Manchester, Rev. Eric Saxon, (undated).
4. It was the threat of demolition which moved Charles Wareing E. Bardsley to record the history of St. Ann's in his book 'Memorials of St. Ann's Church, Manchester, in the Last Century' which he published in 1877.
5. Manchester Courier & Lancashire General Advertiser, Thursday 5 June 1890.
6. A Picture of Manchester, Joseph Aston, 1816.
7. Manchester Mercury, Tuesday 11 July 1818. The requirement upon grave owners to install a stone over their family grave appears to have been common to a number of burial grounds.
8. Manchester Iris Saturday, May 17 1823. This contains a lengthy and detailed description of the removal of the ball and cross and an engraving of the work in progress.
9. Manchester Faces & Places Vol. 1 page 163.
10. Memorials of a Manchester Parish Church (St. John's, Deansgate), Papers of the Manchester Literary Club Vol 5, 1879.
11. Leech's New Manchester Guide, 1815.
12. Discovering Manchester, Barry Worthington, 2002. The disappearance and discovery of Lavinia Robinson was so memorable that thirteen years later it was used in a case at Salford Easter Sessions to specify the approximate time when the defendant had entered into employment (see Manchester Courier & Lancashire General Advertiser, Saturday 5 May 1827).
13. Sussex Advertiser, Monday 21 March 1814. This report is not specific that it is Holroyd, simply a person 'intimately connected' with the death of Lavinia, though this is the impression which is given. That Holroyd was alive and practicing as a surgeon is reported in the same newspaper dated Monday 11 April 1814.
14. Manchester Courier & Lancashire General Advertiser, Tuesday 3 March 1887 This article provides a lengthy retrospective account of the death of Lavinia Robinson.
15. Memorials of a Manchester Parish Church (St. John, Deansgate), Papers of Manchester Literary Club, Volume 5, 1879.
16. Manchester Courier & Lancashire General Advertiser, 11 March 1907.
17. A Picture of Manchester, Joseph Aston, 1816.
18. A Picture of Manchester, Joseph Aston, 1816.
19. The Victorian Celebration of Death, James Stevens Curl, 2000.
20. Manchester Faces and Places, 1893.
21. Manchester Courier & Lancashire General Advertiser, 11 March 1907.
22. Manchester Courier & Lancashire General Advertiser, Tuesday 3 March 1887.
23. Manchester Courier & Lancashire General Advertiser, Monday 11 March 1907.
24. Manchester Guardian, 20 September 1930.
25. GMCRO GB127.M74/32/1 Town Clerk's Papers re. Closed Burial Grounds.
26. www.stjc.org.uk/history.php St. James's Club website.
27. The Guardian, 10 September 1962. The article claims that 'This will be the first Manchester City Centre churchyard of any size to be cleared for secular use'.
28. Manchester and the Textile districts in 1849, Angus Bethune Reach, 1849.
29. Manchester Courier & Lancashire General Advertiser, Saturday 24 February 1838. The advertisement to which this refers was published in the previous Saturday's edition.
30. Manchester Courier & Lancashire General Advertiser, Saturday 17 October 1849.
31. A note in the registers records the discovery in 1833, when building the new vestry, of a brass plaque recording the laying of the foundation stone. This plaque was incorporated in the new building.
32. Manchester Mercury Tuesday 16 September 1817.
33. Manchester Mercury, Tuesday 13 January 1818.
34. A Picture of Manchester, Joseph Aston, 1816.
35. Manchester Courier & Lancashire General Advertiser, Saturday 28 April 1827.
36. Manchester Courier & Lancashire General Advertiser, Saturday 14 July 1827.

37 Manchester Courier & Lancashire General Advertiser, Saturday 27 December 1828.

38 Manchester Times Saturday 17 March 1877.

39 Manchester Courier & Lancashire General Advertiser, Saturday 24 September 1825.

40 Manchester Courier & Lancashire General Advertiser, Saturday 7 June 1884. The article contains an account of Thomas Rothwell Bently's funeral.

41 Manchester Guardian, 7 April 1952. The article notes that the spire '*took an unconscionable time falling*'.

42 Manchester Guardian, 24 June 1840.

43 Manchester Guardian, 16 December 1854. Publishing the appointment of Canon Richson as incumbent of St. Andrew's the report comments: '*Here too he will find an extensive sphere of usefulness in his new functions as the clergyman of a poor and densely populated district.*'

44 Manchester Evening Chronicle, 12 June 1961. Gorton and Openshaw Recorder, 16 July 1961.

45 The Guardian, 3 March 1967 contains a legal notice relating to the proposed removal of tombstones and monuments.

46 A photograph dated 2004 and showing the cross appears on Derek and Daryll Bailey's family web site http://2deebees.net/page29.html

The Working Classes and their Funeral Expenses

The following article first appeared in the Manchester Guardian 22 April 1854 and was re-printed on 24 April 1954 under the heading of '100 years Ago'.

When it is proposed to close a graveyard in the midst of a populous district; those who are interested in the continuance of the nuisance become eloquent upon the hardship that the creation of a suburban cemetery would impose upon the working classes, in the shape of hearse hire, &c.; but those who know the customs of the poorer classes on such occasions. know that any extra cost for the conveyance of the dead would be inappreciable, compared .with the wasteful expenditure consequent upon the enormous eating and drinking of friends. acquaintances, and neighbours, before and after the funeral obsequies. The subjoined statement requires very little comment. It was made-out under the following circumstances:- A working man in this city died a short time since; and his widow received from clubs £9. 14s. 6d. Within a few days, we believe, after the funeral, the widow applied to the poor-law officials for relief; and the statement was given in order to show how the club money had been so quickly expended:-

Coffin & plate	0	18	6
Church dues	0	11	6
Clothing for two boys	0	14	0
Two pairs of shoes for ditto	0	14	0
Two shirts for ditto	0	5	6
Two caps for ditto	0	3	0
Half-yard of crape	0	0	10
Srude (shroud) for coffin	0	6	3
Bands for hats & paul (pall)	0	15	10
By cash to Mrs –	0	10	0
Beef and mutton for the funeral	1	11	11½
Beer for the funeral	1	4	4
Baby's bonnet & boots	0	2	2
Tobacco, tea & lemon	0	3	0
Funeral bread, cheese, sugar & butter	1	17	4½

	£9	19	1

It would thus seem. that for the feast connected with this funeral. about 60lb. of flesh meat, and some 12 gallons of· beer. were considered necessary (and were no doubt nearly consumed), in addition to considerable quantities of bread, cheese, &c.; and that the expenditure for food and drink amounted to £4. 13s. 8d. or very nearly half the sum received from the club, as a return for, perhaps, long years .of subscription! It would. indeed be well. if some influence could be brought to bear. by which to· prevent such a sacrifice of money, of moderation, and .of all that decent solemnity of feeling and conduct which is so fitting, and seems so natural, on the occasion of conveying to the tomb the remains of a relative ·or friend.

Protestant Nonconformist Burial Grounds

Protestant Nonconformist Burial Grounds

Up to now we have only looked at the burial grounds established by the Church of England, who had maintained a monopoly over burial of the dead up to the early decades of the seventeenth century.

Manchester was an active centre of religious nonconformity. Dissenting congregations had been established in the seventeenth century and flourished through the eighteenth and nineteenth. A wide variety of nonconformist denominations established chapels in the town. There are few sects which were not at some time represented.

[portion of text obscured by handwritten annotations] ...tion ...the ...lled ...rian ...the ...his ...rchy ...local ...urch ...was ...d to ...ouse. ...louse ...ed to ...pecif-ically to accommodate his by now large and expanding congregation but died the following year.

Over the next century the congregation at Cross Street was, like many early dissenting sects, subject to a number of schisms. A number of groups of members split away and established new chapels which adhered to a variety of Independent, Congregationalist and Unitarian doctrines. These later foundations included the Cold House Chapel, Cannon Street Chapel, Grosvenor Street Chapel and both an Independent and a Unitarian chapel in Mosley Street.

Most of these later chapels closed as their congregations moved out to the suburbs but the Cross Street Chapel survived, at least in name and location. Although the present chapel is a modern building, it stands on the same site as its seventeenth century predecessor and so can reasonably claim the longest pedigree of any place of worship in Manchester after the Cathedral.

Close on the heels of the Independents in establishing a presence in Manchester was the Religious Society of Friends (Quakers). They had probably been holding meetings in private houses for some years but in 1673 they purchased a plot of land on Deansgate to use as a burial ground. The Quakers were never as numerous as many of the other denominations but have nevertheless maintained a presence to the present day.

The Baptists also attracted followers and built chapels, though at a later date than many of the other sects. Their chapel on Rochdale Road is now the third building to stand on a site which Baptists first occupied in 1789.

A chapel was founded in Peter Street in 1793 by the New Jerusalem (Swedenborgian) Church. Its first minister was William Cowherd. Cowherd's personal beliefs led to increasing theological differences with the Swedenborgians and he eventually left Peter Street and established his own chapel at King Street in Salford. Cowherd's followers acquired the name 'Bible Christians', but they were never a national movement and have no connection with the sect of the same name which developed in Cornwall some years later and which in 1907 became part of the United Methodist Church. One of Cowherd's followers and pupils was James Scholefield, who subsequently left King Street to build his own Bible Christian chapel at Every Street.

The Swedenborgians no longer have a chapel in the city and the last Bible Christians disappeared with the death of Scholefield and the closure of Every Street in the 1860s.

The Methodist Church also had a number of chapels, though like other groups their followers moved out to the suburbs and their city centre chapels were abandoned.

Most of the Protestant nonconformist chapels provided space for the burial of their members. Burial of the dead was an issue which presented some problems for nonconformists. Their beliefs did not exclude them from burial in the parish graveyard but this required the Anglican burial service to be read over the body by an Anglican minister, a practice with which they disagreed. Dissenting ministers would not be legally permitted to officiate at burials in Anglican cemeteries until 1880.

There was also a sound financial reason for chapels to maintain their own burial grounds; the burial fees provided a useful contribution towards the upkeep of the chapel and its minister. This was particularly the case where the chapel had a large congregation and where there was sufficient space to accommodate a large graveyard.

The several nonconformist burial grounds in Manchester varied considerably in size. The smallest accommodated no more than a few graves but the largest recorded up to thirty thousand burials. It was not only the church members who benefited from these burial grounds, there was a benefit to the wider community since the larger burial grounds made a useful contribution to the availability of burial space in Manchester. This took some of the pressure off the parish graveyards.

Many dissenting chapels closed when their congregations moved to new and frequently out-of-town locations. Their burial grounds, if they were still open, usually also closed at the same time. In some cases the bodies were exhumed and removed to graves or vaults at a new chapel. The few which had survived as working graveyards up to 1854 were closed under the new requirements imposed by the Burial Acts of that year. These closures were mostly immediate but a few chapels, notably Every Street Bible Christian Chapel, managed to secure postponements for a few years.

As it became more difficult to find burial space in the town, some of the dissenting congregations worked together to provide burial places for their members by opening the Dissenters' Cemetery at Rusholme Road in 1821. This is discussed at length in a later chapter. Once the smaller burial grounds had been closed, much of their business moved to the Rusholme Road, Ardwick and Manchester General private cemeteries, all of which offered non-denominational burial space where dissenting ministers were free to perform whatever burial rites they felt appropriate or where burials could take place without any ceremony.

Once Philips Park Cemetery had opened in 1867, to be followed by Manchester Southern Cemetery in 1878, nonconformists had access to non-denominational burial space in the new municipal cemeteries. These also are discussed in a later chapter.

There is no trace on the ground today of most of the nonconformist chapels. Only Cross Street Chapel and the Friends' Meeting House in Mount Street survive. Only at Mount Street and Every Street is there any visible indication that there was ever a burial ground, a small plaque at the former and a few preserved ledger stones at the latter.

Manchester's Independent Chapels

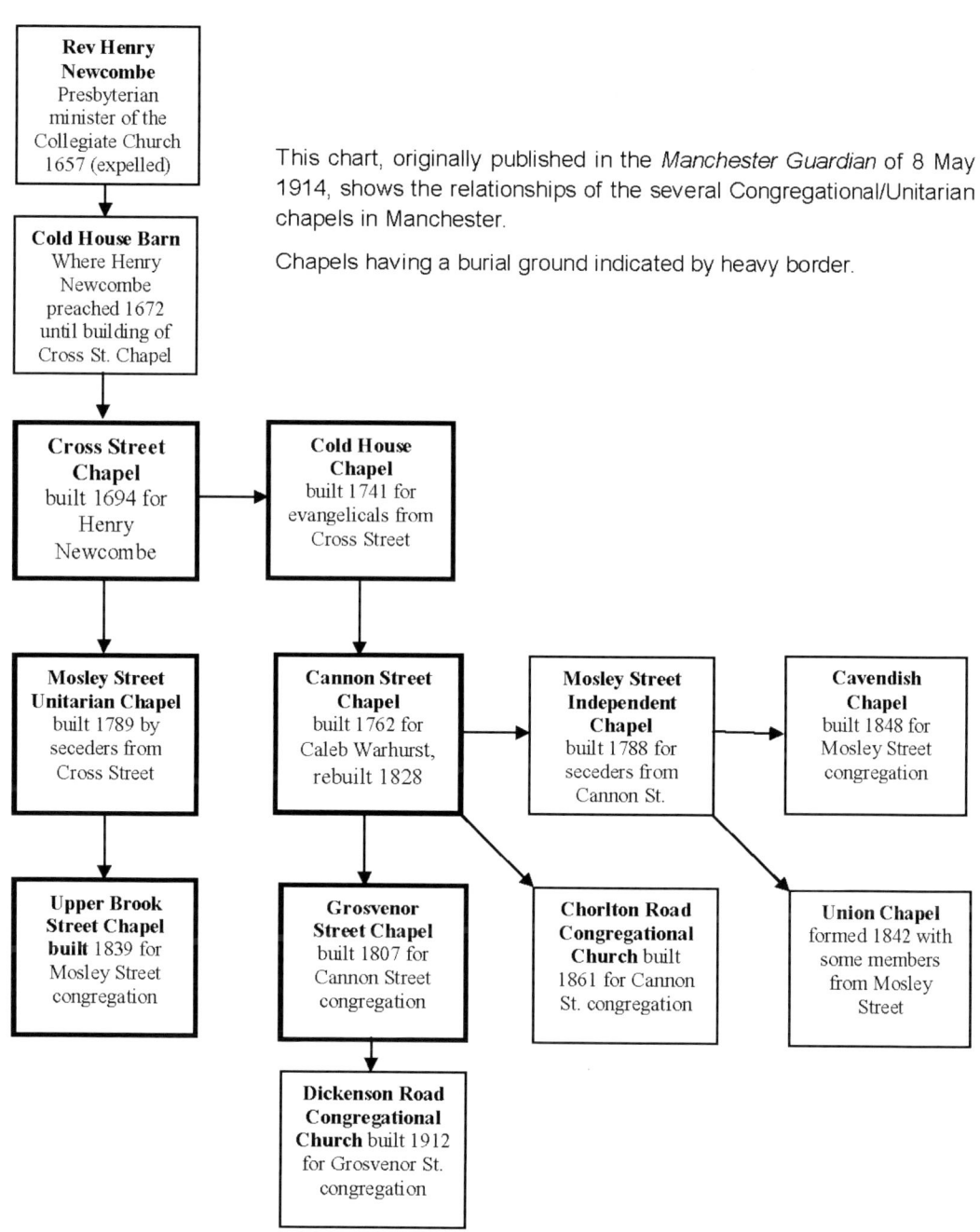

This chart, originally published in the *Manchester Guardian* of 8 May 1914, shows the relationships of the several Congregational/Unitarian chapels in Manchester.

Chapels having a burial ground indicated by heavy border.

Rev Henry Newcombe
Presbyterian minister of the Collegiate Church 1657 (expelled)

Cold House Barn
Where Henry Newcombe preached 1672 until building of Cross St. Chapel

Cross Street Chapel
built 1694 for Henry Newcombe

Cold House Chapel
built 1741 for evangelicals from Cross Street

Mosley Street Unitarian Chapel
built 1789 by seceders from Cross Street

Cannon Street Chapel
built 1762 for Caleb Warhurst, rebuilt 1828

Mosley Street Independent Chapel
built 1788 for seceders from Cannon St.

Cavendish Chapel
built 1848 for Mosley Street congregation

Upper Brook Street Chapel
built 1839 for Mosley Street congregation

Grosvenor Street Chapel
built 1807 for Cannon Street congregation

Chorlton Road Congregational Church built 1861 for Cannon St. congregation

Union Chapel
formed 1842 with some members from Mosley Street

Dickenson Road Congregational Church built 1912 for Grosvenor St. congregation

Cross Street Chapel

The Original Cross Street Chapel

Cross Street Chapel is one of Manchester's few nonconformist chapels to have survived to the present day. Its survival, however, is in name only. The present building, which has the look of a corporate business headquarters rather than a place of worship, dates only from 1997 but stands, nevertheless, on the site on which its predecessor had been erected two centuries earlier.

The original Chapel, which stands today in the heart of the city, opened in 1694 to accommodate Reverend Henry Newcome and his growing congregation. It was built in a field called Plungeon's Meadow, a name which reflects how small Manchester was at that time. Indeed, Cross Street did not exist when the building was erected and the chapel, which was generally referred to in contemporary records as the *'Dissenters' Meeting House'*, would have been described as standing in Pool Fold. Even fifty years later, Cross Street chapel stood very much at the edge of the built-up area of the town.

The chapel was surrounded on its front, rear and northern sides by a small but well used burial ground. This was divided into two parts, known respectively as the 'Higher' and 'Lower' Grounds. The significance of these names is not obvious from the early engraving which gives no hint of the sloping site on which the site stands. There appears to be no surviving plan to show the boundaries of the two sections.

Burials would almost certainly have begun soon after the chapel's opening but the earliest surviving burial register dates only from 1785. There is consequently no record of either the number of burials which took place or the names of those buried in the graveyard before this date.

SHALLOW GRAVES

The burial registers are unusual. Not only do they record the the cause of death (measles and 'decline' feature frequently) but also both the location and the depth of each grave. These details would have been of great value to the sexton. The depths recorded appear to relate to the depth of soil covering the top of the coffin and would have served to tell the sexton how much space was available for future interments.

The depths of the graves tell us much about the nature of urban burial in the early 19th century. The greatest depths recorded are around eleven feet. This suggests that new graves were dug to depths approaching twelve feet – a significant excavation. With each successive interment the depth was reduced by the height of the coffin plus the depth of soil (if any) between successive coffins. Even as early as 1785, depths of three feet or less appear frequently, indicating that some of the graves had become well filled during the previous century.

Burials could be very shallow indeed. John, the twenty-eight year old son of Thomas Hilton of Princes Street, was buried on the first of August 1817 . His grave is recorded as an astonishingly small *nine inches* deep. It is more remarkable that the word '*full*', which appears next to some other entries, does not appear. Did the sexton think that another burial, perhaps of a child, might be possible?

John's was not the only shallow grave. Many other entries show depths of one foot or less. Fortunately, each of the graves would have been closed with a large ledger stone, so there was no danger of the remains being exposed by animals. However, the potential for the release of offensive smells is obvious, particularly if the grave was inside the chapel.

Burial Inside the Chapel

Bodies were buried beneath the floor of the chapel, though the absence of early registers means it is not possible to say how numerous these were. Bodies were buried directly in the earth but there also appear to have been a number of vaults. The first to be buried inside the chapel was probably Henry Newcome himself. He died aged 67 on 17 September 1685, just a year after the Chapel had opened. He was buried three days later near the pulpit of his chapel.

One of the graves belonged to the Birch family and had been in use since 1734. The Birch graves had been marked with brass plaques set into the floor but in 1871 the plaques were removed during a major renovation of the chapel and it was not until thirteen years later that the family had them reinstated. They were fixed to a marble slab which bore the inscription:

> '*These tablets were removed from graves in the centre of the chapel during the alterations of the pews in the year 1871 and were placed here by members of the family October 1884'.*[2]

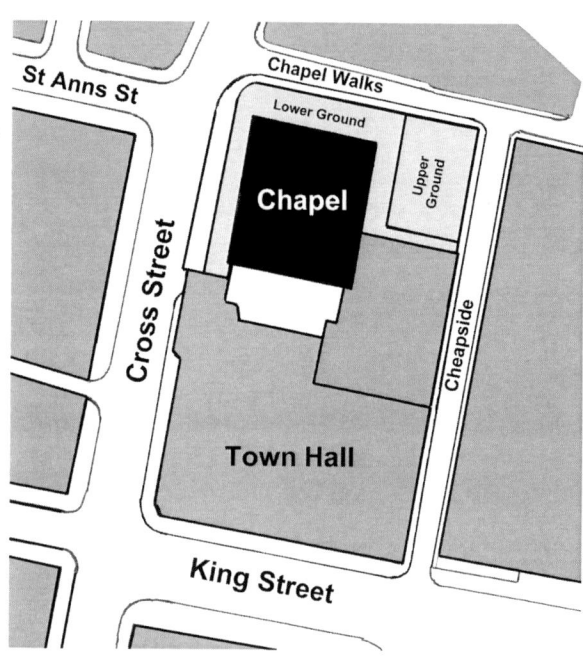

Cross Street Chapel circa 1848

It is possible that the numerous deep excavations for graves both inside and outside the chapel had caused some instability of the structure since in 1883 it proved necessary to construct two additional buttresses to support the south wall.[3]

Road Widening

In 1845 the Corporation felt it desirable to widen Cross Street, which was becoming an increasingly important thoroughfare.[4] To achieve this they purchased a strip of land in front of the chapel, amounting to an area of some 55 square yards. This strip included part of the lower burial ground. The road widening was achieved without disturbing the bodies but left a number of graves under the new pavement. As a condition of sale, the chapel trustees insisted that the Corporation accept a covenant prohibiting them from disturbing the remains. This prevented the Corporation from laying drains, water and gas pipes under the pavement on the east side of the street. Ironically, the covenants which applied to the Corporation did not apply to the Postmaster

General and so telegraph and telephone ducts were at a later date laid between the coffins.

CLOSURE

The surviving burial registers which cover 1785 to 1840 record something over six hundred burials but there might have been two to three times this number during the chapel's first ninety years. Between 1830 and 1840 the annual number of burials averaged about seven and so it is unlikely that the total number of burials after 1840 exceeded one hundred. The last burial reportedly took place in 1852 so the final register may be missing. The graveyard was in any event closed for further burials in 1854 under the Orders in Council issued following the Burial Acts.

CROSS STREET IN THE 20TH CENTURY

As the population of the city centre declined and businesses replaced houses, the congregation attending Cross Street Chapel dwindled. In 1914 it was claimed that only thirty worshippers attended most services, rising to fifty or sixty on Sunday evenings in a chapel which could accommodate up to 1,200 worshippers. Where once the prosperous worshippers had arrived in their carriages, a carriages was now a rare sight at the chapel.

The decline in attendance was cited in 1914 to justify a proposal in the Manchester Corporation Act of that year that the old chapel should be demolished. A clause in the Act granted permission for removal of the bodies from the burial ground and for reburial at the municipal cemetery. This would have two benefits. Firstly it would allow a part of the site to be taken to enable a further widening of Cross Street and to enable underground services to be installed on that side of the street. Secondly, it would allow a commercial building to be erected on the site, which the Corporation considered too small to constitute a useful public open space. The Act was passed later in the year, despite considerable public objection and a whole day's debate by a Select Committee of the House of Lords.[5] In the end, the

argument was hypothetical. The Great War intervened and no more was heard of the proposal.

Following the war, the chapel enjoyed a resurgence of support. The preaching of the charismatic H. H. Johnson attracted a new congregation and the chapel pews were once more filled to capacity. Plans to vacate the site were dropped.

The chapel continued to be well attended between the wars but in the winter blitz of 1940 the building was gutted. Services resumed almost immediately; the congregation assembling in the open air within the remaining walls. A temporary building was soon erected within the shell. This served for nearly twenty years.

A new chapel building was erected in 1959 sitting more or less on the foundations of its predecessor. This short-lived building, however, proved unsatisfactory and was replaced by the present chapel and office building in 1997.

The new building extended across the whole of the old chapel grounds including the burial ground and so it was necessary to exhume the bodies, much as had been proposed in 1914. The remains were removed to Southern Cemetery in January 1996 where there is a plaque which reads:

'Sacred To the Memory Of Rev. Henry Newcombe M.A. Founder of Non Conformity in Manchester, and those other Ministers, Members and Adherents of Cross St Chapel buried in its Graveyard 1695 - 1846. Their remains Now Rest either beneath Cross Street and Chapel Walks or were re-interred in this place in the year of our Lord 1996.'

This inscription implies that widening of Cross Street and Chapel Walks simply extended the streets over the edges of the burial ground without disturbing the remains in the process. This was confirmed in 2013 when exploratory excavations in Cross Street, prior to the exhumation of the last of the remains, uncovered the gravestones under the pavement.

Coldhouse Chapel, Shudehill

In 1741 a part of the Cross Street congregation broke away and established a new chapel which they built in Thornley (or Thorniley) Brow, a narrow street which leads off the north side of Shudehill. This was close to the site of the old Cold House Barn, where Henry Newcome had first preached when he returned to Manchester, and so in memory of this former place of worship they named their new premises Cold House Chapel. This group did not remain long and over the next century the chapel accommodated, at different times, congregations of Baptists, Wesleyan Methodists, Independents and Scots Baptists.

The chapel site included what appears to have been a quite small burial ground though there seems to be little record of it in contemporary sources. The burial ground seems to have only been used for a fairly short time and for a very small number of burials but there are no surviving registers or other records to provide the names or even the number of those who were interred there.

The Cold House Chapel burial ground was not specifically mentioned in the Orders in Council issued under the Burial Acts in 1854 and so it seems safe to conclude that it had probably been inactive for a great many years. Subsequent events suggest that it had been completely forgotten by this time. It was to be rediscovered twenty years later.

THE GRAVEYARD REDISCOVERED

The circumstances surrounding the rediscovery of the Cold House Chapel burial ground are somewhat opaque. On 3 August 1874 builders excavating the footings of an extension to the warehouse belonging to Messrs. Peverley and Blake uncovered two well-preserved wooden coffins about four feet below the ground. Three days later, a further three coffins were discovered and then a further two small coffins, presumably those of children. The coffins were removed to the Oldham Street mortuary and subsequently reinterred at Philips Park Cemetery.

The burial ground appeared to have been long disused since where the coffins lay had been under a wall which formed part of some uninhabited houses described as being 'very old'. There is no mention of the graves being marked by any memorial.

Thorniley Brow showing the back of Rosenfield's warehouse, the site of the former Cold House Chapel.

The only clues to the identities of those buried were initials and dates picked out in iron nails driven into the lids of the larger coffins. The details recorded in this way were: 'NB Ae [aetatis = aged] 21 1772'; 'RB Ae 62 1774'; 'HB 1772'; 'IB 1774' and 'HB 1774'.[6] The common 'B' of the initials suggest that all might have been related.

The identities of the bodies were never established. It was suggested that a former minister of the chapel and his wife had been buried there. The name of Winterbottom was mentioned, presumably referring to James Winterbottom, a Baptist minister who was active at Coldhouse Chapel. However, aside from this suggestion being at variance with the initials on the coffins, James Winterbottom is known to have died in 1759 and so he (and probably other members of his family) can safely be ruled out.

It is not wholly clear why the builders were building on the chapel grounds at all. The fact that the coffins had been discovered underneath later walls suggests that the chapel site had been encroached upon many years before, either with or without the acquiescence of the trustees.

Peverley and Blake claimed that they had tried to purchase the chapel but had been frustrated in their efforts by the trust deed, which required that the chapel remain intact whilever three or more people continued to worship there. They had certainly been in contact with the trustees but it was suggested that the trustees were disinterested and whether interested or otherwise, they were indisputably ineffective. This seems hardly to be surprising. One of the trustees was said to be close to death, while another lived in Liverpool. The third, it appears, lived in London. Some sort of deal, the details of which

have been lost, had been struck between Peverley and Blake and the trustees in which the partners had supposedly promised to renovate the chapel. As a part of the trustees' agreement or perhaps to secure it, they had paid each of the trustees £50. There is a distinct whiff of questionable behaviour on one or both sides.

The builders' encroachment on the chapel grounds was subsequently challenged, but the trustees were unable to produce either deeds or any other evidence to substantiate their claim to the land. The development therefore continued and eventually resulted in the chapel being completely hemmed in by the surrounding buildings. The only access to the chapel and the little that remained of its yard was through a three foot wide passage which the builders had constructed under the new warehouse to provide pedestrian access from Thornley Brow.[7]

Despite this difficulty, worship continued at the chapel but the congregation appears to have been very small. Eventually, at a meeting on 10 March 1899 held in the chapel, now described as 'cheerless and forlorn', it was agreed that the building should be sold to James Thomas Pendlebury for the sum of £550.[8]

The chapel was subsequently demolished and the site redeveloped. The largest of the new buildings to occupy the site was a shop and/or warehouse latterly occupied by D. Rosenfield and Sons.

A proposal was made in 2002 to redevelop the site for housing, but this seems to have come to nothing. The former Rosenfield building, which now stands behind the Shudehill Metrolink platform, is at the time of writing unoccupied.

Cannon Street Unitarian Chapel

Cannon Street Chapel circa 1907

Cannon Street Chapel was founded in 1762 by the congregation of Coldhouse Chapel in a place which was at that time known as Hunters Croft. The chapel, which was built at a cost of £343, opened on 21 April 1762. The first minister was the Reverend Caleb Warhurst, who was succeeded on his death in 1765 at the early age of 42 by Timothy Priestley.

The chapel had a small burial ground but it appears that some of the records have been lost. There is no surviving record of burials before 1786 and the one register which survives contains records of burials only for the three year period up to 1788. It is therefore not known whether there were any burials before 1786. There is also some doubt as to the date of this last burial. The one surviving register contains a final entry relating to a burial in 1788:

'The wife of Dugal Munn who died 6th and was buried 9th of May 1788. The last corpse buried in Cannon Street Chapel'

Dugal(l) Munn was a tape manufacturer with business premises in Withy Grove. The register records just twenty burials over these three years.

The closure of this burial record coincides with a schism in the congregation which took place in 1788 when a large proportion of the congregation broke away to form Mosley Street Independent Chapel. It is uncertain whether burials continued at Cannon Street after this date and were recorded in a new (and now lost) register or whether use of the graveyard was discontinued at this time.

The chapel was enlarged in 1829 but during the 19th century the area became increasingly commercial in character. The congregation drifted away to the suburbs and in 1860 the chapel was sold. The building was still in existence as recently as 1938, at which time the graveyard was used as a depot for storing handcarts[9].

Swindells, writing in 1907, comments that the burial ground *'after years of neglect was the subject of a somewhat animated newspaper controversy a few years ago.'*[10] Unfortunately, I have been unable to find any record of the dispute to which Swindells alludes. It was around this time that the photograph of the chapel was taken, showing it at that time to be the premises of Cooper, Dennison and Walkden's ink manufactory.

The burial ground was finally cleared in 1939, at which time the chapel was demolished to make way for the widening of Cannon Street. The exhumed remains were reinterred at Southern Cemetery.[11]

Mosley Street Unitarian Chapel

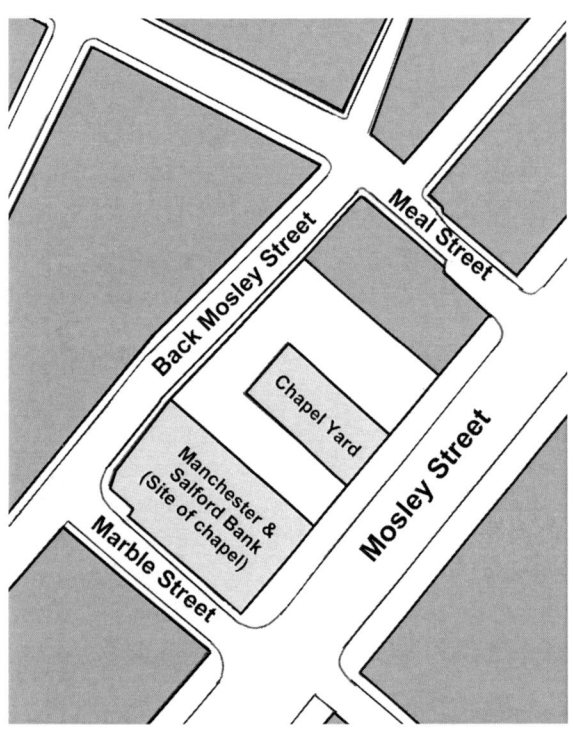

Mosley St. Chapel Yard c1848

At the top of Mosley Street, facing Piccadilly Gardens, stands a branch of the Primark clothing store but occupying this site two centuries ago was a Unitarian burial ground.

Mosley Street Unitarian Chapel was built in 1787 to accommodate a large group of worshippers which had seceded from the Cross Street Chapel. The worshippers at Mosley Street Chapel were some of the most prominent citizens of Manchester and included George William Wood, MP for Lancashire, Edmund Potter, later MP for Carlisle, Robert Hyde Greg, later MP for Manchester, Dr. Henry, the vice-president of the Literary and Philosophical Society and many of Manchester's most prominent manufacturers[12]. Alongside their new chapel, they established their burial ground. Joseph Aston wrote in 1815:

'The burial place belonging to this chapel being small, a very good method has been adopted to make the most of it. Every grave which has hitherto been made, has been lined with bricks and mortar as a common grave. This method keeps each grave separate; it likewise prevents the earth from closing in upon the person who digs; and the neighbouring coffins are not disturbed, a circumstance but too common in crowded cemeteries'.[13]

CLOSURE

As was the case with most of the town centre chapels in the early nineteenth century, the prosperous congregation moved to the suburbs and less than fifty years after it had been built the chapel found itself surrounded by warehouses and other commercial premises.

Mosley Street Chapel closed its doors for the last time around 1834 and was sold, along with its adjacent schoolhouse, to John McConnell for £10,000. The chapel was demolished the following year and the head office of the Manchester and Salford Bank, designed by the architect Richard Tattershall, was erected on the site, opening in 1838. The adjacent burial ground site remained undeveloped for several years and the graves remained undisturbed.

For a short time the Mosley Street congregation dispersed to other chapels but in 1839 they moved into a new chapel in Upper Brook Street, Chorlton-on-Medlock, which had been built with the proceeds of the sale of the Mosley Street building and site.

The Mosley Street burial ground was mentioned in 1839 at a meeting of Manchester ley (parish rate) payers which had been convened to discuss the impending sale of the Walkers Croft parish burial ground. Speaking against the sale, Elijah Dixon cited the Unitarian

Mosley Street Chapel
Shortly before its demolition

burial ground in support of his belief that the sanctity of burial grounds should be respected:

> *'There was a little place, he said, in Mosley Street which formally belonged to a set of men whom perhaps many enlightened dissenters of the present day would term infidels and who were termed Unitarians. There was a little plot of ground belonging to these people in Mosley Street and it appeared that no consideration could induce them to give it up. It was a sepulchre for their dead and the living would not suffer their feelings to be outraged by the removal of the remains of their departed friends.'[14]*

We have already seen that Elijah was on the losing side of the argument about Walkers Croft and his confidence in the Unitarians' attachment to their burial ground seems to have been equally misplaced. A letter to the Notes and Queries section of the Manchester Guardian in 1875 from a correspondent who described himself as *'A Former Schoolboy'* recounted:

> *'The Mosley Street Chapel was pulled down about the year 1835 and sold, together with the school building in Back Mosley Street, attached to the back portion, to Mr. John McConnell for £10,000. The small graveyard, overlooked by the school windows, remained unbuilt upon for a number of years, perhaps 15; it had not been used for interments for a very long period and must have been a dreary-looking dismal place at its best. The remains, such as could be found, were removed to the enclosure attached to the Upper Brook Street Chapel and a full record was kept of the names and dates on the gravestones at the same time, which can probably be seen on application.'[15]*

The memorial record to which he refers has survived in Manchester's archives, though not, it seems, the original burial register.

It appears that the removal of the remains from the Mosley Street burial ground took place in two stages. A note in the Upper Brook Street burial register refers to the interment of four coffins which are described as:

'Coffins removed from the old chapel yard in Mosley Street and deposited in No. 1 vault in the new chapel yard Upper Brook Street, Manchester in the night of Wednesday the 4th May 1842'.

This entry is followed by a transcription of the inscriptions on the coffin plates. The coffins included one containing the remains of William Hawkes, who had been minister of the chapel from its opening until his death in 1820, and two others which appear to contain two of his sons. The fourth coffin contained the remains of George Duckworth, an attorney and prominent Unitarian who had died in 1816.

A second and lengthier record refers to the removal of remains from sixteen graves which had contained a total of forty-three adults and seventeen children. All but three of these burials were dated before 1820, the earliest being dated 1790. These remains were removed in July 1846 and reinterred in eight vaults at Upper Brook Street. As befits such a prosperous congregation, it is noted that several of the coffins were made of lead. Three of the new vaults at Upper Brook Street bore memorials which related to those moved from Mosley Street, presumably members of families which still had a connection with the chapel.

The memory of the 'Former Schoolboy' seems to have been fairly accurate. The burial ground is marked on the Ordnance Survey 60 inch map based upon an 1849 survey but within five years it had disappeared. A letter from 'Antiquarius' speaks of Mosley Street's two dissenting chapels which, the writer remarks, '...have both disappeared'. He adds '...and a burial ground of the Unitarians non est inventus. What has become of it?'[16]

What had become of it was that a warehouse had been built on the site of the former burial ground. In 1875 the warehouse was occupied by George Peake and Co. and around 1884 by Richard Goodair who remained there until well into the twentieth century. The warehouse was subsequently demolished and replaced by an extension to the adjacent Lewis's department store in 1929. In 2008, following the financial collapse of Lewis's, the store became a branch of the Primark clothing chain.

The Manchester and Salford Bank expanded rapidly and in 1862 moved into a new and larger building further down Mosley Street. Tattershall's handsome building, which stood on the former chapel site, was taken over by the clothiers H. J. Nicoll and Co. But today the building, now Grade II listed, has returned to its original use. It is now a branch of the Santander Bank.

Grosvenor Street Independent Chapel

The Grosvenor Street Chapel was established by a substantial part of the Cannon Street Chapel congregation, which built a new chapel on Grosvenor Street in 1807 when Cannon Street Chapel became too small to accommodate their increasing numbers. The congregation was led by the Reverend William Roby and became commonly known as 'Roby's Chapel'. The building occupied a site between Grosvenor Street and Aytoun Street, with the chapel fronting the former and the burial ground the latter. In 1844-5 schoolrooms were erected on the Aytoun Street frontage and these extended over a part of the burial ground The rear part of the new building was supported on pillars so as not to disturb the burials. The Gentleman's Magazine was complimentary of the arrangement, *'level with the street is an open cloister or colonnade intended as a playing place'*.[17] Neither this, nor similar coverage in the Illustrated London News, mentions that the playground was a working cemetery!

It is fitting that on 20 January 1830 William Roby was buried in the graveyard of the chapel he had founded. Roby's was probably the most highly attended funeral the chapel had witnessed. Despite high winds and heavy snow throughout the morning, demand for places was so high that a ticketing system had to be adopted to ensure that regular worshippers would not be excluded. Nevertheless, the chapel was still extremely crowded.

The burial ground was closed by Order in Council of 21 March 1854, though there had not been a burial for several months previous to this. It remained undisturbed for the next half century. In 1910 Manchester City Council agreed to purchase the chapel. school and burial ground. They planned to build a central receiving house for the Manchester Royal Infirmary on the site. The sale was conditional on the Council obtaining Parliamentary permission to redevelop the site and on the remains being exhumed and reburied elsewhere. Permission was forthcoming the following year and in October of 1911 the Council published a statutory notice in the Manchester Guardian. This informed the public of their intention to remove the human remains and informed the heirs of those buried there that up to £10 would be granted to anyone who wished to make their own arrangements for reburial of their loved ones. The remains were subsequently removed to Southern Cemetery later that year.

The former hospital buildings were demolished and in 1998 the site became a sheltered housing development called Aytoun Court. There is no indication that it was formerly the site of a chapel but the name of William Roby has been remembered by the renaming of Grosvenor Street as Roby Street. The burial registers have long been missing and so it is not known how many burials took place there.

Grosvenor Street Chapel

Quaker Burial Ground, Jackson's Row

The burial ground of the Quakers, more properly called the Religious Society of Friends, was the first graveyard to be established in Manchester since the Old Parish Churchyard. Situated at the junction of Deansgate and Jackson's Row, the land was purchased in 1673 specifically for use as a burial ground, though a meeting house was later built on the site.

THE QUAKERS' FOLLY

The early burial registers have not survived but in 1878 John Owen noted the existence of a plaque on the wall, which, although almost completely illegible, carried the date 1674 and it is assumed that this was the year when the burial ground opened. The first burial of which we have a record dates from 1682 and appears in the Collegiate Church burial register. This was noted by Owen:

> 'While passing the remaining portion of the dull brick wall at the corner of Jackson's Row we are reminded of an extract from the Cathedral register proving the antiquity of the first burial ground belonging to the Friends in Manchester: "1682, Nov. 4, Giles Meadowcroft, of Crumpsall, Gent., buried at the Quakers Folly."'[18]

The reference conveys something of the contempt with which the Quakers were regarded by the established church. Between 1695 and 1743 some 89 burials in the Collegiate Church register are annotated 'buried at meeting house' or similar. It is difficult, however, to determine whether the term 'meeting house' refers to the Quaker meeting house or to Cross Street chapel, which was also frequently referred to as the dissenters' meeting house. The description may possibly cover both. These 89 references may be connected with the requirement, under various acts passed between 1660 and 1680, that burial

shrouds should only be made from woollen cloth, legislation which was enacted to stimulate the woollen industry. Persons presenting a body for burial were required to provide an affidavit confirming that the law had been complied with. These laws were repealed in 1814, though they were a 'dead letter' by 1770 if not earlier.

The first Quaker meeting house in Manchester was built on the Jackson's Row site in 1693 but was subsequently replaced with a larger building on the same site in 1732. In 1795 the meeting moved to a new meeting house in Dickenson Street (see below), but the Jackson's Row burial ground was retained and remained in use for burials until 1847.

In 1828 the sexton, Robert Bohannah, described his burial ground when he gave evidence at the trial of John Massey, who was subsequently convicted of stealing a body from the graveyard. His description is brief but suggests a well-tended graveyard: 'The graves are made smooth and flat like beds in a garden with walks between them.'[19]

CLOSURE AND CLEARANCE

Burials at Jackson's Row finally came to an end in 1847 with the burial of Emily Lloyd, an infant from Hulme. The burial ground was later said to be used as a playground by children attending the Free School in Jackson's Row.

John Owen visited the burial ground in 1863. He reported it to be in a lamentable state of repair, with only one surviving gravestone set in the wall and much defaced. He comments, somewhat scathingly:

> 'I am told that there were several more gravestones but such has been the apathy or indifference of the Friends that when the shops were built on the Deansgate side of the graves a few years ago they were removed or destroyed and as yet I have

not found any one, Friend or otherwise, who can inform me of their disposal.'[20]

Between September 1876 and May 1877 the remains were removed at a cost reportedly in excess of £1,000. Excavations were carried out by a team of six to eight men and were taken down until they reached the underlying rock to ensure that all remains were recovered. Contemporary accounts report that 631 bodies were removed from 253 graves, each grave being between nine and twelve feet in depth. What percentage of the total number of burials which had taken place over the preceding two centuries this represented cannot be established, as there is no surviving register before 1763 and doubt as to the completeness of the registers thereafter.

The remains mostly consisted of no more than skulls and the larger bones. Where the remains of coffins were found, the occupants were not identified by coffin plates, but simply by initials and date of death picked out in brass headed nails driven into the lid. This near-anonymity is common in Quaker burials. Each identifiable set of remains was placed individually in a new coffin and the coffins removed weekly to be reinterred in a specially built tomb in the burial ground at the Friends' meeting house at Ashton-on-Mersey.[21] The reburial site is marked with a stone which carries the inscription:

'Within this enclosure were deposited the remains interred in the Friends' Burial Ground, Jackson's Row, Manchester from 1682 to 1847 inclusive. Re-interred 1876-7.'

The Jackson's Row site was redeveloped in 1878. Century Building was constructed on the newly cleared site but this was destroyed in the 1940 blitz. The present building on the site is the rather unexceptional '201 Deansgate' which was built in 1995-6. There is nothing to mark the earlier history of the site.

The Memorial at Ashton-on-Mersey

Death comes even to stone memorials And the names on them.

Decimus Magnus Ansonius Epitaphia xxxii, 10

Quaker Meeting House, Mount Street

Friends' Meeting House, Mount Street

The Manchester Friends' meeting moved from Jackson's Row to a newly built meeting house in Dickenson Street in 1795. Writing in 1815, Joseph Aston commented on the new building:

'It has a small burial-place attached to it … the burial place is still made use of for interment'.[22]

The new meeting house was close to Peter's Field and in 1819 a number of the victims of the Peterloo Massacre took shelter there. It was said that for many months afterwards the floorboards were stained with human blood. This first building was, however, demolished and a new and more substantial building, designed by the Quaker architect Richard Lane, erected in its place in 1828 at a cost of £7,000. The new meeting house, which today presents an impressive frontage to Mount Street, opened in 1830.

The burial place mentioned by Aston is shown at the rear (western end) of the meeting house on the 1849 Ordnance Survey map, though it appears also to have extended along at least one

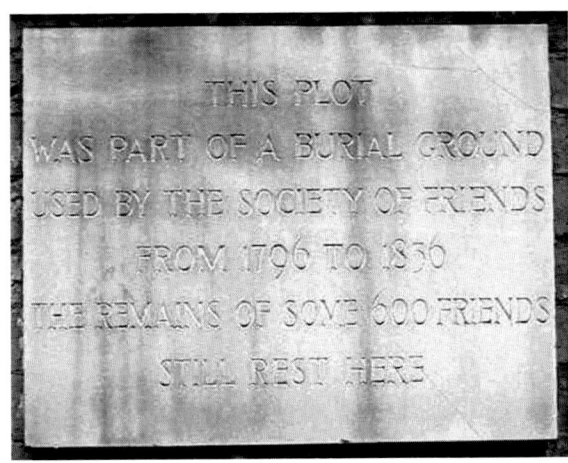

The Commemorative Plaque

side of the building. It was surrounded by a high wall to deter grave-robbers who, as we have seen, had proved troublesome at Jackson's Row. Body snatching was at its peak in Manchester around the time the meeting house was built and so a substantial wall would have seemed a sensible precaution. The wall was reduced in height during building work carried out circa 1961-2 but still remains quite impressive.

DALTON AND BRADSHAW

Two of the more famous worshippers at Mount Street were the physicist John Dalton and George Bradshaw, the creator of Bradshaw's Railway Guide, which has recently come back to prominence as the basis for Michael Portillo's several television series on railway journeys. Neither man was, however, to be buried at Mount Street. Dalton's funeral in 1844 was effectively hijacked by a committee and he was buried at Ardwick Cemetery with a level of ceremony well above that typical for a Quaker (see page 149). Bradshaw died of cholera in 1853 while visiting Norway and was buried where he died.

CLOSURE

Further burials were prohibited by the Order in Council published on 15 April 1854, the prohibition becoming effective from 1 March 1855.

The meeting house has changed little in appearance since it was built but the burial ground has been concreted over and now serves as a car park. The graves remain undisturbed beneath the asphalt but a small number of grave-stones have been retained at the side of the building. These follow the Quaker tradition of simplicity, being small in size and recording no more than the name and the date of death and age of the deceased. The dates on the grave-stones also follow the usual Quaker practice which avoids using the names of the months, many of which derive from the names of pagan deities. Consequently, for example, March - derived from Mars, the god of war - appears as 'the 3rd month'.

A plaque on the rear wall of the meeting house commemorates the former burial ground:

> 'This plot was part of a burial ground used by the Society of Friends from 1796 to 1856. The remains of some 600 Friends still rest here.'

Following the closure of the Mount Street burial ground, Manchester's Quakers have been buried in their burial ground at Ashton-on-Mersey which was established in 1856.

The Remaining Gravestones
in the former burial ground at Mount Street

New Jerusalem Church, Peter Street

New Jerusalem Church, Peter Street
The graveyard is behind the railings to the left

Manchester's New Jerusalem Church opened on Sunday 11 April 1793. It was only the second New Jerusalem chapel in England, the first having opened in Birmingham two years previously. The first two ministers were William Cowherd and Joseph Proud.

The church, a handsome building in brick and stone, was built in what was then called Yates (or Yate) Street, a road which ran down from St. Peter's Church to Deansgate. When St. Peter's Church was consecrated in 1794, Yates Street was renamed Peter Street. Peter Street at the end of the 18th century passed between fields and the New Jerusalem Church was the only building along its length except for a property called 'Cooper's Cottage'. Apart from the addition of a few houses, the street remained undeveloped until after 1830. Joseph Aston, writing in

1816, remarked *'There is a small burying place attached to this church'*. The New Manchester Guide, published the previous year, provided a little more description: *'On the west side of the church there is a burial ground enclosed with a wall and palisades in front'*. This must have proved inadequate since a further plot of land adjoining the church was purchased in 1828 specifically to be used for burials. The whole, however, was not large and presumably sufficed for such burials as the congregation, said to number 276 in 1818[23], required. It was noted that the burial ground *"had for many years been a source of income to the Society"*.[24] It is not known how many people were buried in the graveyard since although the baptismal and marriage registers have survived, the burial register sadly has been lost. Neither was any record made of the memorials which would have once marked the graves.

The burial ground was closed under the Burial Acts in 1854 and in about 1857 schoolrooms were built over the burial ground. This was done without the removal of the remains and in 1892 Joseph Nunn, in a letter to the Manchester Courier, noted that *'For many years the Peter Street School was taught in a building over sinking graves'*.[25]

CLOSURE AND CLEARANCE

The church closed with a service held on 24 July 1888. The premises were sold to the Whitworth Trustees for £10,000 and were used to accommodate the Manchester Technical School Spinning and Weaving Branch. Looms and spinning machinery were installed in the school room and to this end it was necessary to provide substantial foundations. The floor boards were lifted and concrete beds constructed. This required some excavation and a quantity of remains were removed in the process. This seems to have been done quite informally and without the appropriate licence.

The buildings were subsequently transferred to the City Corporation but by 1901 it was decided that the site was no longer required. Permission to demolish the buildings and remove the human remains was obtained in the Manchester Corporation Bill of 1902[26]. I have not been able to determine precisely when the site was cleared but it was probably done in 1903[27].

The Albert Hall now occupies the site, The foundation stone of this large building, designed by W. J. Morley for the Methodist Mission, was laid on 24 March 1909. The Albert Hall opened in 1910 as a building for both worship and entertainment but fell out of use as a Methodist place of worship in 1969.

A LINGERING MEMORY?

In the 1990s the Albert Hall building became the home of a nightclub called Brannigans Bar. In 2003 the premises featured in an episode of the television programme *'Most Haunted'*. Staff had complained of ghostly sightings and poltergeist activity and the medium brought in for the programme claimed to sense the presence of the spirits of a child murderer and two dead children. Much was made of the building's former Methodist chapel on the first floor, but nobody seems to have been aware that the building stood on the site of a former burial ground. Had this been known, who knows what they would have made of it!

Brannigan's Bar closed in 2011 and the building remains unoccupied at the time of writing.

Human Remains Found

The following article appeared in The Manchester Courier and Lancashire General Advertiser on Saturday. 7 February 1846.

On Thursday afternoon, as some workmen were excavating the foundations of the old brewhouse of the King's Arms, Bridge Street, now occupied by Mr. Redfern, the owner, preparatory to the erection of some outbuildings, they discovered under a large flag the full length figure of (from supposition) a fellow creature. The remains had been deposited in a hole cut in the rock about six feet long, a foot and a half deep and about the same in breadth. The recess therefore corresponded in every particular to that of a grave for the reception of a human body, but the spades and picks of the workmen had been applied with such destructive effect that the bones which had been a very long time buried had been severed into bits and so obliterated all immediate evidence of identity.

Christ Church, King Street, Salford

Christ Church circa 1809

Although this book is concerned with Manchester's burial grounds and Salford falls outside my arbitrary boundary, I have exceptionally included Christ Church. This is firstly because it provides the link between the New Jerusalem chapel in Peter Street and Christ Church, Every Street and secondly because a great number of those buried there came from Manchester.

The denomination Bible Christian is somewhat misleading. The churches at King Street and Every Street (which is described in the following section) belonged to a sect peculiar to Manchester and which had no connection to the better-known Bible Christian movement, which emerged in Cornwall in 1815 as an offshoot of Methodism.

Christ Church owed its foundation to William Cowherd (1763-1816). Cowherd had originally served as a curate at St. John, Deansgate but subsequently adopted the beliefs of Emanuel Swedenborg and in 1793 became the first minister of the New Jerusalem Church in Peter Street. He broke away from Peter Street around 1800 as a result of doctrinal differences and established his own peculiar sect of Bible Christians for whom he built at his own expense a chapel in King Street, Salford.

Cowherd's followers were required to abstain both from eating animals and from consuming alcoholic liquor and he is credited as being one of the founding fathers of vegetarianism. The congregation's abstinence from meat-eating earned their chapel the facetious nickname the 'Beefsteak Chapel'.

THE BURIAL GROUND

The chapel was surrounded by a large burial ground. This was in use from as early as 1800 and so apparently pre-dates the chapel. The burial ground included a substantial number of private graves, from which the burial fees would have provided a useful source of income to the chapel.

Burial at Christ Church proved very popular. From the start, it was not restricted to members of his congregation but another reason for its popularity was that Cowherd's church offered inexpensive, sometimes free, burial for the poor, albeit that such burials would be in common graves or 'pits'. The surviving registers record over 10,000 burials during its first fourteen years. This compares to just short of 14,000 burials in the Collegiate Church registers over the same period.

Fittingly, when he died in 1816, William Cowherd was buried in the graveyard of his own chapel. His memorial read:

> 'William Cowherd, the founder and minister of Christ Church, Salford, died 24th of March, 1816, aged 53 years "All feared, none loved, and few understood."'

The verse is taken from the poet William Pope:

> 'He who would save a sinking land
> All fear, none love, few understand.'

William Cowherd's Grave

There had possibly been as many as 30,000 burials up to the closing of the graveyard in 1855 required by the Burial Acts.

JOSEPH BROTHERTON

One of the most prominent members of the King Street congregation was Joseph Brotherton. A life-long follower of William Cowherd, he became the recognised minister of the chapel after Cowherd's death. Brotherton was elected Salford's first Member of Parliament in 1832, a seat to which he was subsequently re-elected a further five times.

Brotherton died suddenly of a heart attack in 1857 but could not be buried in the graveyard of the church where he had both worshipped and ministered for much of his life since it had closed two years before his death. He had, however, been an ardent supporter of the movement to establish municipal cemeteries and so it is perhaps fitting that he was the first person to be buried at the new Weaste municipal cemetery in Salford.[28]

FROM GRAVEYARD TO TIMBER YARD

By 1869 the congregation had moved away from King Street to a new chapel in Cross Lane. The trustees, still saddled with a £100 chief rent on the site, decided to obtain some income from it by leasing the buildings and graveyard for use as a timber yard. The seven year lease which they granted stipulated that the gravestones should not be damaged, that the graves should not be disturbed and that the owners of private graves should have access to them.

The new tenant, a Mr. Bradford, proved cavalier in his interpretation of these terms and stacked an estimated thirty tons of timber on top of the gravestones, breaking several in the process and preventing access to the graves by their owners. Furthermore, he commissioned works including the installation of a sewer which required a six foot deep trench to be opened across the site. This excavation resulted in the removal of large quantities of bones, some of which were removed to a 'tip' in Broughton. Some of the burials were said to be as little as twelve inches below the surface.

Thomas Greenwood, whose parents and brother had been interred at Christ Church, wrote to P. H. Holland, the government's inspector of burial grounds, to demand his intervention. Holland conducted an enquiry and amongst other discoveries found '*a heap of rubbish covering, but hardly concealing, a large quantity of human bones*'. Holland, however, found himself powerless to force a remedy since unconsecrated graveyards were outside his authority. He recommended that the grave owners should meet to work out their own remedy and possibly petition the government for a change in the law. Greenwood replied that the only real remedy left for him was to request a licence to remove the remains of his family members for reburial elsewhere. Holland recommended against this and clearly feared that setting such a precedent would produce a flood of similar requests. It is not known whether Greenwood pursued this course.[29]

In the course of the inquiry, Holland commented that he had been told that the remains of as many as 35,000 people had been buried at Christ Church. Speaking on behalf of the chapel's trustees, a Mr. Peacock responded that this figure was a newspaper exaggeration and that it was quite impossible. Holland concluded that the burial ground contained perhaps 2,500 bodies. This estimate, which amounts to about 10% of the actual total, is breathtakingly inadequate. It seems clear that both Mr. Bradford and the trustees wished to downplay the scale upon which remains were being disturbed. Holland, whose experience should have informed him better, appears on this occasion to have been somewhat naïve.

The site of Christ Church chapel and its burial ground is now a car park. The remains have not been removed and there is nothing on the site to suggest its former use

How soon, alas! how very soon, the dead
Are quite forgotten! In their graves they lie
All quietly embedded, and we walk
Above them and around, and read their names,
And note their length of pilgrimage, then pass
Unthinkingly away. Or, it may be,
If that our friend or father lie interred
In some contiguous nook, we loiter on
And gaze a moment o'er the sepulchre
That hides him from us; then we muse awhile,
And, being melancholy, weep! What more?
Alas, how soon, how very soon, the dead
Are quite forgotten!

Anon.
From Manchester Poetry
edited by Charles Wheeler, 1838

Christ Church, Every Street

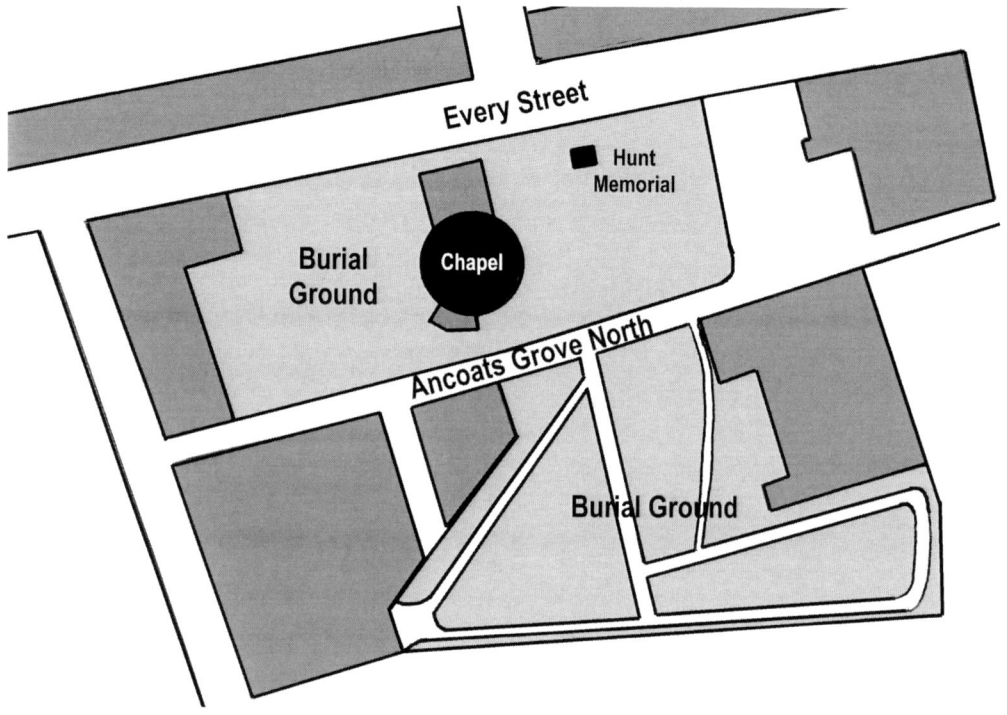

Every Street Chapel and Burial Grounds circa 1851

Every Street Chapel, also known as Christ Church and as the Round House or Round Chapel, was built by James Scholefield who built his house, and unusually shaped chapel, in what had formerly been a corn field on a country lane. The chapel opened for worship on 29 February 1824.

Scholefield was a former medical student, but had never obtained a formal medical qualification. Despite this he styled himself and practiced as a doctor. In the 1851 census he gave his profession as '*Surgeon in practice before 1815*', 1815 being the year after which the Apothecaries Act required qualifications to be obtained. Neither had he received a formal qualification in divinity but he had served as an assistant preacher to Rev. Cowherd at Christ Church in Salford by whom he was ordained to the ministry.

CHRIST CHURCH BURIAL GROUND

From the outset Scholefield established a burial ground to either side of the chapel. The first burials took place nearly two years before the chapel itself was completed. Scholefield did not take a stipend for his work as a minister and the burial fees appear to have provided a significant part of his income.

In the first few years, the registers record around 170-200 burials annually but by the 1830s the number had risen to 600-700. This encouraged Scholefield to extend the burial ground onto an adjacent and larger plot of land behind the chapel on the other side of Ancoats Grove. This increased the area of his burial ground to a total of 9,330 square yards making it similar in size to the Walkers Croft parish burial ground.

The burial ground offered both private graves, and brick-lined vaults, which could be purchased for the exclusive use of a family. These would generally be covered with a flat ledger stone on which would be inscribed the names of those buried beneath. Scholefield's records show that there were 838 family graves by the time the graveyard closed.

Family burials were, however, in the minority. The majority of the burials were in common graves without any memorial. It is not clear how many common graves there were or whether they were as capacious as those which were being used at other graveyards during this period.

Marginal notes in the burial register indicate the fees charged for burials. For burial in a common grave the charge appears to have been four shillings for an adult and two shillings for a small child. The price of interment in a private grave seems to have been between seven and eighteen shillings. This was, on top of the one Guinea fee to purchase the grave in perpetuity and further small charges to remove, inscribe and replace the memorial stone.

Scholefield offered his customers one more service; one perhaps unique to his graveyard. In the 1820s and early 1830s Manchester was plagued with an outbreak of body snatching. For a fee of eight shillings, he would erect a 'Safety Tomb' above the grave. This iron-railed enclosure was fixed in place for sufficient time to ensure that the body had decayed to the point where it would be worthless for medical research. Body snatching is described at greater length in Appendix 4.

THE 1832 CHOLERA EPIDEMIC

The Every Street graveyard and its minister attracted little attention until 1832. Asiatic cholera, was then sweeping the country and had appeared in the poorer parts of Manchester. Scholefield concocted and sold a cholera 'remedy' and there are claims that this was, at least in some cases, effective against the disease. Scholefield's remedy remained on sale long after its creator's death and was advertised as recently as 1941. Whether it was by then produced by one of Scholefield's descendants (his son qualified in medicine) and whether to the same formulation as in 1832 is not known.[30]

Scholefield was summonsed to appear at the New Bailey court in August of 1832. It was not his medical activities which caused concern but a charge that he had buried the bodies of cholera victims in his graveyard. The Local Board of Health, which had been established to manage the response to the outbreak, had issued an order which required all persons certified as having died of cholera to be buried in the parish burial ground at Walkers Croft. Copies of this order had been circulated to the operators of all the local graveyards and this certainly would have included Scholefield.

The Board of Health clearly believed that Scholefield had contravened the Board's order on several occasions. Their minute of 22 August 1832 notes that *'The Board finding that Mr. Scholefield continues to bury parties dying of cholera in his burial ground in spite of the Orders in Council, Mr. Heron be requested to summon Mr. Scholefield before the Magistrates…'*

The proceedings focused on one specific burial. Amelia Statham was a small child, who was said to have fallen ill the day after she had attended the burials of two cholera victims at Every Street. Twenty four hours after falling ill she too died of the disease. Amelia's father brought her body to Every Street for burial. Scholefield, who should have refused the child burial, is claimed to have said: *'I'm making myself liable to a penalty for interring this body; will you indemnify me?'* The father, distressed, agreed that he would, and Amelia's body was buried at about ten in the evening in a grave which had already been opened to accommodate a burial on the following day.

Although Scholefield argued that this was an isolated case and that he had only permitted the burial out of compassion for the distressed father, the court asserted that there had been complaints relating to the burial of at least fifteen or sixteen other cholera victims at Every Street. Scholefield disputed the numbers but finally admitted that he might have buried four victims of the disease. The court was surprisingly lenient and discharged Scholefield subject to his giving an undertaking that he would observe the order relating to the burial of cholera victims in the future.[31] Presumably he did so as there were no further complaints.

CHRIST CHURCH BURIAL SOCIETY

Scholefield found himself back in court in October 1837, this time to answer a summons in the Court of Requests raised by John Leigh, who was seeking to recover £1-14s-9d, his share of the funds of the 'Christ Church Sunday School Sick and Burial Society'. Leigh was a former scholar and teacher at the Sunday school and since 1828 he said that he had been contributing three-half-pence a week to a burial club of which Scholefield was the treasurer. Burial clubs were a popular way for working people to insure their families against the cost of burial by contributing a small weekly sum into a common fund. Leigh asserted that the club had been broken up on 18 June and that Scholefield had subsequently refused to refund his share of the funds. Scholefield replied that the club had not been broken up and hence Leigh was not entitled to any part of the funds. He further asserted that Leigh '...and others, having become stout men themselves, wished to break up the club and rob the little children of their shares.' Following evidence which showed the club to have been very poorly administered and to be operating outside the provisions of the Friendly Societies Act, the suit was dismissed on a legal technicality – in the words of John. Hill, the chief Commissioner of the court, 'I am sorry for it; but I cannot decide otherwise.'[32] Scholefield seems once more to have had a lucky escape.

LEFT WING LEANINGS

James Scholefield was politically well to the left and an active supporter of the Chartist movement. On 17 August 1842 he permitted his chapel to be used for a Chartist meeting. For this he was arraigned at the Lancashire Assizes of 21 March 1843 charged with conspiracy. Once more luck was with him and he was acquitted.

His Chartist sympathies were demonstrated once more in his burial ground, where in 1842 he had promoted the erection of a memorial to Henry 'Orator' 'Hunt, of Peterloo fame. The memorial took the form of a red sandstone obelisk thirty feet tall positioned prominently in front of the chapel. Some 15,000 attended the laying of the memorial's foundation stone by the MP Feargus O'Connor. An address was read saying that the monument was

> '...to perpetuate the memory of Henry Hunt and of those who fell in that action, and thus to show to future generations how the people of these times esteem sterling worth , and how they appreciate genuine patriotism.'

THE FUNERAL OF JOSHUA LYNESS

Every Street was again at the centre of political events in September 1842. A group of men and women had attacked the cotton mill belonging to William Morris in James Street, Oldfield Road. They were workers who had been 'turned out' from Morris's mill some time previously. A large group of Morris's workers emerged from the mill and waded into the crowd and in the course of the resulting melée a weaver called Joshua Lyness was dealt a fatal blow on the head.

Lyness's funeral took place on 19 September and inevitably became a focus for protest. A large crowd of weavers followed his coffin through the town from his house in London Road to the Every Street Chapel. Two bands accompanied the cortège playing suitably sombre music including the Dead March from Handel's Saul.

Lyness was buried close to the recently erected Hunt memorial. Scholefield seems to have recognised the potential for public disorder and conducted the burial ahead of two others which had been scheduled for that day so that the crowd might disperse more rapidly.[33]

STRENGTH TO STRENGTH

In the three decades after 1830 the number of burials at Every Street reached unprecedented levels. In only one year were there fewer than six hundred burials and by the mid-1840s there were typically nine hundred burials annually.

A significant contribution to these numbers came from the unlikely source of the Manchester Poor Law Guardians. A summary account which appears in the burial register shows that between 1842 and 1849 there had been no fewer than 1,146 burials paid for by the Manchester Poor Law Union. These had netted Scholefield a total of £219-10-6, an average of three shillings and ninepence per burial. The numbers, which rose steadily from 26 in 1842 to 413 in 1847, suggest that the arrangement began in the former year. These burials drop off rapidly in 1848 and 1849, probably because the Guardians had set up a contract with Manchester General Cemetery. The loss of this business does not, however, seem to have noticeably reduced the total number of burials.

SCHOLEFIELD'S FINAL YEARS

In 1847 Scholefield was elected as a Borough Councillor to represent New Cross Ward. His political leanings ensured that he had no shortage of enemies and his eligibility to stand for this office was called into question. The basis of the objection was that it was not permitted for a minister of the church to serve on the Council. After some argument the objections were dismissed since it was ruled that Scholefield was not recognised to be a minister of religion '...within the meaning of the Corporation Act'.

Scholefield died in 1855 and was buried, alongside his late wife Charlotte and four of his children, in a grave in his garden, close to the door of his house. At the end he was pragmatic concerning the future of the chapel. According to anecdote his deathbed instructions to his daughters were:

> 'Make what you can of it girls ... use it for a circus if you can – after all, it's round. It has served its time as a chapel'.

THE END OF THE BURIAL GROUND

An Order in Council was issued in 1854 requiring that no further burials should take place in the burial ground after 1 March 1856. In 1855, which should have been its final full year, the registers record their highest ever annual total of 1,215 burials. The graveyard did not, however, close.

Scholefield's executors proved as adept at sidestepping the law as Scholefield and they succeeded in obtaining a succession of postponements using the argument that there was no other burial ground in the district and that closure would be a great inconvenience to those who lived locally. The acceptance of this argument kept the graveyard open over the next decade. The executors' stalling finally came to an end, in July 1867 with an inquiry by Dr. Holland, the Government's Inspector of Burial Grounds, into whether the closure should be enforced. He accepted the argument concerning the lack of local graveyards but noted that with the imminent opening of the Philips Park municipal cemetery this would soon no longer be the case.

Scholefield's executors' accepted that circumstances had changed but now argued that Scholefield's family were dependent upon the income from the burial ground. They would, it was claimed, be ruined by the need to continue paying an annual chief rent of £200 on the land which would not be compensated by income from burials, the only way in which income could be obtained from the property.

The evidence given to Holland's inquiry shows that business had continued very much as usual since the original closure order. The executors' representative, somewhat incredibly, said that he was unable to say how many burials had taken place since the original closure order had been issued. He said that there had been about two hundred each year for the past three years and *'in all probability there had been 2,000 interments since the ground was ordered to be closed'*. The Inspector would perhaps have been surprised to know that the actual total during this time was well in excess of seven thousand.

When questioned about compliance with the requirement that bodies should be buried in individual graves, the executors' representative became evasive and claimed that half of the space was made up of family graves and that multiple interments were therefore permitted. He was equally evasive on the matter of the depth of soil over the final interment[34]. The closure order was subsequently enforced and the final burial, that of two year old Ralph Holland of Tame Street, took place on 6 August 1867. Since it had opened almost half a century earlier, some 28,000 people had been buried there.

THE FINAL YEARS OF EVERY STREET

By the time of the 1857 inquiry the chapel was already disused and the lower portion of the graveyard was described as being *'...in a very wild and neglected condition'*. In 1888 the executors decided to clear the graveyard of many of its memorials and their contractors advertised for those who wished to preserve their gravestones to come forward and claim them. The most notable loss was the monument to Henry Hunt. Despite last minute efforts to save the memorial and re-erect it on another site, it was dismantled and sold for £3 to be used as building stone.[35].

In 1897 the chapel was taken over by the Manchester University Settlement. The settlement was based at nearby Ancoats Hall and was a movement for social improvement. The chapel was used as a recreational building where the Settlement organised dances and staged theatrical events.

The graveyard was cleared of its remaining memorials and a number of the stones moved to the edge of the site along the wall. Mary Stocks describes the site as she remembered it in 1926:

> *'And outside its doors, smooth shale superseded Dr. Scholefield's tombstones which were lined up, backs to the playground wall, to remain there as silent unobtrusive witnesses to its past without impediment to the feet of those who were about to mould its future.'*[36]

Not all of the gravestones had been removed. The Settlement erected a hut on a part of the graveyard and when this was removed in 1940 a further forty-two stones were discovered.

The grounds were further improved in 1958 by a Quaker work camp, a group of about twenty young men and women who spent four weeks at the Settlement levelling and resurfacing part of the old graveyard with tarmac to provide areas for children to play netball, rounders and tennis.[37]

In the same year there was a report of subsidence on Every Street near to the chapel and suspicion was voiced that the road might have been been widened over part of the former graveyard. There seems little concrete evidence to support this suggestion.[38]

The Settlement moved out in 1983 and the chapel was demolished in 1986 despite last minute efforts by the Victorian Society and others to preserve the unique building.

Today the site of Scholefield's Christ Church chapel is a public space. A circular raised flower bed has been constructed on the footprint of the old chapel. Set into the wall of the flower bed is a large stone, which was once fixed high on the front of the building, bearing the inscription *'Christ Church Erected Anno Domini MDCCCXXIII'*. Around the flower bed, set into the grass, are a few of the surviving gravestones. Unfortunately, there is no information board to inform passers-by of the interesting history of this unusual site.

Rochdale Road Baptist Chapel

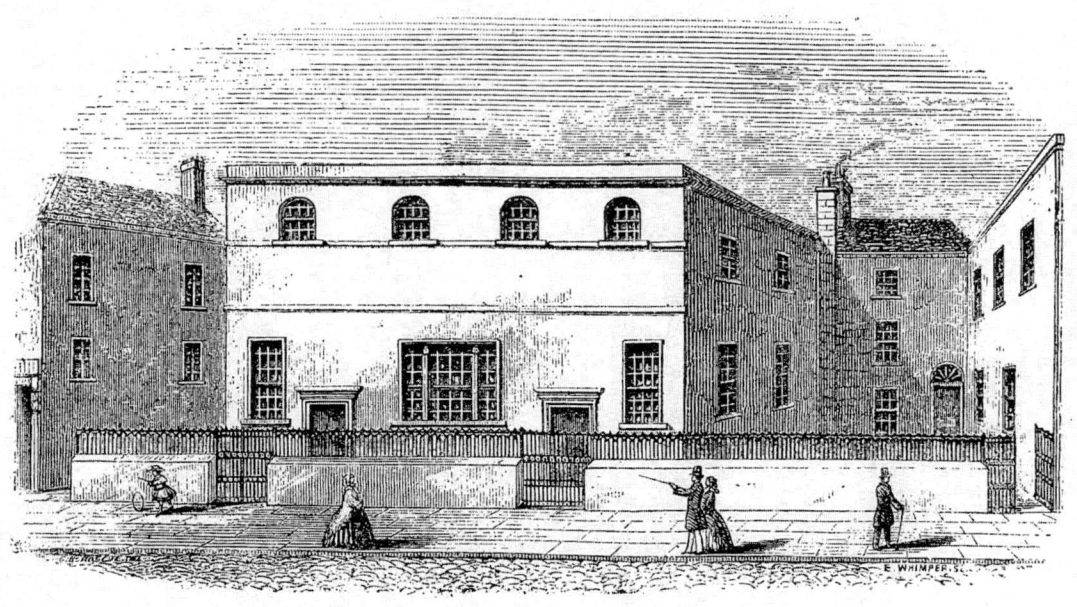

Rochdale Road (Gadsby's) Chapel

Standing on Rochdale Road by the corner of Sharp Street is a particularly fine Particular Baptist Chapel. The building dates from 1907 and is actually the third Baptist chapel to stand on this site.

The first chapel was established in 1789 by John Sharp. It was a small building measuring only about 12 yards by 15, which at this time did not face Rochdale Road but fronted a street then called Baptist Street after the chapel but later renamed Dyche Street. To complete the confusion, the chapel was originally known as the St. George's Road Chapel. Between the chapel and Rochdale Road (formerly called St. George's Road) was the chapel graveyard, a modest 26 by 16 yard plot.

Sharp continued as the minister of the chapel until his death in 1805. His body was buried inside the chapel he had founded, near the foot of the pulpit stairs, under a stone which read simply: '*John Sharp 1805*'.[39]

WILLIAM GADSBY

Following Sharp's death, the congregation invited the thirty-four year old Reverend William Gadsby to replace him. Gadsby came to the chapel in 1805 and remained until his death thirty-eight years later. Gadsby, a former ribbon weaver, was an active promoter of the dissenting cause and an outspoken advocate of the disestablishment of the Church of England. He was also a generous philanthropist and it was said that he would give away as much as £100 of his £280 annual income. Gadsby's name appears frequently in lists of donors to collections for soup kitchens and funds to assist unemployed weavers during the trade recession of the 1840s as well as being mentioned in connection with many other charitable causes. His congregation

William Gadsby

The loss of the little burial space which remained unused was not a great inconvenience to the congregation. Gadsby, five years earlier, had been the chief promoter of the Rusholme Road Dissenters' Cemetery and this offered an excellent and capacious alternative. The new chapel, a plain Georgian building with an austere interior fitted out with straight backed pews, quickly became known as 'Gadsby's Chapel'.

William Gadsby died in 1844 aged 71 years and was buried at Rusholme Road[40]. In 1947, when Rusholme Road Cemetery was cleared his memorial, though not his body, was removed to Charlesworth Strict Baptist Chapel in Derbyshire which he had been instrumental in founding. It is still there to the present day.

THE MEMORIALS

We have no complete record of who was buried in the chapel graveyard since the whereabouts of the burial register are not known but we are fortunate to have a record of the memorials which once covered their graves. The antiquary John Owen transcribed 41 memorials which he found at Rochdale Road Chapel. From these we have the names of of 88 people who were buried there between 1791 and 1821[41]. The last burials clearly took place immediately before the rebuilding of the chapel. Owen could not have visited much earlier than the 1840s or 1850s so it would appear that these memorials had been preserved following the rebuilding.

ANOTHER REBUILDING

Gadsby's old chapel was demolished around 1907 and a new and more imposing chapel built on the same site. This opened on 4 July 1908[42]. I have found no record from this time to suggest that bodies were found under the old chapel or in the old burial ground during the rebuilding of the chapel so it seems possible that they were removed during the 1822 rebuilding.

seems to have been much in need of charity. Gadsby himself had observed that *'The worshippers were a poor set'.*

The old chapel seems to have been poorly built and was already quite dilapidated when Gadsby took up his appointment. In 1822, following some dispute, the old chapel was taken down and a new chapel built facing onto Rochdale Road. Gadsby pushed through the rebuilding despite the concerns of some of his congregation that to accommodate a larger building it would be necessary to build it over the old graveyard, which was by now quite well filled. I have not found any record to show what became of those buried there and it is not inconceivable that the graves were left in place under the new building. It is also possible that they were removed to the Rusholme Road Dissenters' Cemetery, though the surviving cemetery records do not refer to any such removal.

Great Bridgewater Street Methodist Chapel

On 26 June 1800 Manchester's growing Methodist congregation purchased a plot of land lying between Great Bridgewater Street and Trumpet Street on the southern side of the town, an area described at the time as '*a growing and prosperous part of the town*'. The land was purchased from its joint owners, Sir George Philips Bart. and architect Charles McNiven for £52-18s. This seems a remarkably low price and may suggest that it was as much a gift as a sale. Philips was a member of a prominent Methodist family. On 10 April the following year the Great Bridgewater Street Chapel was opened. The chapel was well attended and among the congregation could be found many of Manchester's wealthy and influential families.

THE GRAVEYARD

From the outset, it was planned for the chapel should have its own graveyard. This was one of the largest nonconformist chapel graveyards and surrounded the chapel on its eastern, western and southern sides. It would be the first Wesleyan Methodist graveyard in Manchester and the only one close to the town centre. Hitherto, Manchester's early Methodists would have been buried in a variety of Anglican and nonconformist graveyards in and around the town.

The first burial took place on 17 October 1800, a full seven months before the chapel building was completed. This first interment, appropriately enough in Grave Number 1, was of George, the one year old son of Joseph Winsley, a joiner from Ancoats, and his wife Elizabeth. George had died of convulsions three days earlier. Over the following year, sales of graves netted the chapel in excess of £50 – substantially recovering the amount which had been paid for the land.

During the next half century the graveyard was to be the resting place of many Methodist ministers and missionaries. These included Jonathan Hern (died 1803), James Denton (1809), Benjamin Roberts and Samuel Bardsley (both 1848). One interesting burial is that of James Whittle who died 22 October 1812 aged 65 years. The burial register tells us that he was: '*the architect and builder of Oldham Road chapel and also the architect of this chapel*'.[43]

The burial ground was closed under the Burial Acts by Order in Council dated 16 June 1854. The final burial had taken place just five days earlier. As with the first burial, this was another infant, five month old Sarah Anna, the daughter of John and Sarah Sambrook of Moss Lane Hulme. In just over 50 years the burial registers record a total of 2,417 burials, possibly the greatest number for any of Manchester's nonconformist graveyards.

THE END OF THE BURIAL GROUND

Towards the end of the nineteenth century the more active and influential members of the congregation drifted away to the suburbs and

Great Bridgewater Street Chapel in 1898
The burial ground is behind the railings to the left of the building and the wall to the right.

chapel attendance declined. The chapel found itself in an area which provided an important access route for the expanding railways. The church's school building in Trumpet Street had already been sold in 1873 and demolished to make way for the Cheshire Lines railway. The proceeds had been used to build a new school but in 1898 the new schoolhouse, together with the chapel and burial ground, were sold to the Great Northern Railway Company for £25,000.

The purchase was part of a £1million project to build a railway goods depot adjacent to Manchester Central Station. The impressive Great Northern Goods Warehouse, which was at the centre of this development, still survives.

The final service at Great Bridgewater Street Chapel took place on Tuesday, 7 June 1898[44] and the remaining congregation subsequently decamped to the Bridgewater Hall in Hulme. The chapel was demolished and the bodies were removed from the graveyard in 1898 to be reinterred at Philips Park Cemetery. The inscriptions on the memorials had already been recorded in 1895, prior to the sale. The site of the chapel and its burial ground disappeared under the viaduct which carried the railway into the goods depot.

Central Station and the goods depot both closed in 1969 and the area was redeveloped once more. Central Station was converted into an exhibition centre, formerly called G-MEX but more recently renamed Manchester Central. The Great Northern Goods Warehouse became a leisure complex. The site of the Great Bridgewater Street Chapel and its burial ground is now lost under the 551 foot tall Beetham Tower hotel and apartment building.

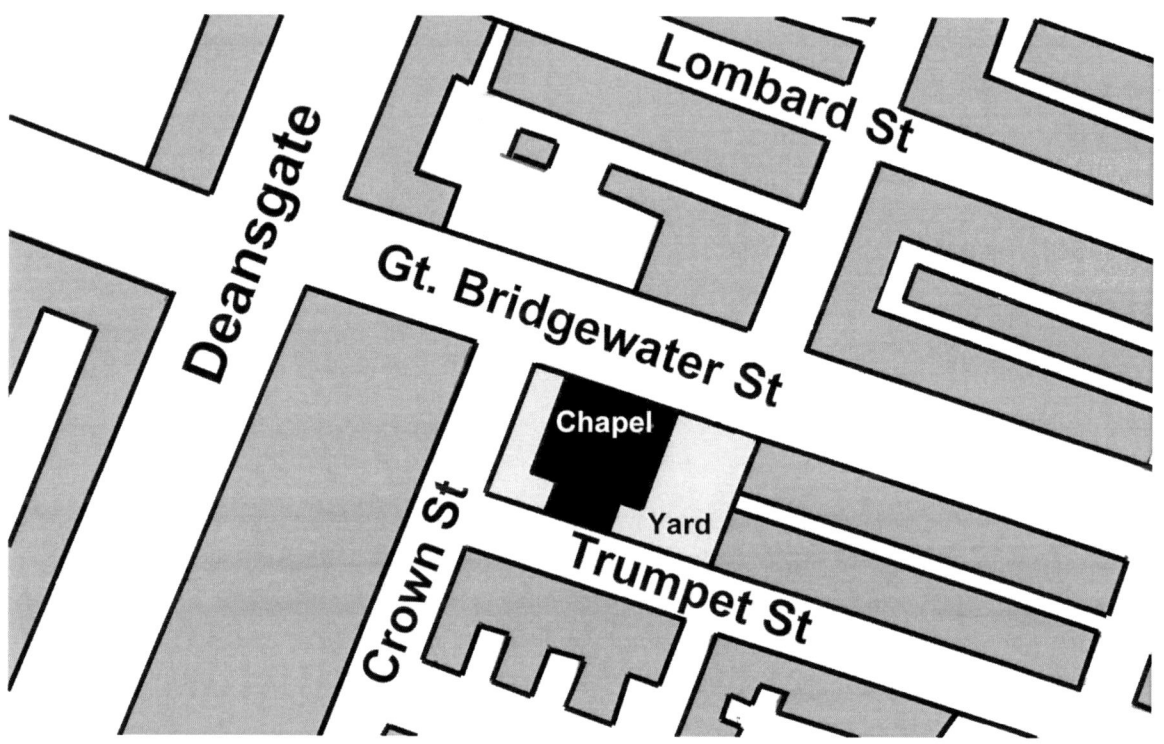

Great Bridgewater Chapel and Yard circa 1848

St. George's Chapel

St. George's Church, Oldham Road was discussed earlier but it appears that there was at one time also a nonconformist chapel close to St. George's Church and that this chapel possessed its own burial ground.

JOHN OWEN'S ACCOUNT

The antiquary John Owen visited the site in 1869 and made the following note:

'Feb 6, 1835 I visited the house of Mr. Cockerham, Goods Department at the Oldham Road railway station. It is situated in what is now called [blank] Street a few yards East of St. George's Church and appears to have been attached to a dissenting chapel which is now a roofless ruin with barely the four walls standing. Behind the buildings is a small burial place which I recollect was rather over forty years ago unenclosed, it appears to me that at that time the brickmakers had encroached so close to the graves that several of the coffins were exposed by the removal of the clay. I remember there were a number of gravestones. On the wall of the chapel there is still an oval tablet inscribed 'St. George's Chapel 1806'. It was subsequently used as I am told as a school attached to St. George's Church. Mr. Cockerham said the chapel belonged to Lady Huntingdon's denomination. There is an enclosed space in front of the house paved with fragments of flags some of which have belonged to grave stones. A portion of one formed one of the steps in the cellar inscribed "Sarah Kenworthy who died May 4, 1821". Mr. Cockerham remarked that it was an uncommon good cellar for keeping, for if he put a barrel of ale in it it would last ten times as long than if it was in any other part of the house, the domestics preferring to go without their ale

than run the risk of meeting Sally Kenworthy. There are two gravestones in the kitchen with the inscriptions downwards but of which he showed me a copy. The first has "In memory of Josiah Thorpe who died Janry. 1, 1823 a. 69y". 2nd "Here resteth the body of John Starrett who departed this life Nov 7, 1821 aged 49 also Jannet his wife who departed this life Dec. 4, 1815 a. 56 years". In Baines History, Directory and Gazetteer of the County of Lancashire Vol 2nd is the following: 'St. George's Chapel near St. George's Church was used by the Swedenborgians for some years but it is now solely appropriated to the reading of the funeral services over those who are interred in the cemetery' (1825).'[45]

Owen's account, supported by Baines's Directory, which was published in 1825 and appears to suggest that there was a chapel separate from St. George's Church but I have been unable to obtain any further information about this chapel. There is no sign of buildings on Roper's map of Manchester, which was published in 1807 but possibly surveyed earlier. However, on Pigot's map published six years later there are two small unidentified buildings to the southeast of St. George's Church. These are perhaps the chapel and house to which Owen refers.

None of the people named on the memorials recorded by Owen appear in the burial registers for St. George's Church either before or after its acquisition by Warden and Fellows of the Collegiate Church. This seems to confirm Owens's account that there was both a separate chapel and probably a separate burial ground attached to it. No registers or other documentary records are known to exist.

Notes for Nonconformist Burial Grounds

[1] The Five Mile Act was one of several laws which were passed, following the restoration of the monarchy, to re-assert the authority of the established church and to suppress religious dissent. The 1665 Act forbade nonconformist ministers from coming within five miles of any incorporated town or the place of their former living. It was not formally repealed until 1812 but was a dead letter by 1689 when the Act of Toleration was passed.

[2] Manchester Courier & Lancashire General Advertiser, Monday 24 November 1884.

[3] Manchester Courier & Lancashire General Advertiser, Thursday 12 July 1883.

[4] Manchester Courier & Lancashire General Advertiser, Saturday 11 January 1845.

[5] Manchester Guardian, 20 March 1914 published a letter from Lawrence Chubb of the Commons and Footpaths Preservation Society opposing the proposal to redevelop the site and remove the remains.

[6] Manchester Guardian, 7 August 1874.

[7] Manchester and the Early Baptists, Ralph Ashton, 1916. Ashton suggests that the coffins may have belonged to members of the Winterbottom family. This is not, however, supported by the initials picked out in nails on the coffin lids.

[8] Manchester Guardian, 11 March 1899.

[9] There is a photograph dated to 1838 in the Manchester Local Image collection

[10] Manchester Streets and Manchester Men – Third Series, T. Swindells, 1907.

[11] Manchester Guardian 3 February 1939.

[12] Reminiscences of Manchester Fifty Years Ago, J. T. Slugg, 1881.

[13] A Picture of Manchester, Joseph Aston, 1815.

[14] Manchester Times Saturday, 11 May 1839.

[15] Manchester Guardian 1 November 1875.

[16] Manchester Courier & Lancashire General Advertiser, Saturday 4 November 1854. *Non est inventus* – was not found.

[17] Gentleman's Magazine Vol. 177 page 418, 1845.

[18] Memorials of Manchester Streets, Richard Wright Proctor, 1974.

[19] Manchester Courier & Lancashire General Advertiser, Saturday 2 August 1828.

[20] Owen Manuscripts Vol. 13, Page 49.

[21] Manchester Guardian 17 May 1877.

[22] A Picture of Manchester, Joseph Aston, 1815.

[23] New Jerusalem Church Repository for the Years 1817 & 1818, 1818.

[24] History of the Peter Street Society of the New Church, Manchester, Francis Smith, 1892.

[25] Manchester Courier & Lancashire General Advertiser, Tuesday 8 March 1892.

[26] Manchester Courier and Lancashire General Advertiser, Saturday 25 January 1902.

[27] A statutory notice stating that the bodies would be removed '…on the first of March next year or soon thereafter' appeared in the Manchester Evening News of Monday 24 November 1902.

[28] Manchester Courier & Lancashire General Advertiser, Saturday 10 January 1857.

[29] Manchester Times, Saturday 28 May 1869.

[30] Notes by E. Bosdin Leech associated with his transcript of the Every Street registers produced circa 1941 include an undated newspaper advertisement for Scholefield's remedy.

[31] Manchester Guardian 1 September 1832.

[32] Manchester Guardian 4 October 1837.

[33] Manchester Courier & Lancashire General Advertiser, Saturday 24 September 1842.

[34] Manchester Guardian 11 July 1867.

[35] Manchester Guardian, 3 October 1888.

[36] 50 Years in Every Street, Mary D. Stocks, 1945.

[37] Manchester Guardian, 25 July 1958.

[38] Manchester Guardian, 18 September 1958.

[39] Manchester and the Early Baptists, Ralph Ashton, 1916.

[40] Manchester Courier & Lancashire General Advertiser, 10 February 1844.

[41] See Owen Manuscripts Vol. 24 pp 18-33, Vol. 32 pp 68-72.

[42] Manchester Guardian, 6 July 1908.

[43] A Souvenir of Great Bridgewater Street Wesleyan Chapel and Sunday School, Manchester and Queen Street Sunday School, Hulme, Edwin Farrow and Chas. J. Wallworth, 1898.

[44] Manchester Faces and Places Vol. ix page 183, 1898.

[45] Owen Manuscripts Vol. 13 Page 14.

Roman Catholic Burial Grounds

Roman Catholic Burial Grounds

Aside from the several dissenting Protestant chapels, the Roman Catholic Church also had a significant presence in Manchester. The Roman Catholic faith was actively and enthusiastically suppressed throughout the seventeenth and well into the eighteenth century but a series of Catholic Relief Acts was passed starting in 1778 and these culminated in the Catholic Relief Act of 1829, which lifted most of the remaining restrictions.

Undoubtedly many of Manchester's Catholics worshipped in secret during the times of persecution. There is the suggestion that there was a chapel and burial ground in the early eighteenth century, but this seems speculative, not to say unlikely, and the first well-recorded Catholic Chapel, which was dedicated to St. Chad, was established in Rook Street in 1774. This was followed twenty years later by St. Mary's in Mulberry Street, which also provided Manchester's first Roman Catholic burial ground.

Further churches were built as the (predominantly Irish) Roman Catholic population grew to reach an estimated 10% of the population of the town by 1841. St. Augustine's was consecrated in Granby Row in 1820, St. Patrick's, Livesey Street in 1832 and (a new) St. Chad's on Cheetham Hill Road in 1847. Each of these had a burial ground and each accommodated considerable numbers of burials.

Following the potato famine of the 1840s the number of Irish Catholics in Manchester increased considerably. The majority of these new arrivals were poor and occupied the poorest and most unsanitary housing, creating substantial local concentrations in such areas as Angel Meadow and the so-called '*Little Ireland*', an area of low-lying land to the south of the present Oxford Road railway station. The burial grounds of the Catholic churches reflect the large numbers of poor parishioners living in these and other deprived areas with considerable numbers of coffins densely packed into large common graves.

The graveyard closures following the Burial Acts of 1854 posed a greater problem for Roman Catholics than for Protestant dissenters. While Protestants simply wished to avoid burial under Church of England rites, Catholics in addition wished to be buried in a graveyard which had been consecrated according to the rites of the Church of Rome. The last of the city's Catholic burial grounds managed to secure an extension of closure date until 1858 but from then onwards there was no Catholic burial ground in Manchester. It seems that most were buried either at the newly opened graveyard of St Mary at Failsworth (The Immaculate Conception) or in the Catholic section of the municipal cemetery at Weaste.

When Manchester's first municipal cemetery opened its Catholic consecrated section at Philips Park in 1866, this became the principal place for Manchester's Catholics to be buried but the choice of site for the Catholic section soon proved disastrous and a better alternative was sought. A dedicated Catholic cemetery, St. Joseph's, was finally established at Moston in 1874, though many Catholics continued to be buried at Philips Park and later at Southern Cemetery.

Smithy Door Roman Catholic Chapel

Smithy Door

There were undoubtedly Roman Catholics in Manchester before their first church was established in Rook Street in 1774 but evidence of where they worshipped is scant. Edward Baines wrote in 1825:

> *'In the early part of the last century the Catholics had a chapel in Smithy Door in a building now occupied by the Grey Horse public house, behind which there is still a large, unoccupied piece of ground then used as a burial ground'.[1]*

Further information appeared in 1834 in a book written by the historian Samuel Hibbert and others:

> *'The ancient chapel, which was founded by Robert de Grelly who flourished in the reign of Henry III and Edward*

I and at the time of the Ecclesiastical survey, was held by Henry Ryle, incumbent of the chantry, is supposed to have been situated between Smithy Door and Old Millgate where a portion of land, which has never been built on still remains, and this plot tradition, often the true vehicle of oral testimony to this day, points out as being the site of a cemetery attached to it ... Early in the year 1829 the cellars belonging to the Grey Horse tavern, Smithy Door, were enlarged and for this purpose the whole north end of this plot in length and in width about four yards was excavated to the depth of about eleven feet. The upper stratum for about four feet in depth was found to be adventitious earth composed of soil, rubbish, bones and other foreign matter. The remaining depth was fine native gravel among which here and there a bone was discovered, but these could not be identified as human'.[2]

These accounts suggest the existence of a burial ground in this location, but neither presents conclusive evidence. If the number of burials was small and there had been none for a century or more, it is quite possible that there would have been little to find, particularly if the excavation was by builders rather than archaeologists.

Whether a Roman Catholic burial ground really existed at this location may never be proved. Hostility to Catholics in the early 18th century was such that it would be highly unlikely that they could have maintained such a visible chapel. Perhaps there was a burial ground but at a much earlier date. If there was a connection to the Catholic Church, possibly this was pre-reformation when Catholicism was the established faith. It seems unlikely that the use of this site as a burial place will ever be proved conclusively.

St. Mary (RC) Church, Mulberry Street

Catholic Chapel Mulberry Street

The small and rather plain church shown above and dedicated to St. Mary, was erected in Mulberry Street in 1794 by Fr. Roland Broomhead on a small plot of land which had been purchased from John Leaf of Pendleton[3]. At this time Mulberry Street was crowded with poor quality housing. Squeezed into a very small site, it was not possible to have an outside churchyard, but the basement of the building was set to use as a burial vault. Joseph Aston, writing in his *'Picture of Manchester'* in 1816 refers to St. Mary's as having vaults which he describes as *'...recently constructed...'*.

The burial registers are incomplete and cover only 1816 to 1825 and 1832 to 1837. It is not possible to say whether burials took place before 1816 (though Aston's comment suggests they probably did not) or precisely how many burials there were in total. The earlier register records 774 burials and the latter about 260, so if a similar average was maintained between 1826 and 1831 then a grand total of something like 1,500 seems possible.

This is a very large number of interments for what is not a very large site – the building occupies a footprint of only about 3,500 square feet.

It is the normal practice for bodies placed in traditional vaults to be enclosed in lead-lined coffins. It is difficult to see that the poor families who worshipped at St. Mary's would have had the money for such coffins and an alternative and more probable scenario is that wooden coffins were buried in the ground under the church. The 1816 burial register is titled '*A list of interments in the Catholic Cemetery, Mulberry Street, Manchester*' which may suggest this to be the case. A similar suggestion comes from the newspaper account of the reopening in 1848 which says '*Many of our readers may be aware that a burial ground existed at St. Mary's (now for a long time closed) which until the building of St. Austin's in 1821 was the only place for the interment of members of the Catholic religion*'.[4] Whatever the method of interment, the vaults would probably have been quite unsavoury.

In 1833, the building was in need of serious repair. Henry Gillow, the incumbent priest, engaged a team of unemployed workmen to undertake repairs and to replace the roof. Unfortunately, Gillow failed to engage a master builder to direct the work. The roof collapsed on 8 August 1835, though fortunately the church was empty at the time.[5] Burials consequently ceased for a period and then briefly restarted towards the end of 1836 after a temporary roof had been erected and the church brought back into use. However, after sixteen further burials over the next year the register comes to an end with the burial of 8 month old Anne Creswel Leeming on 30 April 1837.

The church closed again in 1847 and was completely rebuilt as the splendid building which exists today and which has deservedly acquired the name '*The Hidden Gem*'. The new building was erected over the old burial ground and the remains left *in situ*. It reopened for worship on 19 October the following year. The burial ground is not mentioned in the Orders in Council which closed most of the city burial grounds in or after 1854, so it is probably safe to assume that interments had ceased permanently in 1837.

It is clear that the burial ground was not disturbed during the rebuilding but less clear as to what, if any, measure was taken to seal it. John Marsh, who was born in 1918 and whose father had been a church warden at Mulberry Street recalled playing in the crypt during the 1920s while he waited for his father to finish his duties. He said he clearly remembered playing with skulls down there.[6]

St. Mary, Mulberry Street today

St. Augustine's RC Church, Granby Row

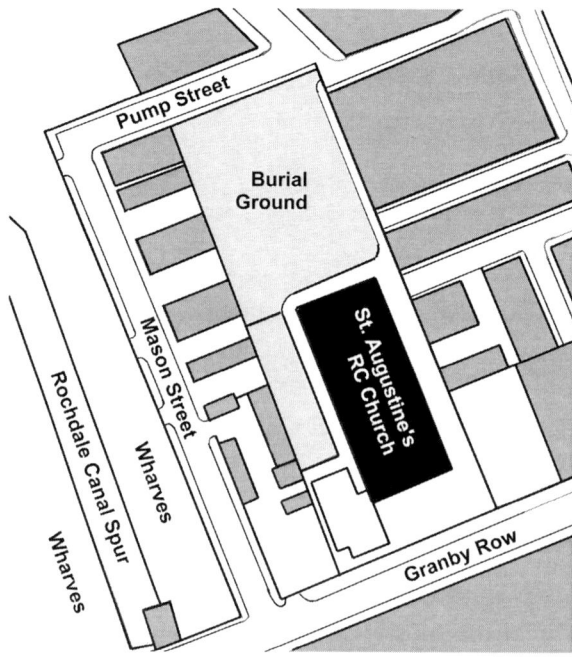

St. Augustine's circa 1849

St. Augustine's was designed by the local architect John Palmer and opened for worship in October 1820. The new church lay just to the north of the River Medlock and was surrounded by fine residential buildings. This was not to last and gradually the area was taken over by warehouses and other commercial buildings.

St. Augustine's had come into being as a result of the efforts of Father Roland Broomhead, whom we have already met as the founder of St. Mary's, but within days of being carried into the new church on its opening day, Broomhead died and became the first to be interred in its vaults. John Palmer, the architect, was to follow in 1846.[7]

There was both a graveyard to the rear and along the westward side of the church together with extensive vaults under the building. Considerable numbers of Manchester's Roman Catholic population were buried at St. Augustine's. The total number buried and their names remain unknown, owing to the loss of the burial registers.

Further burials in the graveyard and interments in the vaults were prohibited by order of the Secretary of State on 21 March 1854 but it seems likely that the graveyard was already becoming filled to capacity by this time.

FRIGHTFUL SCENES

Within a few months following its closure, the burial ground was in the newspapers under a headline of '*Frightful Scenes in a Graveyard*'. A decision had been taken to erect schoolrooms over the section of the churchyard adjacent to Pump Street. There had supposedly been no burials in this part for many years. Neither the church officials nor the builders seem to have been greatly concerned about disturbance to the human remains and deep trenches were being excavated for the foundations. The excavations exposed the remarkable density with which the ground had been filled with the dead..

Witnesses described adult coffins packed in 'shoulder-to-shoulder' and children's and infants' coffins packed into the spaces between them. It was said that it was impossible to put a spade between them. If this was not shocking enough, no fewer than thirteen layers of coffins had been exposed and still the excavations had not

*St. Augustine, Granby Row
Shortly before demolition*

reached the deepest layer. It was estimated that there could be as many as eighteen layers which would have filled pits up to twenty feet deep. Over the whole of this scene of horror was a covering of as little as twelve inches of soil.

What was still more disturbing was that some of the burials had been much more recent than claimed. A claim that the bodies had been buried *'thirty years and more'* seems disingenuous, given that it was only thirty four years since the very first burial had taken place. Witnesses described *'noisome smells'* and noted that *'black unctuous matter oozed out in abundance'*.[8] Both the church officials and the builder must have been aware from the outset that remains would be disturbed and both should have been aware that to remove remains from a graveyard without

a licence was an offence. Astonishingly, not only had they proceeded with the work, but had done so in full public view. Members of the public wandered through the excavations and even small children were seen to be playing amid the remains. Shortly afterwards and following a visit to the site by the mayor, Joseph Heron, the Town Clerk, wrote to Charles Gibson, the solicitor for the Salford diocese. Gibson's reply a week later reported that the Bishop, Dr. Turner, had been unaware of the nuisance being caused and that he had conducted an investigation and stopped the work. The investigation determined that the work had commenced *'under misapprehension of the consequences'*. It had not been appreciated how many graves would be disturbed. Two *'highly respected medical gentlemen'* had been

Removal of remains from St. Augustine's,
Granby Row 1909

consulted before the work commenced and had expressed no concern in relation to the works proposed.[9] No prosecutions appear to have followed the unlicenced disturbance of the remains.

CLEARANCE AND DEMOLITION

The church itself continued in use to 1908 when the congregation moved to York Street. The buildings and graveyard were sold to Manchester Corporation for £39,000 under the Manchester Corporation Act of 1908 to make way for the Manchester Technical College. This in turn became UMIST (University of Manchester Institute of Science and Technology) and is now part of the University of Manchester.

Following publication of the necessary statutory notice[10], the human remains were removed to Moston Cemetery. This was done over an extended period in 1909, the coffins being removed a few at a time on horse-drawn carts.[11] The original estimate for this work was £1,000 but when exhumations commenced, it was discovered that there were very many more bodies than had been thought, both in the graveyard and under the church. This suggests that those planning the work were unaware of the revelations some fifty years earlier. The greater number of remains and the removal of a greater amount of material recommended by the City Surveyor as a sanitary precaution dramatically increased the cost. The matter was referred back to the Corporation, which agreed to allocate a further £5,000 to complete the work.

St. Augustine's had been the burial place of several of Manchester's Roman Catholic clergy and special arrangements were made for their exhumation and reburial in the *Campo Santo* vault at St. Joseph's in Moston. Those whose remains were reinterred were the Reverends Roland Broomhead (died 1820 and founder of St. Mary, Mulberry Street), J. Rickaby (1821), T. Parkinson (1821), J Ashurst (1824), J. Smith (1827), T. Maddocks (1829), Henry Gillow (1837

and former minister of St. Mary, Mulberry Street), John Laytham (1838), J. Parsons (1838), J. Ward (1844) and J. Billington (1845).[12]

A plaque on the present buildings states:

'On this site between 1820 and 1908 stood St. Augustine's RC Church and its parish schools. Known as 'St. Austin's', it was the third oldest Catholic Church in Manchester. By the 1840s it served over 10,000 predominantly Irish parishioners. Between 5,000 and 15,000 people were buried in the Church grounds. In 1908 the Church moved to York Street and in 1940 to All Saints.'

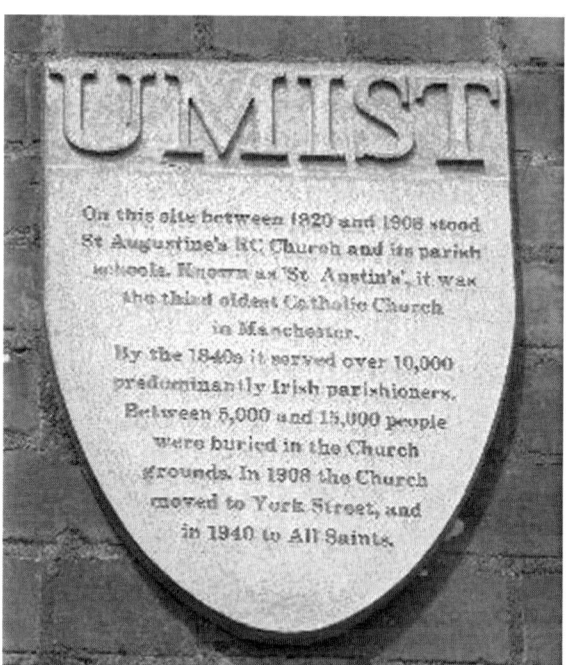

The memorial plaque at UMIST

No burial registers are known to survive and the substantial under-estimate of the number of burials in 1909 suggests that they had already been lost by that time. At the time of clearance a record was made of the gravestones and this is now held by Manchester Archives.

St. Patrick's RC Church, Livesey Street

St. Patrick's Church was founded in 1832, at a time when the Irish Catholic population of Manchester was rising rapidly. The church was built on a three-and-a-half acre site to the north side of Livesey Street, on land which had been purchased from Henry Sudell. The church, built of brick and with seating for 1,700 worshippers, opened in March 1832. Father Daniel Hearne, who had previously been a curate at St. Mary, Mulberry Street, was the first incumbent. The area behind the church, which made up about half of the site, was used to create a burial ground.

It is unclear when the first burial took place since the first few pages of the very fragile burial register have been lost but the burial ground is presumed to have opened at the same time as the church. The first burial for which there is a record was on 10 May 1832. St. Patrick's Nunnery was built adjacent to the church between 1834 and 1836 and there was a small burial ground for the burial of nuns in the north-west corner behind the nunnery.

A DISPUTED FEE

St. Patrick's was the scene of an unfortunate dispute in 1839. On 11 June John White, a hand-loom weaver who lived in Dewhurst Court off St. George's Road, and his wife Mary brought the body of their five year old son James for burial at St. Patrick's. The funeral service was read and the body deposited in an open common grave. After the service the child's parents went to pay the sexton the six shillings burial fee but were shocked to be told that '...*since the child was two or three months over the age of five years...*', they would have to pay the full adult burial fee of twelve shillings. They appealed to the priest (presumably Fr. Hearne), who rather disingenuously said he could do nothing since it was a matter for the sexton. Unable to raise a further six shillings immediately, they offered to return with the money the next day, even offering to leave the coat belonging to another of their children as a surety. Their offer was met not just with a demand for immediate payment but by the sexton removing the coffin from the grave and telling the couple that if they did not remove it from the church, he would call a policeman to remove it for them. Left with no alternative, the parents took the body to the Walker's Croft parish burial ground, where it was buried the following day. The coverage of this incident in the Manchester Courier showed no small measure of anti-Catholic opinion by the newspaper.[13]

THE BURIAL ACTS

The Orders in Council published on 15 April 1854 required the closure of all of the Catholic Burial grounds in Manchester including St. Patrick's. A date of 1 March 1855 was set, after which only burials in existing private vaults would be permitted. However, an appeal would appear to have been submitted and a second Order in Council appeared on 31 March 1855 extending the effective date to 1 March 1856. Further extensions were subsequently secured until a final Order in Council dated 5 June 1858 demanded that burials cease 'forthwith'. The final burial took place a week later on 12 June.

ILLEGAL INTERMENTS

Although extensions were obtained to the 1855 closure date, burials were only permitted to continue subject to a restriction limiting burials to a single body in each grave. Early in 1858 Mr. Fox, the Corporation's Inspector of Nuisances, visited the graveyard to investigate several reports concerning burials at St. Patrick's. As a result of his findings, Dr. Cantwell, then the incumbent of St. Patrick's, was summoned to appear at the City Police Court. When he appeared on 22 January it was asserted that he had permitted burials in his churchyard which contravened the single interment restriction.

On 17 January Fox said that he had seen a total of fifteen coffins, seven of which contained adults and eight of which contained children, laid end-to-end in a single trench with only what he described as a 'feather of clay' between them. It appears that the sexton had found a novel way to minimise the digging required and to optimise the use of space. If this was not an infringement of the restrictions, it certainly stretched them close to breaking point.

Cantwell appears to have escaped on a technicality. His solicitor objected that the Town Clerk's *copy* of the Order in Council which specified the restrictions was inadmissible as evidence. The Town Clerk withdrew the summons, saying that he would issue a fresh summons once he had obtained a copy of the London Gazette containing the original Order.[14] No further summons appears to have been raised and it is possible that the Town Clerk had become aware that the Home Office intended to close the graveyard within a few weeks and so let matters lie.

NUMBER OF BURIALS

The surviving burial registers record something over 27,000 burials during the 26 years the graveyard was active; an average of something over a thousand a year. This divides into two clear periods. From 1832 to 1845 the annual number averaged about 700 while from 1846 onwards it virtually doubled to average about 1,370. It seems probable that this reflects both the large influx of immigrants from Ireland in the wake of the potato famine together with the effects of the closure of the burial ground underneath St. Mary's.

AN UNFORTUNATE ACCIDENT

At about four o'clock on Thursday 3 October 1901, a schoolboy called Martin Scully decided, for reasons known only to a twelve year old boy, to climb over the boundary wall behind St. Patrick's. In doing so he caught hold of one of the gravestones, which proved to be insecure. The boy fell and the stone toppled onto his head and shoulders, crushing him to death.

Martin's body was discovered about an hour later by a scullery maid who worked at the St. Patrick's Convent and was taken to the Royal Infirmary. The boy was initially not identified but shortly afterwards a man came forward and identified the body as that of his son, who had gone missing earlier that day. However, when the man went to the police station to collect the boy's belongings, as soon as he saw Martin's clothing, he realised it did not belong to his son, who turned up safe-and-sound some time later. The dead boy was correctly identified that evening by his father, also called Martin Scully, an ironworks labourer who lived in nearby Bebbington Street[15].

THE END OF OLD ST. PATRICK'S

The original St. Patrick's Church survived to celebrate its centenary but was by now showing its age. A final service took place on 13 January 1935[16] and demolition commenced the following day. A new St. Patrick's, which stands to this day, was built on the same site and consecrated by the Bishop of Salford on 17 March 1937[17]. It appears that the burial ground had been cleared some years earlier prior to the building of a new boys' and girls' school, which commenced in 1924. The remains exhumed were reinterred in the St. Joseph's burial ground at Moston.[18]

Notes for Roman Catholic Burial Grounds

1   Baines History, Directory and Gazetteer of the County Palatine of Lancashire Part II, page 138, 1825.
2   History of the Foundation in Manchester of Christ's Church, Chetham's Hospital and the Free Grammar School, Samuel Hibbert, John Palmer, William Robert Whatton & J. Greswell, 1834.
3   Bancks's Directory of 1800 lists John Leaf Esq. Of Pendleton.
4   Manchester Times, 21 October 1848.
5   Manchester Guardian, 15 August 1835.
6   I am indebted to Lawrence Gregory of Salford Diocesan Archives for this account of his conversation with John Marsh.;
7   Manchester Evening Chronicle, Saturday 19 January 1909.
8   Manchester Courier & Lancashire General Advertiser, Saturday 24 June 1854.
9   Manchester Courier & Lancashire General Advertiser, Saturday 8 July 1854.
10 Manchester Courier & Lancashire General Advertiser, Friday 19 March 1909.
11 Manchester Evening News, 7 September 1909. The article includes a photograph of one of the carts being used to transport the coffins.
12 Manchester Courier & Lancashire General Advertiser, Saturday 24 July 1909.
13 Manchester Courier & Lancashire General Advertiser 22 June 1839. The Courier's coverage of the incident showed a marked anti-Catholic sentiment. A few days later a further article appeared under the title 'More Popish Impudence' and accused poor Catholics of obtaining a coffin from the overseers and then raising large sums for an elaborate funeral at the Catholic Church.
14 Manchester Courier & Lancashire General Advertiser, Saturday 23 January 1858.
15 Manchester Courier & Lancashire General Advertiser, Friday 4 October 1901. The inquest is reported briefly in the same publication dated Monday 7 October.
16 Manchester Guardian, 14 January 1935.
17 Manchester Guardian, 18 March 1937.
18 St. Patrick's Former Pupils' Association web site www.stpatricksfpa.co.uk

The Private Cemeteries

The Birth of the Private Cemetery

By the early 19th century the unsightly and unsanitary condition of city centre burial grounds was becoming an acute problem. Burial grounds operated against a background in which legislation was substantially absent. There were no rules to govern where a burial ground might be situated, no statutory limits to the numbers who might be buried in a grave and no requirements as to the depth at which a body should be buried. There were laws concerning 'nuisance' which might in theory have been used to limit the worst excesses but there seems to have been little effort to enforce standards upon the graveyard owners, who at this time were the local churches.

Manchester does not appear to have experienced quite such appalling conditions as George Walker was to describe in London in 1839[1] but there was, nevertheless, no shortage of horror stories and it was becoming clear that new solutions would have to be found as the city continued to grow.

The Church of England showed little inclination towards improvement. New burial grounds were opened but only when it became virtually impossible to cram another coffin into the old one and when new burial grounds were opened, they were exploited in the same unsatisfactory fashion as those which they replaced. The single goal was to accommodate as many burials in the smallest piece of ground and at the lowest cost possible. That burial fees contributed usefully to church income encouraged the maximum exploitation of the available burial space.

The civil authorities were equally disinclined to provide a better alternative. Up to 1838 Manchester was administered as a manor which regarded the matter as one for the church. Even after the granting of borough status there seems to have been little interest by the Council, who were in any event hampered by a lack of legal authority to acquire land and establish cemeteries. Had they done so, possibly by securing a private Act of Parliament as was done in Leeds, it is questionable whether they would have operated cemeteries in a much more satisfactory way than had previously prevailed.

What neither church nor state would address found a solution in private enterprise. The idea was simply to form a joint stock company, capitalised by the issue of shares. The company would use its capital to purchase a suitable piece of land and open a cemetery. The cemetery would operate on a commercial basis, charging fees for burials and memorials. The fees would be set so as to cover the operating costs and to provide a return to the shareholders by way of annual dividends.

The unique selling point of these new cemeteries would be their aesthetic appeal. Instead of cramped, overflowing plots hemmed in by city buildings, they would be open, airy, landscaped and planted with with trees and shrubs. Plots would be well-spaced so that the opening of new graves would not disturb the occupiers of older ones. The aesthetics of such cemeteries had been described by the Frenchman Bernardin de Saint Pierre (1737-1814) and perhaps the best known early example is the Père-Lachaise Cemetery in Paris which opened in 1804. These first 'garden' cemeteries were to prove highly influential in the design of England's private cemeteries as well as many of their municipal successors.

There is some dispute concerning which was the first English cemetery to be conceived as a purely commercial venture. The Rosary in Norwich was laid out in 1819 but the first burial did not take place there until November 1821[2]. Rusholme Road Dissenters' Cemetery in Manchester was conceived in 1819, somewhat later than The Rosary, but the first burial at Rusholme Road took place in May 1821, some six months before its East Anglian counterpart. While The Rosary was slow to attract business, with only 34 burials in its first six years of operation, Rusholme Road proved immediately successful. It was popular with the public, particularly middle class nonconformists, and consequently proved, at least in the short term, outstandingly profitable for its investors.

By the early 1830s the idea that there was a good profit to be made from operating cemeteries as commercial ventures was becoming established. New private cemeteries opened in several cities including, among others, Birmingham and Sheffield in 1836, Bristol and York in 1837.

Where there is a profit to be made from a new market, there is seldom a shortage of schemes to attract investors and so it was with cemeteries. An editorial appeared in the Manchester Guardian in 1836 under the title 'Joint Stock Mania'[3]. The editorial focused particularly on plans to float companies which proposed to open new burial grounds and commented '...we find that in Manchester alone there are no less than six new cemeteries projected.' The economic viability of these schemes was questioned. It was pointed out that the land for the Rusholme Road Cemetery had been acquired for a fraction of the cost projected for any one of the proposed schemes but even the Rusholme Road company had never produced dividends totalling more than £1,000 in any one year. (This was not quite true as the previous year the total dividend had been £1,200. However this was the high point in its performance and the more general observation is indisputably true). Where was the business to come from which would support six large cemeteries? Was Manchester expecting a new visitation of the plague? The six proposed cemeteries and their intended capitalisation were as follows:

Manchester General Cemetery	£20,000
Salford and Hulme Cemetery	£20,000
Salford, Pendleton, Hulme and Broughton Royal Cemetery	£40,000
Ardwick Cemetery	£20,000
Hulme Cemetery	£30,000
Necropolis	£30,000

That the market might provide a return to investors on a capital investment of £160,000, more than twenty-five times that of Rusholme Road, was completely unrealistic and nothing more was heard of most of the schemes. The Manchester General and Ardwick proposals, however, found backers and were turned into reality.

While many private cemeteries were established using private Acts of Parliament, this formality was only necessary if the proprietors wished to establish a consecrated section within their proposed cemetery. Where the cemetery was to be open to those of all faiths or none, there was no such requirement. All three of Manchester's private cemeteries chose the non-denominational route and it was only in 1848, when Manchester General Cemetery wished to open a consecrated section, that an Act was obtained.

All three cemeteries appear to have adopted a similar business structure in which the terms were set out in a Deed of Settlement signed by the founding shareholders. The assets of the business were vested in a number of trustees and day-to-day operation placed in the hands of a Committee of Directors.

The Manchester General and Ardwick Cemeteries opened in 1837 and 1838 respectively. Both made much of the appearance of their buildings and, as at Rusholme Road, adopted the then fashionable Greek Revival style for their mortuary chapels, offices and other buildings. They were clearly aimed at the middle classes whose revulsion at the condition of the city graveyards was matched by an ability to afford something better when it was available. Both of the new companies soon recognised, however, that the predictions of the Guardian's editorial had been close to the mark and that even in a growing city like Manchester the available business would be insufficient to provide anything like the hoped for return on their shareholders' capital. Investors took note and there would be no further investment in private cemeteries for Manchester. The attraction to investors in other cities, nevertheless, remained and further private developments included cemeteries at Sheffield, which opened in 1836, Hull (1845) and Northampton (1846).

The stories of Rusholme Road and Ardwick Cemeteries can be reconstructed in some detail from the extensive company records held by Greater Manchester County Record Office. These include the original Deeds of Settlement together with annual accounts, shareholder registers and the directors' minutes. Unfortunately, the corresponding records for Manchester General Cemetery appear to have been either mislaid or destroyed and so it has been necessary to depend chiefly upon newspaper articles in order to chart its history. Although newspapers are informative about consecration and other newsworthy events, they are less helpful in providing a detailed picture of the cemetery's financial performance.

Each cemetery has its individual story, but all share a common theme of early promise which was not ultimately fulfilled.

Rusholme Road Dissenters' Cemetery

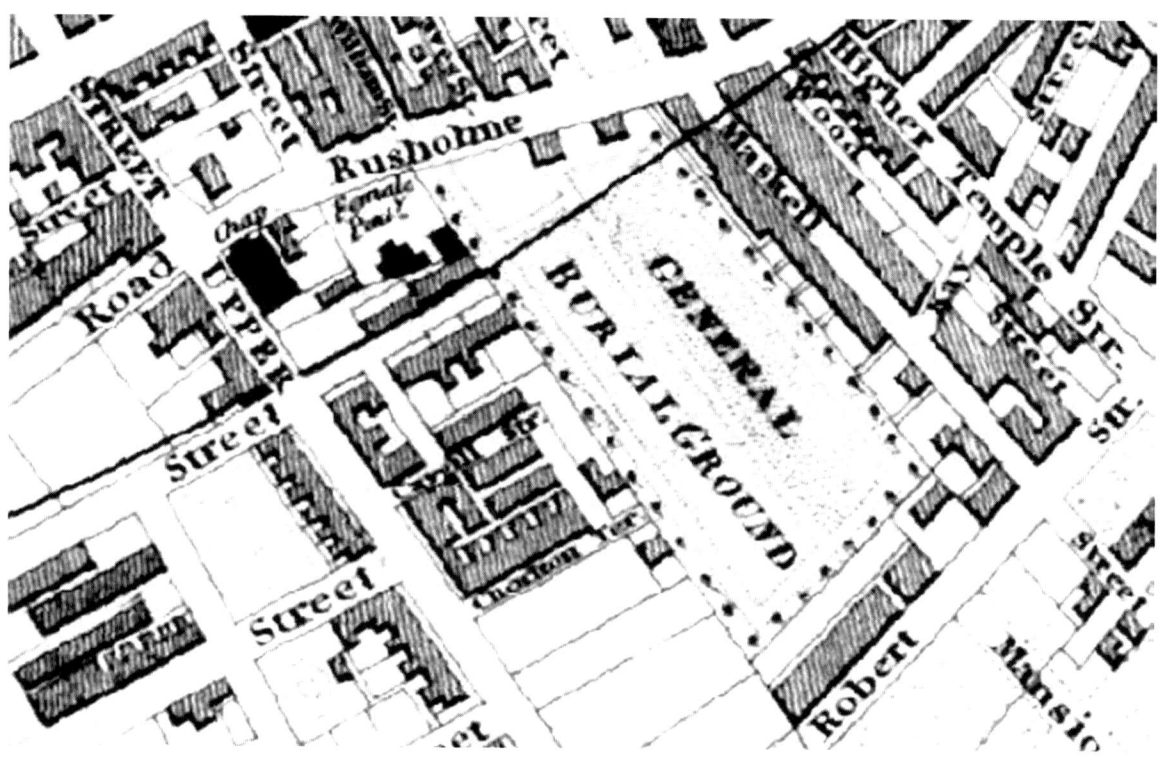

Rusholme Road Burial Ground 1836

In 1819 William Gadsby, the minister of Rochdale Road Baptist Chapel, was becoming increasingly concerned at the condition of the several burial grounds in the town which he described as *"intolerably full"*. Gadsby had a direct interest in this problem since the small burial ground at his own chapel had no space for any further burials and he was at this very time planning to re-build his chapel and to extend the building over the graveyard (see page 100).

Up to this time, individual dissenting congregations had each established their own burial ground, where members could be buried without the requirement for the Anglican burial service to be read at the funeral. Many of these were small and most were full or filling up rapidly. Few of the chapels, which were frequently hemmed in by surrounding buildings, had space to extend their graveyards.

With the assistance of the local Member of Parliament, George Hadfield, Gadsby developed a proposal to establish a cemetery suitable for the burial of religious dissenters and which would be available for the burial of those of any religious persuasion or none.

The new cemetery was established as a joint stock venture. It was proposed to raise £6,000 capital by issuing a total of 600 shares priced at £10 each. Shareholders would receive a dividend arising from the net income received from burial charges.

It does not seem to have taken long to attract the necessary investors. The shares were taken up by a total of 115 shareholders, whose holdings extended from a single share to fifteen shares. Some of the larger shareholders also purchased one or two shares in the names of each of their children. Seven of these original shareholders were women, who held 31 shares between them.

The capital subscribed by the shareholders was used to purchase a four and a half acre plot of land, called Cock Meadow. The purchase, from the executors of the late John Kearsley, was completed on 1 & 2 May 1821 for a price of £3,878.

Rusholme Road Cemetery (also known as Chorlton Row Cemetery, the Dissenters' Cemetery and, in its early years, as the General Cemetery) opened on 16 May 1821 with the burial of 31 year old Martha, the wife of James Wood of Chorlton Row, who appears to have died in childbirth.

This first interment took place barely two weeks after the completion of the purchase and so it appears that the 'cemetery' was, at this point, little more than an open field. It was, however, soon transformed. High red brick walls, topped with a plain flat coping, were erected around the perimeter and offices, a chapel and a house for the sexton was built at the northern end of the plot. A public footpath bisected the site. This was, to say the least, something of a nuisance, so the proprietors applied to the Quarter Sessions for the path to be closed. An order to this effect was granted on 17 January 1822 without any opposition being voiced.[4]

The new cemetery at the time of its opening was surrounded by open fields. It was at the time described as:

'The most beautiful cemetery ... it is laid out in the manner of a most beautiful garden, planted with shrubs, interspersed with evergreens, with pleasant water, margined with grass and flowers'.[5]

Not only did the cemetery provide pleasant surroundings but the proprietors were also at pains to set the minds of potential customers at rest::

'... to prevent so distressing an occurrence as the robbing of graves, which has been carried on to an alarming extent, a faithful watchman, who has been several years in the employ of one of the committee, walks over the ground in the night, accompanied by a large dog.'[6]

IMMEDIATE SUCCESS

The new cemetery proved an immediate success. Many of Manchester's leading businessmen were dissenters and so had no reservations about burial in ground which had not been consecrated by the Church of England. Indeed, they welcomed the freedom to have their own ministers conduct the burial service, something which would not be possible in a Church of England burial ground until 1880. What is more, these were people who could afford the high charges levied to purchase perpetual burial rights in private graves and vaults. This is not to say that the cemetery catered exclusively for the use of the wealthy. Less costly burial was also available in public graves. The fee for this was eight shillings, considerably higher than in other city graveyards but still much cheaper than the cost of a private grave.

Following the burial of Martha Wood in May, a further 45 burials had taken place up to the end of 1821. The following year saw this leap to 336 burials, then to 851 and 930. In 1825 the total number of burials reached 1,169 and it would not fall below one thousand for the next 30 years.

Over the ten years 1825 to 1835 the annual average was 1,740 burials. This was a considerable number and it is instructive to compare it to the number of burials in the parish burial ground which over the same period averaged 1,332 per annum. It is clear that one of the side effects of the new cemetery was that it took significant pressure off the other cemeteries in the city. The number of burials peaked in 1837 at 2,526.

Income from burial fees was supplemented by the sale of graves and gravestones. Prices for the cemetery's services in 1837[7] were:

Purchase of a grave	£2-14-6
Opening of an existing grave	14-6
Purchase of a vault	£12-0-0
Opening of a vault	£1-2-6
Purchase of a gravestone	£1-15-0

Even accepting that many burials would have been in public graves, it is clear that Rusholme Road was an almost instant commercial success. Unfortunately the minutes and accounts for this early period have been lost and so it is not possible to assess the business directly. An indication of profitability can be inferred from the dividends paid to shareholders. In 1841 it was noted that the dividend on each £10 share had averaged £1-7-0, which represented an annual return of 13.5% on the original investment, and that the dividend had never been below £1-5-0 (12.5%). It is little wonder the price of the shares, if one could obtain them, had risen to £16 by 1837. This is not to say that many shares were traded. The shareholder register shows that many only ever had one owner and most did not change hands more than three or four times over a period of fifty years or more.

The scale of these returns to investors can be seen as a persuasive argument to potential shareholders in other private cemeteries, both in Manchester and further afield. The performance of shares in Rusholme Road Cemetery was directly quoted in the prospectus for a private cemetery for Stockport as an inducement to potential investors.[8]

The opening of two further private cemeteries at Harpurhey and Ardwick in 1837/1838 does not appear to have had an immediate impact on business, which continued in excess of 2,000 burials per annum until 1841. By this time, the share price had fallen to £9 10s, slightly under the issue price, perhaps in anticipation of the more competitive market which was emerging[9]. Over the next ten years business declined steadily to around 1,500 burials per annum as the increased competition began to bite but Rusholme Road remained a very profitable undertaking, nevertheless.

THE RIGHT TO VOTE?

In 1835 about thirty of the shareholders appeared before the Revising Barristers' Court for South Lancashire. The court consisted of a group of barristers tasked with revising the electoral roll for the southern division of the county. The shareholders claimed that their shareholdings in the cemetery entitled them to vote in Parliamentary elections. At this time one of the voting qualifications was ownership of real estate to the annual rental value of 40 shillings. The shareholders argued that since each share in the cemetery represented a share in the ownership of freehold land, the receipt of dividends in excess of £2 constituted the equivalent of a '40 shilling freehold'. After a lengthy legal argument the court concluded that '...the cemetery is an association joined together for the purpose of making a speculation or trade' and further that the return upon which the claim was made was of a casual nature and not guaranteed. The shareholders' claim to the franchise was consequently rejected.

This experience did not prevent shareholders from returning to the court in 1837 to present (and once more lose) a similar argument. They made one final attempt in 1841 on which occasion the court dismissed the application without further discussion.[10]

HYDROPHOBIA

On Saturday 4 January 1834 seven year old Thomas Pitt was bitten by James Peers's dog and his father wisely took him to the Infirmary, where the wound above his eye was cleaned and dressed. Shortly afterwards the dog also bit its owner. James Peers visited Thomas's father, William, and told him that he believed the dog to be mad and that he felt he and Thomas should seek medical advice. They went to see Thomas Grindrod, a surgeon, who opened their wounds and applied poultices, presumably to draw out any infection. On Wednesday Thomas became ill. He experienced convulsions when given drinks and showed considerable agitation when a bowl of water was brought to wash him. His father took him to see physicians, who administered medication, but his condition deteriorated and at 3am on 11 January Thomas died. He was subsequently buried at Rusholme Road. Thomas did not, however, rest long in his grave. The Manchester Coroner became aware of the death and insisted upon investigating. Thomas's body was exhumed for examination and an inquest held at the George IV public house in Great Ancoats Street. After hearing the evidence the jury returned a verdict of *'died by hydrophobia, caused by the bite of a dog'*.[11]

Awareness of the risk of contracting hydrophobia, more commonly known today as rabies, from a dog bite would have been high. In 1830 there had been a 'mad dog' panic. The panic had led to calls for all dogs to be muzzled or even destroyed. In reality, the number of cases was relatively low and the disease persisted, with fewer than a hundred cases a year, throughout the 19th century.[12]

Only about one in twenty bites from an infected animal results in infection, which might explain the very different outcomes for James Peers and Thomas Pitt, but once contracted it was invariably fatal without immediate and radical treatment such as cauterisation of the wound. It was not until 1885 that Louis Pasteur developed an effective vaccine but even this had to be administered (as it does today) during the dormant period between the bite and the appearance of symptoms.

But did Thomas really have rabies? The incubation period for the disease is usually three or more weeks and exceptionally nine or ten days. It would be unusual for symptoms to appear within as little as four days. Perhaps this was the reason for the Coroner's interest. Given the limited capabilities of medical science in the 1830s, it is difficult to see how a reliable diagnosis could have been made. It seems quite possible that Thomas died from some other cause, possibly even unrelated to the dog bite.

The last case of rabies in England resulting from an animal bite was in 1902, though the disease is still endemic in many countries.

THE 1837 INFLUENZA EPIDEMIC

By the mid-1830s the cemetery was undertaking a weekly average approaching 50 interments but in 1837 the Manchester Guardian reported *'...at the Rusholme Road Cemetery there were no fewer than sixty-seven interments last Sunday ... a much greater proportion has been of aged persons than was ever known before'*.[13]

The cause of this sudden increase was an epidemic of influenza, which had apparently arisen in Russia and swept across Europe. It was at its worst in England in the first quarter of the year. All burial grounds saw an increase in business. The parish burial ground recorded almost double the number of burials from January to March as had been performed during the same period in 1836. However, what was an unwelcome financial burden to the parish provided a grim windfall for the proprietors of Rusholme Road Cemetery.

ANOTHER LEGAL DISPUTE

Rusholme Road Cemetery was at the centre of another legal struggle in 1840, when the proprietors appealed against the assessment of the cemetery for payment of poor rates. The proprietors argued that since burial plots were 'sold' to the public in perpetuity, it was unreasonable to levy a rate on the cemetery for land which had been given over to graves and so was consequently of no further commercial value to the cemetery.

After listening to lengthy arguments from both sides, the Arches Court came down on the side of the Chorlton-on-Medlock Overseers of the Poor, who had argued that despite the grant of exclusive use, the freehold of the land used for a grave or vault was retained by the proprietors and as such was subject to rates in the normal way. At this time it was noted in passing that about one third of the cemetery was already occupied by private graves and vaults. This matter rumbled on for some years, with the company making successive attempts to obtain a reduction in valuation. Despite their best efforts the proprietors remained unable to obtain a ruling in their favour.

SOME PROMINENT BURIALS

Rusholme Road was the last resting place of a number of Mancunians who were well-known in their time but who are today largely forgotten.

John Edward Taylor founded the Manchester Guardian and was its first editor. Taylor was not a Mancunian. He was born in Ilminster, Somerset in 1791 but had moved to Manchester with his father, a Unitarian minister, after his mother's death. He began to publish the Manchester Guardian as a weekly newspaper in 1821. It became a daily in 1836 and remains in print (since 1959 renamed The Guardian) to the present day. Taylor died in 1844 and was buried at Rusholme Road alongside his first wife Sophia Russell Scott who had died some years previously.

Also to die in 1844 was the founding father of the cemetery, the Reverend William Gadsby. Gadsby died on 27 January 1844 and was buried in the cemetery which he had founded. Following the closure of Rusholme Road and during the clearance of the memorials in 1955, Gadsby's gravestone was removed and relocated to the burial ground of the Baptist Chapel at Charlesworth in Derbyshire, where Gadsby had preached at the opening of the chapel in 1837. The stone bears an epitaph which Gadsby had composed himself:

'Here rests the body of a sinner base
Who had no hope but in electing grace;
The love, blood, life and righteousness of
God
Was his sweet theme, and this he spread
abroad.'

John Rylands, the cotton manufacturer, married three times. His first two wives were both buried at Rusholme Road. Dinah, the daughter of W. Raby of Ardwick and the mother of his six children (none of whom survived him), died of epilepsy and was buried at Rusholme Road on 18 August 1841 at the early age of 41. In 1848 John married Martha, the widow of Richard Carden. She died of heart disease and was buried on 16 February 1875. John's third wife, whom he married eight months later, was Enriqueta Tennant who had been Martha's companion up to the time of her death. John Rylands himself was buried at Manchester Southern Cemetery. By the time of his death in 1888, Rusholme Road Cemetery had become decidedly run down and was no longer a fashionable burial place for one of Manchester's leading businessmen. Enriqueta, who built the John Rylands Library in John's memory, died in 1908 and was cremated.

There were many black professional boxers in nineteenth century England. One such was James (or Jemmy) Robinson. Robinson's grandfather was described as a 'Moor' who had come to Scotland some time around the late seventeenth or early eighteenth century. James's father John was born in Paisley but had moved to Manchester where he practiced as a herbalist. James, the first of his four sons, was born on 8 August 1828.

He made his professional debut as a bare-knuckle boxer in 1846 at Madeley in Staffordshire against the Birmingham fighter James Evans for a purse of £50. Robinson won by a knockout after flooring Evans several times in the 56th round.[14] He never lost a fight and his prowess as a featherweight gained him the nickname *'the ebony phenomenon'*. A promising career was, however, cut short in 1849 at the early age of 20. Robinson was one of the many victims of the epidemic of cholera which struck Great Britain in that year.

The circumstances of his death were reported by Mr. Grainger, the Medical Officer of the Board of Health. It was said that Robinson and some of his friends had been in Liverpool from Tuesday the 5th to Friday the 8th of June. He returned to Manchester and fell ill with diarrhoea the following Saturday. He sought medical attention on Sunday but died at his lodgings on Monday morning[15]. James Robinson was buried at Rusholme Road the next day.

It seems probable that he contracted cholera during his time in Liverpool since it was reported that the keeper of the lodging house where he had stayed in Liverpool had also died of the disease shortly afterwards.

He was survived by his younger brother, George, who was also a successful fighter.

THE IMPACT OF THE BURIAL ACTS

In 1854, in common with the other city cemeteries, Rusholme Road became subject to the Burial Acts and they proved particularly onerous. The cemetery was prohibited from undertaking further burials except in existing family graves and vaults. Even in these circumstances burials were only permitted subject to a minimum depth of soil over the final interment.

The company protested against these restrictions vigorously. The rules would, they argued, leave Manchester General Cemetery in virtually a monopoly position and one which they had already exploited by announcing two price increases within a fortnight. They complained that the restrictions prohibited any new graves being created in the one third of the cemetery which at that time remained unused. It was, of course, the sale of new graves which contributed a substantial part of their income. They also protested that the requirement of a minimum of 4 foot 6 inches of earth over any burial would

prevent further interments in more than half of the existing family graves and vaults. To these practical objections, the cemetery registrar H. H. Jones, writing to the Manchester Guardian, added his own somewhat plaintive objection that he *'...should be forcibly and suddenly plunged from a state of comparative competence and comfort into a state of pauperism.'*[16]

The company's representations secured a temporary respite. The prohibition on making new graves was deferred until 1 April 1855, provided they were not dug within 20 feet of any dwelling house and that only one body was interred in each new grave. However, after this date the full restrictions would come into force.

The impact on business was immediate and dramatic. In 1852 and 1853 business, which had previously been declining, had picked up to approaching 2,000 burials per annum. The imposition of the new restrictions virtually halved this to 1,084 in 1854 and further reduced it to 384 in 1855. For the next six years, the average number of burials fell to 197[17].

THE BEGINNING OF DECLINE

The suddenly reduced income undoubtedly forced the company to implement some drastic economies and standards seem to have slipped as a result. *'A Lover of Decency'* wrote to the Manchester Guardian in 1859 complaining that at a funeral he had recently attended the sexton had been *'...so drunk he could hardly stand'*. The graveside had collapsed and to assist him in clearing it, the sexton brought a man *'..more drunk than himself who absolutely tumbled into the grave...'*[18]. Four years later a Mr. M. Scarnell wrote to the paper concerning the recent funeral of a member of the Order of Oddfellows, at which the grave had been made too small. It had taken three attempts at widening it before the coffin would fit – all this in front of the grieving wife and friends of the deceased and amid cries of *'Shame!'*.[19]

A Temporary Upturn

Just as it seemed that Rusholme Road Cemetery was in terminal decline, its fortunes seemed to change. In 1862 the number of burials picked up to 319, with much of the rise occurring in the latter part of that year. The following year numbers rose above 1,000 once more and remained at this high level to the end of 1868, reaching a high of 1,663 burials in 1867. What could account for this unexpected improvement?

The answer seems to lie in two letters which survive among the cemetery records. Both come from Phillip Holland, the government's Inspector of Burial Grounds. The first, dated 12 February 1863, refers to a complaint from a Mr. William Weston of Salford in which he claims that bodies have been buried in family graves with as little as one foot of earth over the coffin. The letter also refers to burials in public graves, something specifically prohibited by the restriction imposed in 1854. Holland asks for an explanation but unfortunately there is no copy of the proprietors' reply. The matter does not seem to have been taken any further.[20]

The second letter, dated 3 September 1868, is more informative. It strongly implies that the 1854 limitations were being ignored, or at least interpreted in a way which was not intended. Holland writes:

> 'It is, I think, desirable to avoid proposing a new and more stringent Order in Council which may perhaps be avoided if I am formally authorised by you to report that the present one shall be in future strictly observed in the sense that burials be limited to those in the family graves then existing to be used only as family graves i.e. the burial of strangers in them not to be permitted'[21]

Although there is no other evidence, it seems clear that the increase in business had been achieved by continuing to inter bodies in public graves and by interring 'strangers' in family graves. It also seems possible that the requirement to have four and a half feet of earth over the final burial was being ignored. Holland's implied threat of a more stringent order, possibly one even more restrictive, seems to have been sufficient to stop the infringements.

A Conflict of Interest?

The Government Inspector's willingness to accept the proprietors' assurance rather than pursue a more formal order is not untypical of Holland's style. He seems to have been pragmatic in seeking workable solutions rather than wielding his official powers. In this particular case, however, there might be another reason for his wish to avoid a fuss.

Phillip had a brother Francis Waverley Holland, some years his junior. Francis was an oil merchant but another of his business interests was the Rusholme Road Cemetery. His precise capacity in 1868 is unclear but by 1880 he is described as the 'President' of the company. Phillip can hardly have been unaware of his brother's interest in a company whose activities he was investigating. There is no suggestion that Phillip bent any rules in this case but he must have had some concern at the possibility of a scandal were the relationship to be questioned.

Years of Decline

The return to the 1854 restrictions once more hit business hard. Annual burials fell again in 1869 to around 200 and from 1877 onwards the number declined rapidly to fall below one a week after 1880.

The reduction in income brought about a neglect of maintenance. In 1889 Mr. Newton Wilson wrote to the Manchester Guardian to say that he had visited the cemetery after many years absence and that he considered that *"A more God-forsaken God's acre it has rarely been my lot to see"*. He describes plaster falling from the buildings in cakes, ironwork perishing in the absence of paint and an untrained growth of vegetation. He ends his letter with an appeal to the Council or some other body to take it over.[22] Mr. Wilson's sentiments were taken up again by several correspondents two years later, and once more in 1905, when J. Collins wrote to the Manchester Guardian to complain '...*never did I see a more deserted place*' and to recommend that it should be redeveloped as a children's playground.[23] These appeals, however, fell on deaf ears.

From around 1880 the cemetery was no longer a viable business. The income from interments and the sale of memorials no longer covered the running costs. It did not, however, collapse. The proprietors had found a new source of income in leasing out the unused part of the cemetery for business use. One part was leased to Walter Carter for £100 per annum. Carter was a carrier and removal man and used a building he had erected on the site for storage. A second part was leased for a further £70 per annum to the building contractors Worthington and Pownall for use as a timber yard. They later erected a saw mill on the site and by 1920 were paying £240 per annum, the major part of the cemetery company's income. Other smaller sums were raised by making the chapel available to a band to use as a practice hall and by renting the cellars out for storage.

Not only did this new source of income enable the cemetery to continue but between 1872 and 1918 the company's cash reserves grew from £200 to £1,200. They even managed to pay a dividend. This peaked at twelve shillings in 1876 but declined to two shillings and sixpence two years later. It remained at this level until 1899 after which dividends ceased.

By the 1880s the shareholders had clearly lost interest in the company. Increasingly the annual general meetings failed to attract a quorum of shareholders. The shareholders were even failing to claim their dividends, a failure which in 1888 caused the Registrar to express "*his anxiety about continuing to declare dividends until some special effort was put forth in order to find the*

whereabouts of the missing shareholders".[24] Many of the missing shareholders would by this time have been dead. The shareholder register shows many of the shares which were issued in 1821 never to have been transferred to new holders. Very few transfers took place after 1880. The shares had either been lost or were viewed as having little value.

In 1890 the Registrar declared that '*the life of the cemetery as a burial ground is annually decreasing and its income consequently failing*'.[25] The proprietors sought to unload the problem onto Manchester Corporation. Their initial approaches to the City Treasurer's office seemed promising and they indicated that the Corporation might be prepared to take over the cemetery. Discussions continued but by November of the following year it was clear that the Corporation had no intention of proceeding. There were further efforts along the same lines in 1896 but again the Corporation appears to have expressed little interest in bailing out the company.

THE LAST BURIALS

Although the cemetery continued to operate into the 20th century, from 1900 onwards the number of burials had fallen to single figures. No burials whatsoever were recorded in 1923, 1926 and 1932. Finally, on 6 February 1933, 78 year old Elizabeth Morris of Withington became the last person to be buried at Rusholme Road Cemetery.

It is clear from the last few pages of the burial registers that the last people to be buried were a few elderly grave owners who had clung on to the deeds to their family graves, perhaps for more than half a century. The last burial of a child took place in 1893, a far cry from the early years of the cemetery when 56% of burials were of those less than ten years old[26]. The last burial of anyone who could be described as 'young' was that of 36 year old Frank Jowett, who had taken his own life in 1899. Of the 125 burials recorded in the register after 1900, no fewer than 86 give 'old age' as the cause of death. The grave owners had simply died or moved away.

CLOSURE AND A NEW FUTURE

The cemetery, during its 112 years of continuous operation, had proved incredibly popular and its registers record a total of 68,241 burials[27].

Because of its increased income from leasing the spare land, it was possible for the proprietors to provide some level of maintenance for the cemetery and its buildings. They still continued to employ a caretaker, though the cost was slightly offset by the £13 annual rent he paid to occupy what had formerly been the sexton's house.

In 1938 Manchester Corporation published a proposal to drive a new road directly through the middle of the cemetery as part of a traffic relief scheme.[28] Had it gone ahead, the Corporation would have almost certainly compulsorily purchased the whole cemetery and landscaped the areas to either side of the new road. The proposal did not, however, proceed any further, presumably owing to the outbreak of war the following year and did not re-emerge after hostilities ceased.

The process of decline continued and accelerated when on 23 December 1940 a German bomb fell about fifteen yards from the chapel and the caretaker's house, badly damaging both. The caretaker appears to have suffered serious injuries as a result. A measure of compensation for the damage was obtained from the War Damage Commissioners and temporary repairs were made so that the caretaker could continue to occupy a part of the house.

Further serious damage was done on VJ Day when a large gang of youths removed the boards from the windows of the house and proceeded to strip out floorboards and other woodwork, presumably for bonfires. The caretaker was threatened with violence by some of the mob and was unable to prevent the pillage.

Both the war damage and the later damage were finally repaired and the caretaker's house was re-occupied on 6 December 1947. The repairs had cost around £650, much of which had come from the company's now dwindling reserves.

By this time the cemetery itself had fallen into a very poor state. Hooliganism was reportedly common and there were unsubstantiated stories that tombs had been entered and rings and other items stolen from coffins. The cemetery was said to be '...decorated with dead cats, broken [bottles?], filthy rags and old iron'.[29] Following two articles in the Manchester Guardian about the

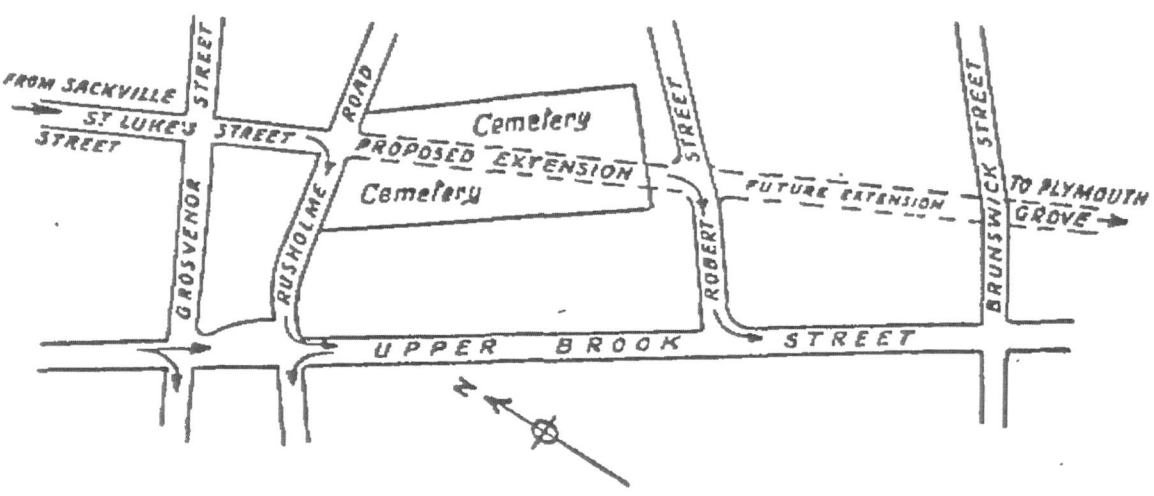

The road scheme proposed in 1938

state of the cemetery and the feral children whose behaviour was of great concern, several readers wrote to the paper to suggest that the cemetery should be purchased by the Corporation. Many suggested that it should be converted into a children's playground to address both the dilapidated state of the cemetery and the lack of proper places for local children to play. It was, however, to be another decade before their wish was to be granted.

There were moves to take over the cemetery from about 1950 but these ran into legal difficulties. The cemetery was finally acquired from the shareholders by Manchester Corporation in 1954 under the provisions of the Manchester Corporation Act of that year. There was an unexpected bonus for those who still held shares in the company. The Act stipulated that compensation of £15 per share should be paid to anyone who could prove ownership at the date of the Act. This was a remarkably generous provision since the cemetery was little other than a liability and no dividend had been paid for half a century.

It is not known how many shareholders came forward to claim compensation but it is noticeable that in the two to three years before the Act a number of shares were transferred into the name of George Edward Beattie. Beattie was at this time nominally the cemetery company's Treasurer and one suspects that he was aware of the possible compensation and sought to obtain such shares as he could in order to turn a profit. Today this might be regarded as blatant insider trading but Beattie's questionable dealing seems to have passed unnoticed.

In 1955 the Corporation published a notice informing persons who had family members buried in the cemetery that if they did not come forward before 22 September to claim any tombstone or memorial, these would be removed, broken up or otherwise disposed of. They were further informed that should they wish to claim a memorial its removal and relocation would be at their own expense.[30] It is not known whether any

memorials were relocated other than that of William Gadsby, which was mentioned earlier.

The now derelict Greek Revival style buildings were demolished and the gravestones and monuments were removed. The bodies were, however, left *in situ*. Exhumation on such a massive scale would have been an expensive undertaking. The grounds were landscaped without disturbing them.

The former Rusholme Road Cemetery was opened as a public park on 14 May 1957 by Harry Sharp, the Lord Mayor of Manchester. As many had wished, it included a children's playground. The issue of whether it was appropriate to permit a former cemetery to be used for children's play had been the subject of much discussion and to avoid any dispute this use was specifically recognised in the 1954 Manchester Corporation Act.

Gartside Gardens, the former Rusholme Road Cemetery

The new park was named Gartside Gardens in memory of John Henry Gartside, a former chairman of the Calico Printers' Association, who had died on 12 November 1906. Gartside had left a bequest of about £33,000 to the Corporation towards *'providing and maintaining, or maintaining such as already exist, parks, squares or open spaces within ten miles of the Town Hall'*[31] but nothing had been done to utilise this generous bequest in nearly fifty years.

Gartside Gardens today is a well-used public park but sadly, given its importance as the site of the first private burial ground to open in England, the park contains nothing to inform visitors about its history.

PHILIP HENRY HOLLAND (1811-1886)

The name of Philip Henry Holland appears several times in this book in his role as the Government Inspector of Burial Grounds.

Philip Henry Holland was born in Manchester on 8 April 1811, the son of Thomas Holland and Elizabeth (née Robson). He was a direct descendant of Philip Holland, a prominent Presbyterian/ Unitarian minister from Bolton and was baptised at the Bank Street Unitarian Chapel in Bolton by his uncle John Holland who was the minister there.

Philip received most of his education in Manchester but moved to London to study medicine at Guy's Hospital. He was granted a certificate at Apothecaries Hall in 1832 and accepted as a Member of the Royal College of Surgeons the following year.

Once qualified he returned to Manchester where he established a practice in Grosvenor Street, Chorlton-on-Medlock. He also served for a period as the Registrar of Births, Marriages and Deaths for that district.

He married Lucy Copland Sothern at Norwich in 1847 and returned to London where he had a practice first at Upper Stamford Street in Lambeth and subsequently in Brixton.

In 1850, he was appointed as one of the Government's Inspectors of Burial Grounds. He served in this capacity for some thirty years during which time he travelled the country holding numerous inquiries into reported abuses and infringements of the rules imposed by the Burial Acts. He paid several visits to Manchester for this purpose during his career, holding enquiries into the conduct of business at Every Street Chapel, Rusholme Road Dissenters' Cemetery and Philips Park Cemetery among others. Accounts of the inquiries which he undertook show him to have been fair in his assessments and pragmatic in his proposed remedies.

He was clearly viewed as a competent public official since in 1862 he was appointed to a committee of inquiry tasked with looking into the health and safety of workers in mines. This appointment may have been prompted by a pamphlet on the subject of accidents in coal mines which he had written some three years previously.

He was politically a Liberal, an intimate friend of Richard Cobden and a supporter of the repeal of the Corn Laws. He was also a believer in self-help and in 1838 published an *'Essay on Dispensaries'* which advocated self-providence in preference to dependence on charity.

He died at his home in Willow Road, Hampstead in November 1886.

Manchester General Cemetery

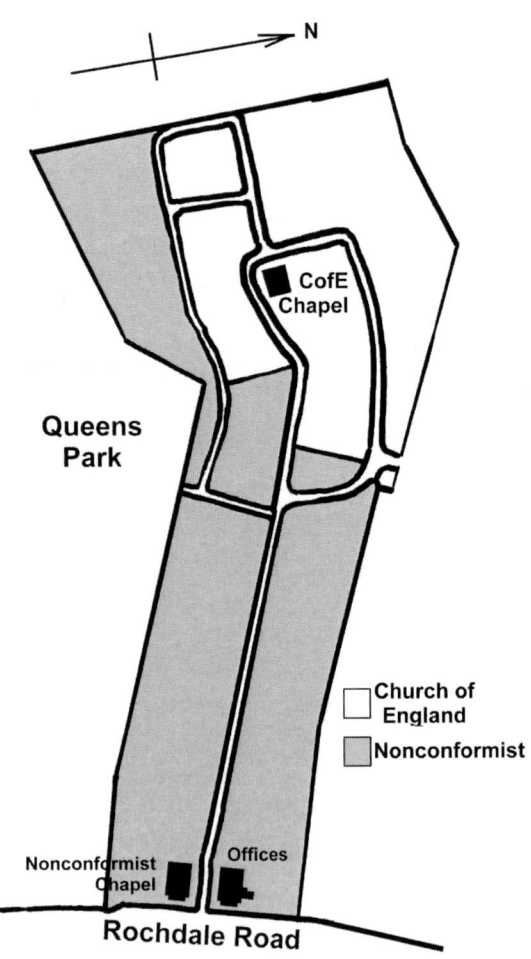

The cemetery was established by a Deed of Settlement dated 2 May 1836[33] and in the same month an 11 acre plot of land was acquired in Harpurhey. Work began to convert it into a cemetery the following September. By the spring of 1837 the company was advertising for a clerk of works to superintend the building works and the setting out of the grounds.[34]

The architect chosen to design the buildings was a Scotsman, William Lambie Moffatt (1807-1882), who had recently moved south from Edinburgh to establish an architectural practice in Doncaster. Moffatt's design included matching lodge and chapel buildings in the Greek Revival style with tetrastyle porticos. These he placed on either side of a main driveway, which descended a gentle slope from the main gate in Rochdale Road to the far end of the cemetery.

The formal opening ceremony took place on 1 September 1837 and was attended by around 150 shareholders and friends, together with the ministers of many of the city's nonconformist chapels. The party were taken to the cemetery in a convoy of twenty coaches which processed to the cemetery from Stevenson Square in the city centre[35]. After the group had walked around the grounds, a service in the chapel was followed by a cold buffet luncheon in a nearby schoolroom.

The cemetery was, however, far from finished and it was not until precisely one year later on 1 September 1838 that the the stillborn child of a couple by the name of Topham was the first to be buried in the new cemetery. A few weeks later the company was advertising:

'The splendid buildings for this burial ground are now long finished and the tastefully laid-out grounds open for interments. Applications for the same or for vaults and graves may be made to the Rev. Jonathan Wood, the Registrar; Mr. John Lessey, chemist, Piccadilly; or to Mr.

Manchester General Cemetery, also known as Queen's Park or Harpurhey Cemetery, was first proposed in 1833. A report in the Manchester Guardian announced:

'We learn that the shares in this new undertaking are fast filling up and that in the course of a month or two the projectors intend to advertise for a piece of ground in the neighbourhood of the town. The capital proposed to be raised is £20,000 in 2000 shares at £10 each'[32].

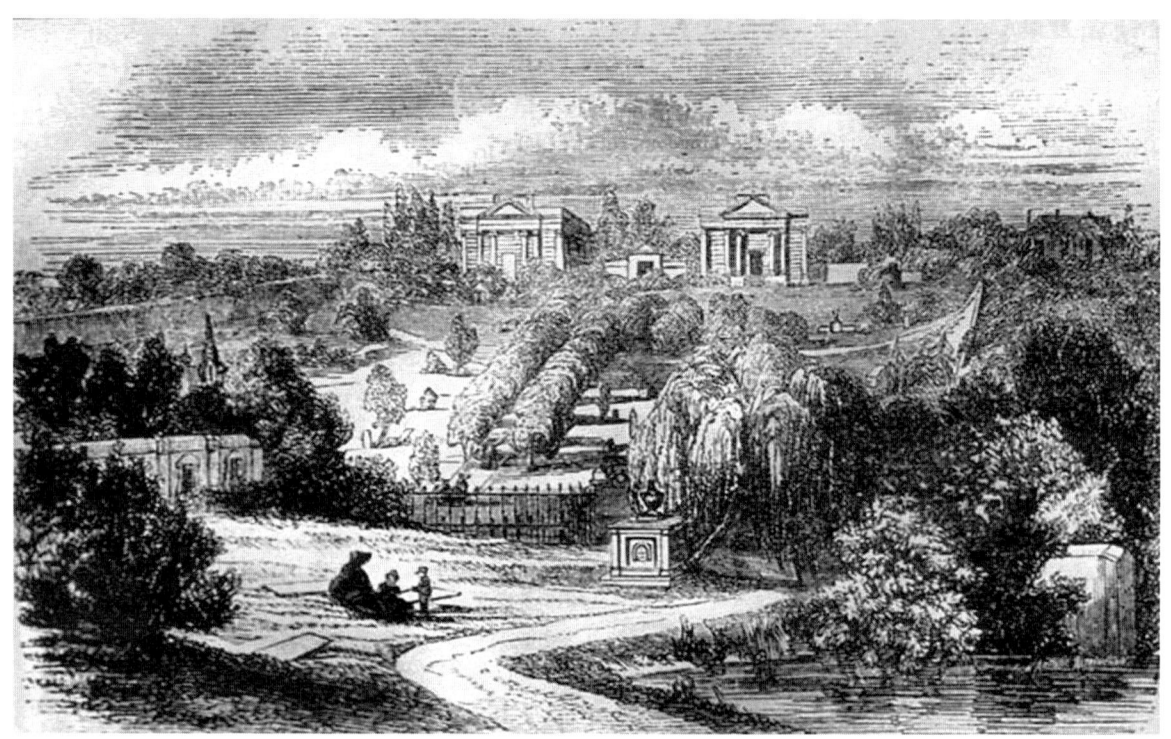

Manchester General Cemetery
(From an early print)

M'Williams, chemist, St. George's Road.
(signed) James Frost, Hon. Sec.'[36]

The new cemetery did not prove to be the instant commercial success which its projectors had undoubtedly wished. The number of burials was disappointingly low. In 1839, the first full year of operation, only 116 burials took place, the following year 262. By 1842 the number had risen to 427, encouraging but still short of the number needed for financial viability.

In 1844, at an Extraordinary General Meeting of the shareholders, there was a proposal to *'...set apart a portion of the cemetery for the exclusive use of persons of a Jewish persuasion'*.[37] Nothing, however, appears to have resulted from this proposal, which may have been an attempt to develop a new (albeit modestly sized) market.

It was not until 1847, in which year the number of burials had risen to 843, that the directors felt confident in declaring a dividend. The payment of two shillings and sixpence per share on the paid up value of the shares (£6-12-6) was a return of less than two percent, considerably lower than the investors might have wished.

Manchester General Cemetery had been unfortunate in opening almost simultaneously with the Ardwick Cemetery. Ardwick, much closer to the city centre and the increasingly prosperous southern suburbs, had a significant advantage in attracting lucrative middle class funerals. The two cemeteries were not just competing with each other, but also with the established Dissenters' Cemetery at Rusholme Road, for a market which, although very profitable for one cemetery, was not sufficiently large to generate a substantial return for three.

The problems were only too evident to the directors. At the Annual General Meeting in April 1848, the chairman reported that the committee

'...had wisely come to the conclusion that [the cemetery] would never be remunerative as it stood and had taken the necessary steps to secure a different result'.[38] The 'necessary steps' to which the chairman referred involved a proposal that Manchester General Cemetery should take over the responsibility for parish burial from the Collegiate Church.

BURYING THE PARISH POOR

In November 1847 it was reported at a parish vestry meeting that the Manchester General Cemetery Committee had submitted a proposal to the churchwardens. They proposed that, given the impending closure of the Walkers Croft parish burial ground and in the absence of any immediate alternative, such burials could be undertaken at Manchester General Cemetery. The company proposed very economical rates. The fee would be four shillings for each adult burial, three shillings and sixpence for each child between the ages of two and ten years and one shilling and sixpence for each infant under two years, of age.[39]

The closure of the Walkers Croft parochial burial ground was imminent but nothing had been done towards establishing a replacement parish burial ground. The churchwardens were clearly desperate to make alternative arrangements. Negotiations proceeded quickly and positively and the General Cemetery Company's chairman was able to report to the Company's 1848 AGM that '...they had received the approbation of the Collegiate body, with whom they had made satisfactory arrangements as to the fees for all burials within the consecrated part'[40]. It is clear that the directors had been thinking along these lines for some time, since as early as 1845 an Extraordinary General Meeting had been held to seek the shareholders' agreement to establishing a consecrated portion with its own chapel.[41]

There were benefits to both parties in this arrangement. The Collegiate Church would at a stroke solve the problem of where to bury the large number of poor people who died in the parish each year and whose burial was their responsibility. They would also not have to invest any capital in the venture. The cemetery for its part would acquire a reliable, if not necessarily highly profitable, source of business. Perhaps uppermost in the company management's thoughts was that by establishing a consecrated section, they would be able to attract private customers whose religious sensibilities would not allow them to consider burial in the unconsecrated ground of their private competitors. There was, however, a potential problem. To establish a consecrated area in a private cemetery required a private Act of Parliament.

The necessary Parliamentary formalities commenced in 1847 and proceeded without serious opposition. The only sticking point was the issue of fees. The Collegiate Church had long exercised an unpopular right to charge fees for baptisms, marriages and burials conducted at other Church of England churches within the parish. As a condition of their agreement to the consecration of part of Manchester General Cemetery, the Collegiate Church clergy sought to have this right, which they claimed had been granted to them by a previous Act of Parliament, embodied in the proposed legislation. Clearly they recognised the potential loss of income if more well-to-do parishioners chose to be buried at the General Cemetery. Their efforts appear to have been successful since discussions at the company's 1848 AGM suggest that the company had acceded to this demand.

Although Anglican burials could not take place until a consecrated area was available, there was no reason why those who were followers of dissenting faiths could not be buried in the unconsecrated part of Manchester General Cemetery, so in this respect, the contract could begin without any delay. The first burial of a workhouse inmate took place on 4 February 1848, about three weeks before the Walkers Croft burial ground was finally closed. This was the burial of 40 year old Harriet Burke, whose name suggests

138

that she was Irish and so possibly a Roman Catholic.

The '*Act for the consecration of a portion of the Manchester General Cemetery*' obtained royal assent on 9 June 1848[42] and a five acre portion of the cemetery was consecrated by the Bishop of Manchester on 4 November following.[43]

The cemetery now had a consecrated section but it still lacked an Anglican chapel. The 1848 Act required a chapel to be erected within five years, but until it was built a temporary arrangement was necessary. The original intention was for a portion of the existing dissenters' chapel to be consecrated for Church of England use but this seems not to have been possible and so the first Anglican funeral services appear to have been conducted at the nearby Christ Church in Harpurhey. Eventually in 1849 a temporary chapel was created in one of the existing cemetery buildings and this was consecrated on 10 April.[44] This temporary chapel served for over six years until the permanent chapel, in the Gothic style, was completed adjacent to the consecrated section. The new chapel was consecrated in December 1855.[45]

Given the large number of burials for which the parish was responsible, the parish burial contract provided a timely lifeline for the struggling company. The Wardens of the Collegiate Church were still proposing to establish a new parish burial ground and so saw the contract as temporary but the benefit to the cemetery in having secured a consecrated portion would continue even if the arrangement ceased. In the event, the *temporary* contract would continue for nearly twenty years until the opening of Manchester's first municipal cemetery at Philips Park.

Overnight, the number of burials increased. It rose from 843 in 1847 to 1,301 in 1848. There was an unusually large total of 1,946 in 1849, the year in which for the second time a cholera epidemic struck the city. Deaths from cholera and diarrhoea during the epidemic totalled 1,156[46] and many of these would have come from the poor end of Manchester society. This 'blip' aside, the number of burials continued to rise steadily, reaching 1,654 by the time the Burial Acts were passed in 1854. The true increase in business was higher than these figures indicate. The register for burials in the consecrated section for this period has been lost and so the numbers relate to the unconsecrated section only.

THE COST AND MANNER OF PARISH BURIALS

A letter to the Manchester Guardian in 1854 throws some light on the cost of parish burials. John Bolton Rogerson, the cemetery's registrar, in answer to criticisms voiced by an earlier correspondent concerning the amount being paid for parish burials, states that in the preceding year there had been a total of 484 interments at the expense of the parish, for which the cemetery had received fees totalling £74-13s-6d. This equates to an average of three shillings and one penny per burial.

To carry out a burial for such a small sum could only have been achieved through the use of common graves containing large numbers of coffins. The Board of Health's inspectors noted in their 1850 report that '*In the Manchester General Cemetery they bury in pits about eleven feet deep*'.[47] This is reflected in the burial register, which contains many examples of graves against which large numbers of burials are recorded. For example, grave number 414 appears alongside 76 entries dating between 24 October and 9 December 1848. This is followed by Grave 211 with 47 entries between 12 December 1848 and the following 7 January. This seems little different to the practice which had been described at Walkers Croft thirty years earlier with the pits being left open for as long as six weeks while sufficient bodies accumulated to fill the space.

THE BURIAL ACTS

Manchester General Cemetery was located outside the city boundary and consequently was not even mentioned in the first tranche of Orders in Council issued under the Burial Acts in March 1854. Business at Harpurhey continued much as before and indeed for a short time improved dramatically. Immediately prior to the Burial Acts there had been around 1,400-1,500 interments annually but in 1855 the number leapt to 3,576. Virtually all of the other burial grounds in Manchester had been prohibited from opening new graves and those which had not been closed were made subject to limits on the number of interments which each grave might accommodate. The most serious restriction related to public graves in which the new regulations permitted only a single interment. This immediately forced cemetery operators to increase their prices. Manchester General Cemetery, subject to none of these restrictions, had a considerable price advantage, particularly when it came to the burial of poorer people and they even alluded to this in their advertisements which announced *'This place of burial upon which no restrictions have been placed...*'[48].

This advantageous situation was not, however, permitted to continue for long. On 26 August 1856 the London Gazette carried a notice of restrictions which had become effective on 9 August:

> *'Now, therefore, Her Majesty, by and with the advice of Her Privy Council, is pleased to order, and it is hereby ordered, that no new burial ground shall be opened in any of the undermentioned parishes without the previous approval of one of Her Majesty's Principal Secretaries of State; and that burials in the said parishes shall be discontinued, with the following modifications, from and after the fifth day of September next (except as is herein otherwise directed), as follows, viz.:*

MANCHESTER.- In the Manchester General Cemetery at Harpurhey, except in vaults and walled graves which can be opened without the disturbance of soil that has been buried in, and in which each coffin shall be embedded in charcoal and separately entombed in an air-tight manner; and in other graves, except so far as is compatible with the observance of the following regulations, viz: No coffin to be buried less than four feet below the surface; one coffin only to be buried in a grave.; no grave to be re-opened unless to bury another member of the same family, in which cases half a yard in thickness of earth shall be left above the previously interred coffin, no undecayed remains to be disturbed, no new grave to be within half a yard of any other grave, no grave or vault to be used which is not free from water'.[49]

The Order effectively required a separate new grave to be dug for each and every burial unless the body was to be buried in a private family grave. This involved considerably more work for the gravedigger and required a lot more land to be used for each burial. Like its competitors, Manchester General Cemetery was forced to increase its fees. This had an almost immediate impact.

Catharine, the wife of an impoverished Irishman called Dennis Lane from the Angel Meadow district, died in September 1856. Lane's wages as a brush maker were only 14 shillings a week and like most of Manchester's labouring poor he had no savings or burial insurance to fall back on. He had, however, managed to borrow money from his workmates and had purchased a coffin, leaving sufficient, he believed, to pay the cemetery fees. He arrived at Manchester General Cemetery and asked them to bury his late wife. He was both shocked and distressed to find that he was met with a flat refusal. The five shillings which he had expected to pay for the burial was insufficient since the minimum fee had increased to twenty shillings (£1). Lane secured offers of further loans amounting to another five shillings but the registrar continued to refuse to carry out the burial for anything less than the full fee. He referred Lane to the Receiving Officer of the Poor Law Guardians who arranged for Catharine to be buried at public expense.[50] Lane's surprise at the charges is understandable. A few weeks earlier five shillings would probably have sufficed.

It was not just those arranging a private funeral who were affected by the increased fees. The price of parish burials also increased. The fee for an adult burial leapt to one pound with reduced charges of fifteen shillings for children aged between seven and fourteen years and ten shillings for those under seven. John Bolton Rogerson[51], the cemetery registrar, explained that new regulations resulted in '...an increase of

labour and expense...' He added that the parish still paid the cemetery a shilling less than was paid by the poorest who paid their own burial fees and that the fees were '...barely sufficient to afford an adequate interest to the shareholders for their outlay'.

If the new restrictions created problems for the cemetery, they created a nightmare for the Poor Law Guardians. Not only did they face a three to four-fold increase in the price of each pauper burial, but poorly paid workers like Dennis Lane, who might previously have paid for their own family funerals, would now find it necessary to turn in increasing numbers to the Poor Law Guardians.

At their meeting following the Lane incident, the Poor Law Guardians investigated their options. One of them reported that he had found a consecrated burial ground in which burials

Entrance, Lodge and Nonconformist Chapel c1958

could be provided in single graves, in accordance with the regulations. This burial ground would, he claimed, charge three quarters the price of Manchester General Cemetery. The Guardians resolved to discontinue burials under the General Cemetery contract. The Guardians give no clue as to which burial ground was supposedly able to undertake burials in the numbers required.[52] The burial registers of St. John and St. Mary, the two largest nearby consecrated graveyards still permitted to open new graves, record no burials from the workhouse. The burial ground of St. Michael's Church had been closed the previous year and could not be re-opened. Neither the Rusholme Road nor Ardwick private cemeteries possessed a consecrated section and even if they had it is unlikely that they would have been able to greatly undercut Manchester General's price. A church outside the city (and the provisions of the Burial Acts) seems the most likely. Whatever the location, this could have been no more than damage limitation since the potential increase in costs was still likely to be considerable.

A month later, the problem was more satisfactorily resolved. The Guardians were now able to report that they had obtained a variation in the regulations to allow the re-opening of a grave '...in accordance with the 17th of the new regulations for burial grounds.'[53] This meant that common graves could be treated in the same way as family graves, thus permitting multiple interments subject to appropriate depth of burial and separation between coffins. This allowed the relationship with the General Cemetery to be restored. The new fees are not known but a reduction should have been possible.

Aside from generally increasing costs and consequently increasing prices for burials, the demands of the Burial Acts do not appear to have had any long-term effect upon the level of business. The number of burials declined in 1856 to 2,361 and then in 1857 declined further to 1,123. However, from 1858 to 1871 burials averaged

around 1,700 per annum, a level which was significantly higher than it had been before the Burial Acts.

The substantial increase in the number of burials was not reflected in the share price. By 1855 this had fallen to £6-5s[54] and by 1858 to £4-10s,[55] which suggests that the increased business had been achieved at the cost of profitability. A new high point was reached in 1865 with 2,053 burials but from this point a steady decline set in with a noticeable downward step in 1868 when the municipal cemetery opened at Philips Park. There was a second if smaller reduction in 1879 with the opening of Southern Cemetery. However, there were still many burials recorded of workhouse inmates, so this business had not completely dried up. The company was, however, now back where it had been thirty years earlier and never really recovered. By 1893 the shares were quoted as trading at 35 shillings.[56]

RESTRUCTURING

Manchester General Cemetery continued to operate as a private company until 1926, when, following agreement at an Extraordinary General Meeting the previous year, the old company was wound up and a new company, Manchester General Cemetery Limited, was formed.[57] Since there are no surviving company records it is difficult to determine the background to this but it was probably intended to protect the shareholders from liabilities in the event of insolvency. The directors of Ardwick Cemetery were undertaking a similar restructuring around the same time for this specific reason.

PURCHASE BY MANCHESTER CORPORATION

The new limited company continued to operate as before but the volume of business declined steadily until it was becoming clear to the directors that the cemetery was no longer a viable business. Only about a hundred burials were now taking place each year, with about ten sales of new graves. No dividend had been paid on the shares since 1938 and in 1955 the company had registered a loss of £250. In 1956 the directors approached the Manchester Town Clerk to ask if the Corporation would be prepared to take over the cemetery. This was not their first attempt to dispose of the cemetery. They had previously approached the Corporation in 1949 but the Corporation had decided that the time was 'not opportune'. This time, however, their approach received a more positive response. Acquisition of the cemetery was agreed in principle, *provided the Corporation are not required to pay any money for the actual acquisition of the cemetery*.[58]

The Parks and Cemeteries Committee spent several months looking into the proposal and by the following spring they had agreed to take over the cemetery and the directors had accepted that no compensation would be paid to shareholders. The committee's plans divided the cemetery into three sections. The lower part had not seen any interments for many years. Here, the proposal was to level the site and incorporate it into the adjacent Queens Park (this did not ultimately come to pass). The middle section was to remain open for interments in existing graves for an unspecified period. In the upper six to seven acres it was proposed to remove the kerbs and flat stones, so as to simplify maintenance, and to demolish the buildings. A total expenditure of over £18,000 was anticipated.[59]

Manchester General Cemetery was taken over by Manchester Corporation under the Open Spaces Act of 1906. The fabric which they inherited was clearly in a very poor state of repair. Soon after taking over the cemetery the Corporation were inviting tenders for *'repair and partial rebuilding of [the] brick boundary walls'*.[60] They were clearly worried by both safety and security, one section of the wall being described as *'very dangerous'*. Their concerns did not extend to the cemetery buildings. The Corporation committed one of those not infrequent acts of municipal vandalism by demolishing Moffat's chapel and lodge which the architectural historian James

Stevens Curl described as *'...probably the finest "Grecian" work in Manchester'*.[61] One of their more creditworthy undertakings was to support Herbert Morton of Stockport, who took on the considerable task of transcribing the inscriptions on the gravestones, by providing a typist to type up his pencil notes.[62] Morton completed his work towards the end of 1959 and his transcripts were deposited at Manchester Archives. The cemetery ceased to undertake burials in new graves in 1961, although further interments in existing family graves continued thereafter and the occasional burial still takes place. The cemetery today is maintained but cannot be recommended as a place to visit unaccompanied.

NOTABLE BURIALS

Nobody with a national reputation appears to have been buried at Manchester General Cemetery. It never achieved the social cachet of either Rusholme Road or Ardwick. It is nevertheless the final resting place of several people of more local prominence. One of the best known is Ben Brierley.

THE CREATOR OF AB O'TH YATE

Ben Brierley was a well-known local writer. Born at Failsworth in 1825, Brierley was a hand-loom weaver and of limited education, though from an early age he showed a talent for writing. He developed his literary skills without formal instruction and by the age of thirty was submitting articles to local newspapers. By the 1860s he was writing longer articles and books and in 1869 began to publish *'Ben Brierley's Journal'*, first monthly and then weekly. He continued to publish this magazine for over twenty years. He was elected to Manchester Council in 1875 and served for six years. In that same year his only child Annie died of tuberculosis aged eighteen and was buried at Harpurhey four days after her death. She had been due to serve as a bridesmaid at a cousin's wedding and the dress which she was due to wear became her shroud.

Brierley visited America in 1880 and again in 1884, where he delivered public readings from his books and articles. He fell on hard times towards the end of his life but his followers raised significant sums towards the support of Ben and his wife.

Much of his work was in dialect, perhaps the best known being his humorous Ab o'th Yate stories. The following lines from one of his dialect songs might describe Ben himself:

Aw care no' for titles, nor heawses nor lond,
Owd Jone's a name fittin' for me.
An' gie me a thatch wi a wooden dur latch
An' six feet o' greawnd when a dee-e.[63]

He died on 18 January 1896 and found his '*six feet o' greawnd*' at Harpurhey. His grave, which is next to his daughter's, is marked by a substantial memorial. A statue of Brierley, paid for by public subscription, was erected in nearby Queens Park two years after his death. Unfortunately, in the 1980s the statue was removed to Heaton Park, and while there was accidentally destroyed. A new bronze statue was erected at Failsworth in 2006.

THE KILLING OF SERGEANT BRETT

Sergeant Charles Brett, aged 52, was killed on 18 September 1867 while riding inside a police van accompanying prisoners to Belle Vue Gaol. While the van was in Hyde Road, a band of about forty Fenian supporters attacked in an attempt to release two of their colleagues, Thomas Kelly and Timothy Deasy. During the successful rescue Brett was shot and fatally wounded, the first Manchester police officer to be killed on duty since the formation of Manchester Constabulary in 1839. Three of the attackers were later hanged for his murder, though there is dispute as to which, if any of them, fired the fatal shot. Brett's funeral at Harpurhey the following Sunday was a major event. The route of the funeral was lined by an estimated 40,000 to 50,000 people. About 250 police officers walked ahead of the hearse and the funeral party was met at the cemetery by the

144

Lord Mayor.[64] Brett's grave was marked with a simple headstone (sadly fallen and broken) bearing the inscription:

'In affectionate remembrance of Sergeant Charles Brett of the Manchester Police Force who died in the discharge of his duty at Hyde Road on September 18th 1867 in the 52nd year of his age. Dare not I must do my duty.'

There is also a memorial to Brett in St. Ann's Church.

OLD MORTALITY

We have already come across the writings of the antiquary John Owen when discussing the memorials in Manchester Cathedral. John Owen (not to be confused with John Owens, the founder of Owens College) was born in Bolton in 1815 but later moved to Hulme, where he lived for many years. He made his living as a corn dealer but it is for his recording of the local history of south east Lancashire and east Cheshire for which he will be remembered. He acquired the nickname '*Old Mortality*', probably after Robert Paterson, a Scotsman who in the eighteenth century decided to travel around Scotland re-engraving the tombs of 17th century Covenanter martyrs. Over his lifetime Owen filled no fewer than 89 large manuscript volumes in which he recorded churchyard memorials and extracts from parish registers and other records as well as notes on families, institutions and buildings. He was also a talented artist and many of his notebooks contain sketches of buildings or coats of arms. After his death the collected manuscripts were purchased by the Manchester Free Reference Library and are now in the care of Manchester Archives and Local Studies. Owen seems to have declined dramatically in his final years. The 1901 census shows him as an inmate of the Stockport Union Workhouse, where he is described as a pauper and as an imbecile. The latter description suggests that he was suffering from dementia. His occupation was recorded as '*retired general labourer*'. Did this mean that he had worked as a labourer in his latter years or that the workhouse did not know of his real history? He died, still in the workhouse, on 18 January 1902. Despite the loneliness and apparent obscurity of his death, he received an appreciative obituary.[65]

A WATERLOO VETERAN

Samuel Hyde was buried at Harpurhey in 1876. Born at Leigh, he moved to Manchester, where he joined the army in 1806, enlisting with the First Foot (Grenadier) Guards. He saw action in the Peninsular War, taking part in battles at Nive, Nivelle, Corunna, Badajos and Salamanca. In 1813 the regiment was stationed at Oporto and Samuel re-enlisted for a further period of service. He took part in the Battle of Waterloo after which he was discharged, with a pension of a shilling a day, in 1817. After leaving the army he returned to Manchester and to his old trade as a weaver. He and his family lived for many years in Failsworth. He moved to Newton after the death of Mary, his wife of over fifty years, in 1861. He was buried alongside Mary on Thursday 18 May 1876. A short obituary in the Manchester Times noted his military record.[66]

THE MANCHESTER MUMMY

There can be few stranger funerals than that of Hannah Beswick. Hannah, the daughter of John Beswick of Failsworth, was a prosperous spinster who died in 1758 aged 70. Her body was not buried but was embalmed by her medical adviser Dr. Charles White and thereafter kept at his home at Sale Priory. There are conflicting stories as to why this was done. The most popular account is that Hannah had a fear of premature burial and asked White to keep her body above ground and periodically check it for signs of life. An alternative explanation was that in her will she left White the sum of £400, the balance of which, after funeral expenses had been deducted, he could retain. By not having a funeral, White could, by implication, keep the whole sum. Following White's death in 1813, Hannah's body was given to the Manchester Natural History Museum where it remained on show to the public until 1868. She was finally laid to rest in an unmarked grave at Harpurhey on 22 July of that year.

TOTAL NUMBER OF BURIALS

The surviving registers of Manchester General Cemetery are now deposited at Manchester Archives and Local Studies and show a total, up to the most recent burial recorded in 2003, of 96,059 burials, an average of over 580 per annum. However, this includes many post-war years in which there were relatively few burials. Over its first century the number of burials averaged around 920 per annum and in some of its peak years in excess of 2,000. The above total is, however, not the whole story. Separate registers were kept from 1848 until 1886 for the consecrated and unconsecrated sections of the cemetery. From 1886 onwards, all burials were recorded in a common register irrespective of whether in the consecrated or the unconsecrated sections. The registers specific to the consecrated section for the period 1848 to 1886 have been lost and so it is only possible to guess at the number of burials which they recorded. In 1885 the number of burials recorded in the unconsecrated section alone was around 400 while from 1886 onwards the number recorded in the combined register was around 1,200. This suggests that there might have been as many as 800 burials each year in the consecrated section at this time. It is therefore quite possible that anything up to 30,000 more burials took place than appear in the surviving registers.

MANCHESTER GENERAL CEMETERY TODAY

As with so many Victorian urban cemeteries, time has not been kind to Manchester General Cemetery. The loss of the lodge and chapel buildings and the replacement of Moffat's imposing gateway by a couple of brick piers destroyed the sense of grandeur with which it once faced Rochdale Road. Sadly, it has also suffered both neglect and vandalism and appears to be the haunt of drug users.

There is, however, a small light on the horizon with the recent Manchester General Cemetery Transcription Project. Although this will do little in itself to halt the decline of this neglected cemetery, the project aims to photograph and transcribe the memorials so that at least a record has been taken before time, theft and vandalism cause even more to be lost. It is a goal of which John Owen would have been proud.

Death's shafts fly thick! Here fall the village swain,
And there his pamper'd lord! The cup goes round,
And who so artful as to put it by?
'Tis long since death had the majority,
Yet, strange, the living lay it not to heart!
See yonder maker of the dead man's bed,
The sexton, hoary-headed chronicle!
Of hard unmeaning face, down which ne'er stole
A gentle tear; with mattock in his hand
Digs through whole rows of kindred and acquaintance,
By far his juniors! Scarce a scull's cast up
But well he knew its owner, and can tell
Some passage of his life. Thus hand in hand
The sot has walk'd with Death twice twenty years;
And yet ne'er younker on the green laughs louder,
Or clubs a smuttier tale: when drunkards meet,
None sings a merrier catch, or lends a hand
More willing to his cup. Poor wretch! he minds not
That soon some trusty brother of the trade
Shall do for him what he has done for thousands.

From 'The Grave' by Robert Blair (1699-1746)

Ardwick Cemetery

Ardwick Cemetery

Ardwick Cemetery, like its close contemporary, Manchester General Cemetery, was established as a purely commercial venture from the outset. Investor interest ran at a very high level and the proprietors found themselves massively oversubscribed, receiving applications for a total of 17,000 shares, a 600% over-subscription. Despite the projectors' efforts to select committed investors, a number of the purchasers were clearly speculators and even before the cemetery was open for business the directors commented that *'many [of the shares] had changed hands'*[67].

The proprietors of the Ardwick Cemetery chose to establish their cemetery by forming an Association under a Deed of Settlement rather than seek a private Act of Parliament. This precluded its consecration for Church of England burials but clearly they believed that this would not be a major handicap.

The Deed of Settlement authorised the Association to raise up to £30,000 through the issue of 3,000 shares of £10 each but it did not prove

necessary to raise this much capital. Only 2,100 shares had been issued at the time the deed was signed on 10 November 1837[68] and no further shares were issued. The shares were floated at an initial price of two pounds ten shillings each payable by 2 May 1836 with further calls of two pounds ten shillings on 29 September 1836 and one pound ten shillings on 30 May 1837, making six pounds ten shillings in all. There would be no further call on the unpaid capital for ninety years.

The deed vested ownership of the Association's assets in six trustees, all of whom were also named as directors. A board consisting of the trustees and three additional directors was appointed to manage the business on behalf of the 120 founding shareholders who had attached their signatures to the deed.

A rumour seems to have arisen, even before the shares were allocated, that the future of the venture was in question. This forced the directors to take out a newspaper advertisement:

'Ardwick Cemetery – A rumour having been circulated to the effect that an injunction had been obtained from the Court of Chancery to stay the proceedings in the above undertaking, the Directors deem it their duty to the proprietors to give this public notice, that the Report is a calumny, unsupported by any shadow of truth. – By order of the Directors. Barrett and Ridgway, Solicitors. Committee Room, 26th April 1836.'[69]

The company procured about eight acres of land from Robert Henry Wilson. This was made up of five discrete but adjoining plots and was purchased for a total price of £12,619. The Deed of Settlement makes it clear that only 10,053 square yards (a little over two acres) was to be developed as a cemetery and that the greater part of the land was to be let out on lease or otherwise exploited with a view to raising sufficient income to support the upkeep of the cemetery, particularly at some time in the future when it was full and unable to generate income on its own account.

The directors quickly proceeded to develop the cemetery. They remarked that *'no plot of land near Manchester could have been chosen so favourable for a cemetery'*. They were unfortunate that the winter of 1836 was severe and so rather than incur the cost of working in adverse conditions they postponed building work until the spring of 1837. Work thereafter was proceeding well and it was expected that the cemetery would open on 1 January 1838. There were, however, further delays owing to another severe winter.

OFF TO A SLOW START

The cemetery finally opened on 13 April (Good Friday) 1838 and an advertisement subsequently appeared in the Manchester Guardian:

'Ardwick Cemetery – Applications for Vaults, Graves and Interments to be made to the Rev. Jas. Bradley, resident minister and registrar or to Mr. Fras. Robinson, bookseller, 109 Piccadilly, corner of Lees-street. John Hall, Hon. Sec.'[70]

Business was at first slow and the directors commented towards the end of the first year *"the public have not yet patronised the undertaking to such an extent as the directors could wish"*. The total income from interments and the sale of graves up to 31 December 1838 amounted to only £151-3-0.[71] Over the next few years business picked up steadily, though not spectacularly. At subsequent annual general meetings the minutes frequently report increases both in the sales of graves and the numbers of interments carried out. Income grew steadily and by 1844 had risen to £380-12-6, sufficient to cover expenses and produce a modest profit.

If the shareholders had hoped for an early return on their investment they were to be disappointed. There was to be no dividend until 1844 and even then the payment only amounted to three shillings per share, representing a return of about 2% on the £6-10-0 paid-up value. The

Ardwick Cemetery Chapel

share price also reflected this lacklustre performance. In 1843 shares in the cemetery were being quoted at £2-8-9 each.[72]

The cemetery would undoubtedly have built up its business over time but after seven relatively unimpressive years there was a significant change in their fortunes. Two funerals in particular secured for the cemetery a reputation as the burial ground of choice for the aspiring middle classes.

THE BURIAL OF JOHN DALTON

John Dalton, the famous chemist and physicist and pioneer of atomic theory, died on 27th July 1844. The arrangements for Dalton's funeral were made by a committee of the Manchester Literary and Philosophical Society, of which he had been President at the time of his death. Dalton had been a life-long member of the Society of Friends and so the obvious place for his burial would have been the Quaker Meeting House on Mount Street. The Committee, however, wanted Dalton's body interred '... *at such a place as will afford to the public, generally, the opportunity of showing their veneration and respect for the memory of so distinguished an individual'*[73]. One also suspects that they wished to be able to erect an impressive memorial, something which would have been anathema to the Quakers, who deplored such public displays. The committee initially sought a burial place inside the Collegiate Church but this was refused so it was decided that Dalton should be buried in one of the public cemeteries. The committee members were evenly divided in their preferences between Ardwick and Rusholme Road and in the end Ardwick was chosen on the Chairman's casting vote.[74] In response to the committee's choice, the Ardwick Cemetery directors offered to provide the space for Dalton's vault and all of their services free of charge.

Dalton's body lay in state in Manchester Town Hall over the weekend preceding the funeral and it was estimated that during this time some 40,000 people filed past to pay their respects.

The funeral took place on Monday 12 August and ninety-five carriages are said to have made up the cortège, which also included about one thousand people on foot.

Dalton's last resting place was in a substantial vault, sealed with a single large stone slab. His oak coffin was sealed in a lead casing with a copper plaque describing his achievements attached to the lead. The casing was then enclosed in an outer decorative coffin of curled

John Dalton 1766-1844

Spanish mahogany. A brass coffin plate simply recorded '*John Dalton DCL FRS &c &c Born September 5th 1766, died July 27th 1844'*.[75]

A public appeal was launched, inviting donations towards the cost of raising a memorial. The appeal raised £125 but it was not until 1855 that the memorial, an Aberdeen granite sarcophagus on a three tier platform three feet high, was erected over the vault.

When the cemetery was being cleared in the 1960s Reverend G. W. Dixon proposed that

Dalton's remains might be removed for re-burial at his birthplace of Eaglesfield in Cumberland where Dixon was Vicar.[76] Dixon's proposal came to nothing and Dalton's body remained at Ardwick. Part of his memorial was, however, preserved. The portion of the red granite slab bearing Dalton's name was preserved and in 1962 installed in the foyer of the rebuilt Literary and Philosophical Society building in George Street. The stone was transferred to the Friends' Meeting House on Mount Street in 1980 and finally in 1997 to the Museum of Science and Industry, where it is now on display in the Manchester Science Gallery[77].

THE FUNERAL OF SIR THOMAS POTTER

The choice of Ardwick Cemetery as Dalton's burial place had provided a major publicity coup and the reputation of the cemetery was further boosted the following year by the funeral of Sir Thomas Potter. Potter was a Unitarian and a wealthy linen merchant. He had had a long association with Liberal causes and had been a supporter of the founding of the Manchester Guardian. He was elected to Manchester

Sir Thomas Potter's Memorial

Borough Council in 1835 and following Manchester's incorporation in 1838 became the city's first Mayor. He was knighted in 1840.

Potter had been associated with the Ardwick Cemetery Association from its beginning. He was one of the original trustees and served as treasurer until the time of his death on 20 March 1845. It was therefore unsurprising that he chose to be buried there.

Potter had personally selected the site for his own vault. He had chosen a plot within a few yards of Dalton's grave and at 328 square yards this would be the largest single plot in the cemetery. The total cost of the plot and the construction of the vault was £42-2-6 and this did not include the cost of the large memorial subsequently erected over the vault. This was to be the most lucrative single burial that the cemetery would ever undertake.

Sir Thomas Potter

Potter's funeral was another large public event. As with Dalton's funeral the previous year, Potter's funeral, with its lengthy cortège of 98 carriages, received extensive newspaper coverage.

IMPROVING FORTUNES

The funerals of one of England's most prominent scientists and one of Manchester's most prominent business and civic figures sent out a message which no amount of advertising could have achieved. Ardwick was Manchester's premier cemetery for the wealthy and would-be-wealthy. Between 1844 and 1845 annual income almost doubled from £380 to £727 and from 1848 to 1852 it exceeded £1,000. This allowed the payment of a slightly larger dividend of four shillings per share, rising briefly to five shillings in 1852.

COMMON GRAVES

Ardwick Cemetery was undoubtedly building its appeal to the middle classes as the fashionable place to establish a family vault but the directors did not ignore the income to be derived from providing a simple burial service for the poor. For a relatively modest fee the deceased would be buried in a common grave. These graves could be extremely deep. In 1843 the directors' minutes record their approving the making of a grave no

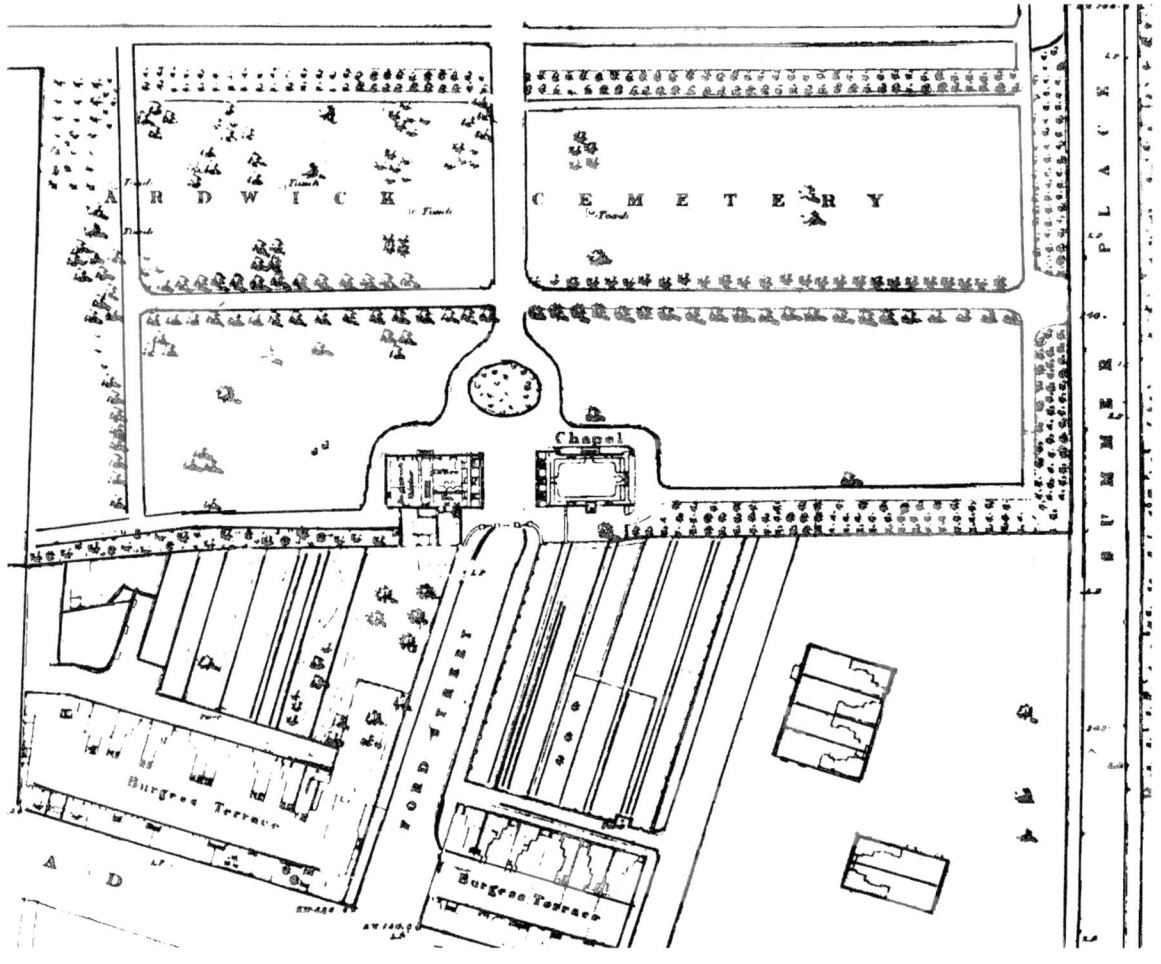

Ardwick Cemetery in 1849

less than 32 feet deep. Directors' approval for the making of *'large graves'* is a regular entry in the minutes of their meetings, a reflection of the level of this business they were undertaking.

The Board of Health undertook an investigation in 1850 into the state of burial grounds and focused much of its comment on Manchester. Their report touched upon Ardwick's common graves:

> 'At the Ardwick Cemetery there was a "pit" open, about 30 feet deep, in which the dead would be piled up to within about three feet of the surface, and the final covering of earth would not be placed over this mass of corruption until some three weeks or a month had elapsed from the deposit of the first coffin'.[78]

Although more than three decades had passed since Joseph Aston's harrowing description of pauper burials at Angel Meadow, conditions equally squalid were being reported at what might at the time have been considered Manchester's most prestigious burial ground.

The Board of Health's revelations possibly took a little of the shine off Ardwick's public image but they did not seem to affect business or dampen the spirits of the shareholders, who presented the Chairman with a silver salver and tea service to the value of £110 *'...in grateful testimony of the ability, perseverance, economy and success, with which as chairman he has conducted the affairs of the association for a period of 14 years.'*[79] The report was, however, a sign of change in the air.

THE BURIAL ACTS

The Board of Health's investigations were a precursor to change and soon after this the government passed the first of the Burial Acts, which imposed restrictions upon urban burial grounds.

An Order in Council was published on 18 April 1854.[80] The Order presented both challenges and opportunities for the cemetery directors. The restrictions imposed on the cemetery could have been more severe — closure would not have been out of the question — but they still had an impact. The first requirement of the Order was that each coffin should be covered by a minimum of four and a half feet of earth. This limited the number of interments which could be made in a family grave but really posed more of a problem for the grave owners than the cemetery. If a family grave could not accommodate any further burials, then the cemetery would be more than happy to sell the family another grave or vault.

The second requirement proved more troublesome, since it demanded that no more than one body be interred in any single public grave. At a stroke this outlawed the use of deep common graves which might contain thirty or more bodies. The requirement would not only produce a considerable increase in work for the gravediggers but it would also dramatically increase the rate at which the available land would be exhausted. The company appealed against this second restriction, deploying the not unreasonable argument that there was no qualitative difference between burying several related people in a family grave and burying several unrelated people in similar fashion. Change was slow in coming but eventually in 1860 the rules were relaxed to permit the burial of up to four bodies in a common public grave. The minimum covering of soil over each burial was at the same time slightly reduced from four and a half to to four feet.[81]

The Burial Acts were not wholly unwelcome to the directors. Taking a positive view, they commented *'...in consequence of the closing of other burial grounds it is presumed that a considerable increase of this description of funeral [i.e. in public graves] will take place during the present year in this cemetery'.*[82] Their confidence was justified. The number of burials, which had dipped dramatically following the introduction of restrictions in 1854, began to increase steadily. It had returned by 1865 to its previous level in excess of 1,000 burials per annum and continued to rise dramatically to reach 3,447 burials in 1871. This was, however, to be a peak from which numbers would subsequently decline year-on-year.

The restrictions inevitably resulted in a significant increase in the fees charged for public burials. The fee to bury an adult in a common grave had last been set in 1840 at six shillings. This now increased to fifteen shillings. For the burial of a stillborn child the increase was still greater, from two shillings to six shillings.[83] The higher charges and increased volume of business improved profitability and each year from 1861 to 1884 a dividend of five shillings per share, representing a return of about 4% of their paid-up value, was distributed to shareholders.

THE GREEK ORTHODOX SECTION

Although Ardwick Cemetery remained broadly non-denominational, this was modified in 1872. Manchester had a small but significant Greek community and several members had been buried at Ardwick. In February 1870 Lycurgus, the Greek Orthodox Archbishop of Syra and Tenos, visited Ardwick and said prayers over several of the graves. The Greek community were desirous that their members should be buried in soil consecrated by the Greek Orthodox Church and a small portion, consisting of a block of twelve graves, was subsequently set aside and consecrated for burials with Greek Orthodox rites.

RISING TENSIONS

Half a century after the cemetery had opened, Ardwick was a very different place. The cemetery, which had been laid out in open fields, was now increasingly becoming surrounded by new buildings. This brought the desirability of having a working cemetery in close proximity to homes and places of business into question.

In 1871 a complaint was investigated by the Corporation's Inspector of Nuisances, Mr. Wilkinson. The identity of the complainant is not known but the complaint clearly related to suspected failure to observe the limitations imposed in 1860. Wilkinson paid at least five visits to the cemetery between 26 October and 3 November and identified a number of irregularities, mostly concerning the failure to maintain a minimum of four feet of earth over each burial. Wilkinson said that he had examined a number of open graves before they were filled-in and claimed that in most cases the depth fell between six and nine inches short of the legal requirement. As a specific example, he claimed that the coffins of two stillborn children would have been buried under as little as two feet two inches of soil. He also reported that more than one body was being interred in a single public grave at the same time, also in contravention of the 1860 regulations, which permitted up to four burials in a public grave but did not permit these burials to take place simultaneously.

The Corporation sent Wilkinson's report directly to Philip Holland, the Government Inspector of Burial Grounds, who wrote to the directors demanding an explanation. Holland pointed out that the report appeared to demonstrate regular breaches of the conditions relating to public graves and went on to point out that if such practices were to continue, he would apply for an order for the complete closure of the cemetery.

In the meantime Wilkinson made two further visits to the cemetery on 21 and 23 November and catalogued further infringements. He also complained that on these latest visits he had been obstructed in the course of his work by the cemetery's workmen.

The chairman of the cemetery directors rejected the claims that they had failed to observe the depth requirements and in particular refuted the allegations relating to the depth of the children's grave. This, they claimed, Wilkinson had measured while the children's coffins were resting in the partially opened grave while the workmen opened out the grave to accommodate them at the requisite depth. In respect of a claim

153

that two smallpox victims had been buried simultaneously in the same grave they responded that this was not the case since the first had been buried on 24 October and the second three days later (a very liberal interpretation of the regulation). The chairman conceded, however, that simultaneous burials in public graves had been their practice but he defended it on the grounds that '... *as the same practice was followed at the Corporation cemeteries I believed it to be correct'*.[84] The directors assured Holland that they would in future adhere strictly to the rules as agreed in 1860 and Holland took no further action.

The cemetery directors, however, did not drop the matter. They complained to the Manchester Town Clerk that his Inspector had been incompetent and mistaken in his findings and furthermore, far from obstructing Wilkinson, they had given him every assistance. The result of the subsequent Corporation hearing was less than conclusive but the Corporation were somewhat lukewarm in support of their Inspector who did not emerge as fully vindicated from the directors' criticisms.[85]

In 1876 a new complaint arose. This time it was alleged that the cemetery was the source of unpleasant smells in nearby houses. Once more, the Town Clerk bypassed the directors and referred the matter directly to Government Inspector Holland, who chaired an enquiry on 17 March. Two local residents, Joseph Hardy and a Mrs. Vickers, each complained of smells which they believed came from the cemetery. However, their complaints were refuted by a Dr. Aspland, who owned nine houses in the vicinity of the cemetery, and by Joseph Worsley, who said he had lived immediately adjacent to the cemetery for eighteen years. Both rejected any suggestion that the cemetery created a nuisance. The complaint that the cemetery was the source of the smells was not upheld and it was suggested that any offensive smells were much more likely to be due to defective drains at the premises concerned.

There seems to have been no further significant complaint but nevertheless in 1887 the Corporation appointed a sub-committee '*to consider the question of intramural interments with special reference to the use of Ardwick Cemetery as a burial ground'*. The sub-committee members complained that they found it difficult to obtain satisfactory information from the cemetery directors and once more complained to the Home Office. The Inspector, Dr. Hoffman, who had replaced Philip Holland some years previously, spent all of thirty minutes at the cemetery during which time he had three graves probed with an iron rod to establish their depth. Hoffman pronounced everything satisfactory and departed. He made two further visits, on 6 December 1888 and 5 September 1889, and on each occasion found everything to be in order. During his December visit he commented to the registrar that '*there was considerable animus on their [the sub-committee's] part'*.[86] Despite Hoffman's failure to find fault, the Corporation sub-committee recommended that there should be no opening of new graves in the 2000-3000 square yards of ground which then remained unused and that burials should only be permitted in the 6,000 family graves and 260 family vaults then existing.

THE END OF PUBLIC BURIALS

Although the Corporation did not have the power to impose this recommendation on the Association, it appears that the directors recognised the inevitability of legislation and decided to act voluntarily before being required to do so, perhaps calculating that by doing so they might avoid an order for the closure of the cemetery. At the Association's AGM on 13 March 1891 the directors reported '*As and from the 1st November 1890 your committee unanimously decided to close the cemetery for public interments, reserving the ground for family graves only'*. This decision was financially damaging since the number of burials was virtually halved from 1,293 in 1890 to 661 in 1891. Income from burial fees fell broadly in proportion from £839 to £464 but operating expenses were reduced by only a small amount. The reduced profitability of the cemetery was reflected in the dividend, which had since 1887 fallen to three shillings and sixpence and now fell to one shilling and sixpence.

In 1892 Mr. Reid, the Governor of Nicholls Hospital, petitioned the Home Office for the

Nicholls Hospital

cemetery to be closed down completely. The hospital had been built in 1880 on land between the cemetery and Hyde Road. The name is misleading since Nicholls Hospital was not a medical establishment but a school '*for the sons of poor persons*'. Reid had been one of the instigators of the unsuccessful complaint in 1887 and clearly regarded the cemetery as an unacceptable neighbour.

The Governor's complaint was that some of his pupils had experienced a problem with a particular type of sore throat which responded poorly to treatment and he believed the cause of this to be connected with the cemetery, possibly from the contamination of drinking water. At the subsequent enquiry held by the Government Inspector, Dr. Hoffman, Reid's complaint was supported by Dr. Tatham, the Medical Officer of Health for Manchester who, while unwilling to confirm the cemetery as the cause, said that the presence of a large number of decomposing bodies in a populated neighbourhood constituted

a danger to health and that both the Ardwick and Rusholme Road Cemeteries should be closed.

The cemetery was not without its defenders. Henry Davies, who lived at 28 Ford Street, close to the cemetery gates, said *"...he did not think there could be a healthier street for a town."*[87]

Reid failed in his bid to close the cemetery but the outcome of the inquiry was the publication of an Order in Council on 30 January 1893 restricting burials to existing family graves and vaults only.[88] Since public burials had been voluntarily discontinued two years earlier, the Order merely formalised the status quo.

BALANCING THE BOOKS

The cemetery was still able to undertake burials in family graves but business continued to decline steadily. During the thirty years following the cessation of public burials the number of burials had gradually declined from 661 in 1891 to 202 in 1900, 123 in 1910 and 55 in 1920. It is clear that following the cessation of public burials in 1890 the cemetery was a decreasingly viable business. The dividend, never high, declined steadily from three shillings in 1892 to nine pence in 1916 and ceased completely in 1920.

Had the company relied solely on income from burials it would have quickly become insolvent but from the outset it had been the intention that income from the surplus land should provide funds to maintain the cemetery. Aside from the sale of two small plots which amounted to less than one acre and small sums from the sale of grazing rights on the unused land, very little income seems to have been raised from the surplus land until around 1898. At this time the directors' minutes refer to a Mr. James paying an annual rent of £112-19-8 for what is described as a 'shop'. By 1905 this had risen to £205-7-0. Several further tenants were found over the next fifteen years but rental income struggled to keep up with the increasing cost of maintaining the now little used cemetery.

In a letter in reply dated 13 June 1921 the directors refused Reverend W. Cooper's request for an increase in the fee for performing burial services saying that *'the cemetery is being carried on at a loss'*. The directors sought to provide funds for maintenance by making a fresh call on the unpaid share capital but the one shilling per share call raised little over £100 and provided no more than a short breathing space. There are references in the minutes around this time to a suggestion that Manchester Corporation might be prepared to take over the cemetery. The sticking point appears to have been the unwillingness of the directors to dispose of the entire undertaking. They appear to have wished to unload the liability, which was the cemetery, while retaining the property which was producing rental income. Discussions went no further.

RESTRUCTURING

On 19 April 1923 Thomas Watts, the Conservative MP for Withington, asked the Home Secretary whether he was aware that permission was being sought to close Ardwick Cemetery. His chief concern was to secure assurances that the rights of those who owned graves there should be suitably protected. The Home Secretary replied that he had received no such representations.

Watts had apparently been mis-informed. The directors were not seeking to close the cemetery but to change its structure from an Association into a Limited Company. It was clear by this time that there was a distinct possibility the cemetery might become insolvent and in this event the shareholders would be exposed to any liabilities which might be incurred. Limited liability had not been available at the time the cemetery was floated and when the formation of limited liability companies became possible in 1855 the cemetery was in good financial health and a change of structure probably seemed unnecessary. Changing the structure was no mere formality since it required the unanimous agreement of all of the shareholders but given the possibility of personal liability for debts, the shareholders did not appear to raise any serious objections and all

156

thirty-seven signed the indenture which brought the Ardwick Cemetery Co. Ltd. into being on 30 July 1925. The new company was formed by exchanging each of the 2100 £10 shares in the old Association for one £1 share in the new limited company.

By the time the new company was formed the number of burials had fallen to fewer than one per week and would continue to fall as some graves became full and the owners of others died off or moved away. The price of a typical burial had by the 1930s risen to between £4 and £5 but the increase in price fell well short of compensating for the reduced numbers.

Under the new company structure a more aggressive approach was taken towards exploiting the unused land. Reginald Larmuth was appointed Managing Director in 1926 with a salary of £50 per annum for what was clearly a part time position. Larmuth's salary was money well spent. Between 1928 and 1932 he raised the substantial sum of £2,450 by selling the freeholds of land which had been some years earlier leased to Great Universal Stores and Associated Newspapers to the lessees. Had this windfall been retained within the company and invested for income, it would have been possible to maintain the cemetery in good order. However, the directors chose to continue to cut maintenance to the bone and distribute the surplus to the shareholders. Between 1927 and 1958 almost £5,000 was distributed in dividends. Meanwhile, the fabric of the cemetery deteriorated year on year.

CLOSURE

By the start of the Second World War the number of burials had dwindled to around one a month. The cemetery was untouched in the December 1940 blitz,[89] though a great number of incendiaries and some high-explosive bombs caused damage to buildings to the west of the cemetery. Part of the unused land on the eastern side of the cemetery was loaned to the War Office to be used as a bayonet assault practice ground by soldiers billeted in Nicholls Hospital and a further part was given over in 1942 as the site of a static water tank for use by fire-fighters. Aside from these minor inconveniences the cemetery had an uneventful war.

With the restoration of peace, the Corporation turned its attention to reconstruction and once more questioned whether the cemetery should close. Representatives of the Parks and Cemeteries Committee visited on 19 October 1948 and again on 14 October 1949. On both occasions they complained that the terms of the 1893 Order in Council were being disregarded, in particular that bodies were being buried in family graves of persons not related to those interred previously. By the latter date, however, the Corporation had already decided to seek closure and the directors had signalled that they would not oppose this. The closure of Ardwick Cemetery was mandated by the Manchester Corporation Act, which passed into law on 28 July 1950. On 27 May of that year sixty-seven year old Lily Bagshaw of Fallowfield became the last person to be buried in Ardwick Cemetery.

THE FINAL YEARS

Closure of the cemetery made little difference to the Ardwick Cemetery Company since by 1950 little of its modest income came from burials. The bulk, around £390 in 1948, came from property leases. Little was done by way of maintenance beyond the most essential repairs and it is clear that the boundary walls and buildings were deteriorating badly. There were unsuccessful efforts to rent out the long-disused chapel, first in 1951 as storage space for groceries and then in 1954 to the Manchester Unity Theatre Club, who were considering converting it into a rehearsal theatre. A structural survey by the latter brought to light extensive dry rot and the cemetery directors decided to call it a day. Although the chapel was listed as being of special or historical interest, the Corporation agreed to its demolition. The chapel was demolished on 5 August 1954 by Wellington Haulage and Demolition Ltd., who not only removed the building free of charge but actually paid the Cemetery Company £50 for the materials which they would salvage.

The last Cemetery Registrar, Henry Cawthra was interviewed by the Manchester Guardian in 1957.[90] Then aged 72, he had worked at the cemetery since 1926 and both of his parents were buried there. Although the cemetery was by this time badly overgrown with weeds over six feet high, he was able to report that little vandalism had taken place. That it was overgrown was unsurprising as he commented that '... they used to have a gardener ... before the war'. The efforts of one elderly man could hardly be expected to control weeds on a three acre plot.

The the Guardian interview had been prompted by Manchester Corporation's announcement of their intention to purchase the cemetery company and to redevelop the cemetery as a public amenity.

PURCHASE BY THE CORPORATION

The Corporation having decided to purchase the cemetery, the Town Clerk, Philip Barrington Dingle, opened negotiations with the company. The directors understandably sought to maximise the purchase price and suggested £4 per share to reflect the value of the company's assets, which included investments to the value of £3,800 and rents amounting to £277 per annum.[91] Dingle's response was that the liabilities of clearing the site or putting and keeping it in proper order exceeded the asset value and that if any compensation at all was awarded to the shareholders this would be generous. He was, however, prepared to offer £1 per share, the nominal value.

The directors dug in their heels insisting that a price not less than £2 was more realistic. It is instructive at this point to note a letter in the company's files dated 18 November 1954 in reply to an enquiry concerning valuation of the shares for probate. The directors had responded that there had been *'no transactions for some considerable time and it would appear under present circumstances little value can be attached to the* shares. *We consider, therefore, that a fair price for probate purposes would be 2/6d per share'.*[92]

In an attempt to break the impasse, Dingle wrote directly to the thirty to forty shareholders. He proposed an offer of £1 for each of the 2,100 shares and implied that the Corporation would otherwise seek permission for compulsory acquisition, which might mean they would receive nothing. Dingle's approach was, to say the least, unorthodox but the company felt that it was both improper and misleading since in their view the proper negotiations had not been completed.

Matters escalated from this point onwards. The company complained that the Town Clerk's offer to shareholders was improper and possibly fraudulent. The police were called in and the CID interviewed both company board members and the Town Clerk. Two debates were held in Parliament, which was at the time considering the Manchester Corporation Bill. The proposed purchase was a very small part of this bill but dominated the debates. The bill was considerably delayed through 1958 and it was not until late December that it went for Royal assent with compulsory purchase authorised at the original price of £1 per share.

This was not the end of the matter. In the course of the dispute, an article in the Daily Mail had injudiciously accused Philip Dingle of fraud. Dingle brought a suit for libel against Associated Newspapers, the Mail's publishers, and after a protracted hearing, at which the Solicitor General appeared as a witness, Dingle was awarded £1000 in damages with costs. Not satisfied, he

Ardwick Cemetery shortly before the gravestones were cleared

appealed one part of the judgement in which he felt a further libel had been incorrectly dismissed and subsequently secured increased damages of £4,000.[93] The Appeal Court judgement was in turn unsuccessfully appealed by Associated Newspapers before matters were finally brought to an end. Philip Dingle received a Knighthood in the 1960 New Years Honours and retired in 1966 after 22 years as Town Clerk.[94]

The Council, having finally completed the purchase, set about clearing the site. The memorials were removed (though summary records of the inscriptions were made) and the remaining buildings demolished, the protected status of the lodge and gatehouse having been removed some time previously. What had for nearly 170 years been Ardwick Cemetery was turned into a public a park and renamed Nicholls Field after the adjacent Nicholls Hospital. The graves were left undisturbed, the ground simply levelled and grassed over. A plaque in the park briefly records its history:

> 'Nicholls Field was opened on 16th June 1966 by Sir Philip B. Dingle C.B.E. LL.D Town Clerk of Manchester 1944 – 1966. The field was formerly ARDWICK CEMETERY where between 1838 and 1950 the remains of over 80,000 people were interred including John Dalton, scientist 1766 - 1844. Sir Thomas Potter, first Mayor of Manchester 1773 - 1845. Ernest Jones, the Chartist 1819 – 1869, Bugler Robert Hawthorne 52nd Light Infantry who won the Victoria Cross at Delhi in 1857. And many others of all walks of life who served God and the City in their day and generation. Councillor F. Hatton J.P. Chairman, Education Committee J. K. Elliot, Chief Education Officer'.

The plaque understates the numbers buried. The cemetery registers record a total of 95,639 burials. The true total is possibly somewhat higher since many stillborn babies were not included in the running totals in the registers.

POSTSCRIPT

It is difficult, from the dry minutes and correspondence, to understand the motivation of those involved in the running of Ardwick Cemetery over its long history. It is evident from the original Deed of Settlement that it was founded by men who believed that a much needed public service could be provided within a commercial framework. It is clear too that, unlike many others, they foresaw the day when the cemetery would be full and sought to provide for this by establishing a second source of income from the surplus of land which they were able to procure. The directors, all part timers, seem to have been incapable of managing this valuable asset effectively and only began to exploit its potential when the decline in the burial business made this absolutely necessary. Their efforts proved too little and too late. Following the conversion into a limited company in 1925 and the appointment of Reginald Larmuth as Managing Director, a more hard-nosed approach prevailed and there was briefly a possibility that the company might generate sufficient income to maintain the cemetery as its founders had wished. Unfortunately, the shareholders, now only thirty-seven in number and dominated by the Lees family, who between them owned about one third of the shares and controlled the company board, chose to squeeze unrealistic dividends out of substantially worthless shares.

Had the £5,000 paid out in dividends over the final thirty years been invested in maintenance, perhaps the Corporation would have been less inclined to compulsorily purchase a well-maintained cemetery. More possibly, had the chapel and lodge been properly maintained, their listing as being of special or historical interest might have encouraged their preservation and today's park might be graced by a fine pair of Georgian Greek revival buildings. We shall never know.

The Private Cemeteries in Retrospect

For around three decades the private cemetery seemed to offer an answer to the growing problem of urban burial. By the time Rusholme Road Cemetery opened in 1821, the pressure on burial space in Manchester was becoming significant but a general lack of burial space was not the principal reason for the undertaking. Only six years earlier the parish had opened its latest burial ground at Walkers Croft and this would provide burial space for the poor for another twenty-five years. The problem was more the lack of burial space for nonconformists. Most of the graveyards of any size were owned by the Church of England and burial there meant to be buried with the reading of the Church of England funeral service. This was something which Manchester's growing nonconformist congregations found unacceptable.

Many of the nonconformist chapels had small burial grounds but these were inadequate to meet the growing demand. It was a logical development, therefore, that the various nonconformist churches should get together to establish an unconsecrated burial ground in which individuals could be buried according to the rites of their own church or without any religious ceremony whatsoever.

The adoption of a joint stock model to finance a capital intensive venture was by this time well established and so a natural, if novel, choice for financing a cemetery. It is difficult to determine the extent to which the investors were motivated by faith or by profit but even those who viewed the venture as a pure investment must have been surprised at the substantial profits and consequent dividends which quickly followed the Rusholme Road Cemetery's opening. Those who invested in a £10 share had received dividends exceeding the value of their investment within a decade and would continue to receive dividends, albeit at a reduced level, for a further sixty years.

There is far less uncertainty concerning the motives of those who had invested in the Ardwick and Manchester General Cemeteries. These were outright commercial ventures whose investors were attracted by the impressive returns which had been received by the Rusholme Road shareholders. Neither venture succeeded to the same extent. To establish Ardwick Cemetery had required twice the capital of Rusholme Road and to establish Manchester General Cemetery three times the amount. To achieve similar returns demanded both a higher volume and a higher value of business. The market for burials is, however, somewhat inflexible. It may be expected to grow with population but commercial success can only be achieved by winning a larger and more lucrative share of the market than one's competitors.

The success of Rusholme Road Cemetery came about because there were prosperous middle class dissenters looking for a place where they might be buried but which was not under the control of the Church of England. The arrival of Ardwick and Manchester General Cemeteries did nothing to expand this market and both initially struggled to win sufficient business from their established rival. But Rusholme Road, with its low capital base, could not easily be undercut for price, at least if those undercutting were to turn a profit. For Ardwick Cemetery salvation came with the funerals of John Dalton and Sir Thomas Potter, which brought with them the social kudos necessary to attract a middle class clientele. For Manchester General it was a harder struggle since they were located well away from the more prosperous residential areas. Their lifeline came in the securing of a consecrated section and a contract for parish burials following the closure of Walkers Croft. This was considerably less lucrative at the level of each individual funeral but had the virtues of both volume and reliability.

All three cemeteries were impacted to some extent by the Burial Acts in 1854. None of the cemeteries was closed, though given the locations of Rusholme Road and Ardwick Cemeteries, this might have been a possibility. Rusholme Road, the most centrally located of the three, suffered the most severe restrictions and was effectively limited to burials in existing family graves. This was a death sentence but one which would play out over seven decades. Commercially Rusholme Road was no longer in the game. Ardwick Cemetery to some extent gained from the Burial Acts. Whilst the number of interments permitted in any individual grave was now limited, their principal competitor for the sale of new graves had been effectively removed. The prohibition on multiple burials in common graves initially had a severe impact on the number of public burials at Ardwick, since the same prohibition was not initially imposed on Manchester General Cemetery, their main competitor for this business. Manchester General Cemetery was not even mentioned in the 1854 Orders in Council and continued with business as usual. Because no limitations had been applied to multiple burials in common graves, the volume of their business more than doubled in the wake of the Acts. This anomaly was not, however, permitted to continue and in 1856 the same limits were placed upon them as had been applied to Ardwick Cemetery. Ardwick and Manchester General, now the only significant players in the market, enjoyed a period of relative stability and success. It was not to last. A new and serious competitor was soon to appear.

Manchester Corporation was slow to open its own cemeteries; Philips Park did not open fully until 1867 and Southern Cemetery until 1879. It might have been expected that this would result in reduced business for the private cemeteries and so it proved. Manchester General Cemetery saw business decline from around 2,000 to around 1,200 burials over the twelve years from 1866 to 1878. By contrast, over the same period, Ardwick Cemetery more than doubled its business from around 1,200 to around 2,700 burials annually. Location was probably a factor. Philips Park was closer to Manchester General Cemetery than Ardwick Cemetery and Ardwick was better placed to serve the expanding southern suburbs. A further factor seems to be that Ardwick competed more aggressively on price.

When Southern Cemetery opened in 1879, the positions were reversed. Manchester General Cemetery's level of business was little affected while at Ardwick, which drew on similar population centres for its business, the decade after 1879 saw numbers more than halved to around 1300 burials.

The municipal cemeteries had a significant effect on price. Financed through low cost government loans, underwritten by the municipal rates and with no shareholders to satisfy, they could cut prices to the bone. They were in a position to dictate market prices and under ratepayer pressure to keep prices as low as possible. Southern Cemetery's basic fee for an adult burial in a common public grave was thirteen shillings. This is two shillings less than the fee which Ardwick Cemetery had been charging twenty-five years earlier for the equivalent burial. In 1864 the average fee which Ardwick Cemetery received for a burial was sixteen shillings, in 1876 it had fallen to fourteen shillings and by 1886 it was less than thirteen shillings. Even though Ardwick Cemetery had maintained and even increased the volume of its business for a period, these depressed prices left them with little profit.

Ardwick Cemetery was forced to withdraw from public burials in 1890 and this halved the volume of their business overnight. Like Rusholme Road, Ardwick also was now at the start of a long and terminal decline. As the twentieth century opened, Manchester General Cemetery was the only private cemetery carrying out any significant level of business; still around 800 burials per annum.

All three cemeteries were purchased by Manchester Corporation during the 1950s. Rusholme Road had been closed for over twenty years and Ardwick had finally closed its doors in 1950. Both were erased from the landscape and found new uses as public parks. Manchester General Cemetery was still a going concern and although some of the graves were levelled and landscaped, it continued as a working cemetery into the twenty-first century.

Early in the nineteenth century it had appeared that the private cemetery would provide a practical solution to the problems which were beginning to arise from urban burial grounds while at the same time providing a good investment for shareholders. This turned out to be a false dawn. Some key factors which undermined them were:

There was significant over-provision – Manchester could probably have supported one, at the most two, profitable private cemeteries, but not three.

They faced subsidised competition – Before the Burial Acts of 1854 there was competition from church burial grounds which carried neither financing burdens nor shareholder pressures. After 1867 competition arose from cheaply financed municipal cemeteries. They were not, therefore, always in a position to set a market price at which they could operate profitably.

They were built in the wrong place – Both Rusholme Road and Ardwick were too close to the city centre. Consequently they were soon surrounded by houses and eventually this gave rise to public health concerns.

One further factor was a failure to provide for the future. A cemetery, however it is established, is somewhat like a pyramid investment. Money is borrowed or invested by shareholders and used to purchase land and erect buildings. Once open, burial fees provide income to fund running costs and to pay interest (or dividends) on the sums invested. This can work well but a problem arises when the cemetery is full and income from fees ceases. Running costs continue to be incurred, even if only to provide basic security and maintenance. These costs can still be significant and have to be provided for. The three cemeteries adopted different approaches to this problem.

Manchester General's approach was simply to buy a piece of land which was sufficiently large that the problem of the cemetery becoming full was pushed well into the future. This worked, at least as far as the company was concerned, and the burden of maintenance was ultimately shouldered by the Corporation. Rusholme Road Cemetery made no provision but some income was raised after the cemetery had closed by renting out both land and buildings. The promoters of Ardwick Cemetery anticipated the problem and endowed the cemetery with a substantial holding of investment land. They expected this to generate income to manage the cemetery properly once it had closed. It is unfortunate that the directors seem to have managed this asset very poorly for most of the cemetery's history. When finally the value of the land was recognised and converted into cash, the twentieth century directors effectively stripped the asset by distributing the proceeds (in large part to themselves) as dividends. In all three cases it was left to Manchester Corporation to sort out the mess.

We should not, however, conclude that Manchester's private cemeteries were a failure. Between them the three cemeteries accommodated well in excess of a quarter of a million burials, burials which would have to have been accommodated elsewhere. Without the private cemeteries Manchester's churchwardens would have had to provide the necessary burial space and their track record in this had not been a good one.

The private cemeteries also provided a model which influenced the later development of municipal cemeteries and without their example it is possible that municipal cemeteries would have developed along utilitarian rather than aesthetic lines, much as had been the case with urban churchyards and burial grounds.

Many critics of private cemeteries had predicted that the eventual outcome would be profits for the shareholders while the ratepayers would be left to foot the bill and at a simple level this proved to be the case. Had Rusholme Road and Ardwick Cemeteries never existed, it is almost certain that the land would have been developed commercially and extremely unlikely that the Corporation would have bought up developed land to provide public parks in these areas.

In this scenario, local residents would not today enjoy access to the large open spaces of Gartside Gardens and Nicholls Field.

Private cemeteries were effectively killed off by the Burial Acts, not so much because of the restrictions which the Acts introduced, but because the Acts led to the opening of municipal cemeteries with which it was difficult, if not impossible, to compete. They staggered on into the twentieth century but the future was to be in public ownership.

Notes for Private Cemeteries

1. Gatherings From Grave Yards, George Alfred Walker, London, 1839.
2. For a useful history of The Rosary Cemetery, see www.heritagecity.org/research-centre/social-innovation/rosary-cemetery.htm
3. Manchester Guardian, 30 April 1836. Around the same time, there was a further prospectus to raise £12,000 for a new cemetery for Stockport. As an inducement to investors, it specifically referred to £10 shares in Rusholme Road Cemetery as trading at £37 each. I have been unable to find any record of them trading for even half this sum.
4. Greater Manchester County Record Office GB127.M74/3/1/16.
5. William Gadsby, B. A. Ramsbottom, 2003.
6. Manchester Guardian 27 April 1822.
7. Manchester Guardian, 26 September 1837.
8. Manchester Times, 30 April 1836.
9. Manchester Times, 8 April 1841.
10. Manchester Guardian 26 September 1835, 27 September 1837, 2 October 1841 respectively.
11. Manchester Courier & Lancashire General Advertiser, Saturday 18 January 1834.
12. Mad Dogs and Englishmen, Neil Pemberton and Michael Worboys. Published in History Today, Volume 57, Issue 9, 2007.
13. Manchester Guardian 1 February 1837.
14. Bell's Life in Sydney and Sporting Reviewer, Saturday 8 December 1849. This Australian newspaper contains the most comprehensive account of James Robinson's family background and boxing career.
15. Manchester Times, Saturday 7 July 1849. The Medical Officer's report is incorrect in stating that Robinson first showed signs of cholera on Saturday 16 June. It is clear from the cemetery register that he was buried on Tuesday 12 June and from the details given he must have shown the first signs on Saturday 9 June.
16. Manchester Guardian 5 July 1854.
17. All statistics relating to the number of burials are taken directly from an analysis of the burial registers.
18. Manchester Guardian, 18 February 1859.
19. Manchester Guardian, 25 June 1863. The author of the letter was Mark Scarnell, an estate agent of 181 Every Street, Ancoats.
20. Letter P. H. Holland to Rusholme Road Cemetery dated 12 February 1863. GMCRO GB127.M74/3/12/2.
21. Letter P. H. Holland to Rusholme Road Cemetery dated 3 September 1868. GMCRO GB127/M74/3/12/3.
22. Manchester Guardian 1 October 1889. The correspondent lived in Liverpool.
23. Manchester Guardian, 28 August 1905.
24. Minute Book 1872-1910, GMCRO, GB127/M74/3/2 Proprietors' meeting 23 February 1888
25. Minute Book 1872-1910, GMCRO, GB127/M74/3/2 Proprietors' meeting 24 February 1890
26. Mr. Robertson on Infant Mortality in Manchester published in the London Medical Gazette, Vol. 15 for session 1834-1835, 1835. Robertson compares infant mortality as recorded in the burial registers of Rusholme Road Cemetery, representing a middle-class clientele with infant mortality recorded in the parish burial ground registers and representing the poorest members of society. His conclusion unsurprisingly points to lower infant mortality among the middle classes.
27. The total is popularly quoted as 78,143 this being the register number of the final burial. However, the 'running' numbers in the cemetery register contain two errors. On 1 December 1865 number 60,999 is followed by 70,000 and on 27 May 1898 number 77,099 is followed by 78,000. The number of actual burials is therefore 9,902 fewer than suggested by the running number of the final entry.
28. Manchester Guardian 8 October 1938.
29. Manchester Guardian 14 May 1947.
30. Manchester Guardian, 2 September 1955.
31. Manchester Guardian 15 May 1957.
32. Manchester Guardian, 24 November 1833.
33. The Deed of Settlement appears to have been lost. It is mentioned in the directors' advertisement in the Manchester Guardian, 30 October 1847 concerning their intention to seek consecration of a part of the cemetery.
34. Manchester Guardian, 15 March 1837.
35. Manchester Courier & Lancashire General Advertiser, Saturday 2 September 1937.
36. Manchester Guardian, 17 November 1838.
37. Manchester Guardian 31 August 1844.

38 Manchester Times and Gazette 8 April 1848.

39 Manchester Guardian, 27 November 1848.

40 Manchester Times and Gazette, 8 April 1848.

41 Manchester Guardian, 14 June 1845. The proposal was signed by 75 proprietors or shareholders so the meeting was probably no more than a formality.

42 London Gazette, 25 July 1848.

43 Manchester Courier & Lancashire General Advertiser, Wednesday 15 November 1848.

44 Manchester Courier & Lancashire General Advertiser, Wednesday 11 April 1849.

45 Manchester Courier & Lancashire General Advertiser, Saturday 22 December 1855.

46 History of the Cholera in Manchester in 1849, John Leigh MRCS and Ner Gardiner, Superintendent Registrar of Manchester, 1850.

47 Reported in the Manchester Guardian, 11 March, 1850.

48 Manchester Guardian, 16 August 1854.

49 London Gazette 26 August 1856 page 2909.

50 The burial register records that Catharine. Lane, aged 30 of 34 Mason Street, Rochdale Road was buried 16 September 1856.

51 John Bolton Rogerson is remembered more as a poet than as the registrar of Manchester General Cemetery, a position which he held towards the end of his life. One of his earlier works was 'Lines on a Tomb, the Inscription of which was Effaced by Time'. The final lines are prophetic of the decline of the cemetery where he worked: *'Thou relic of a once-proud tomb;/Crumbled to dust thou soon wilt lie,/No more wilt fix th' observing eye,/And the inquiring gaze will pass/O'er thee, as o'er a worthless mass'.*

52 Manchester Guardian, 19 September 1856.

53 Manchester Guardian, 30 October 1856.

54 Manchester Guardian, 31 March 1855.

55 Manchester Guardian, 20 April 1858.

56 Manchester Guardian, 18 April 1893.

57 London Gazette, 28 May 1926.

58 Manchester Corporation, Parks and Cemeteries Committee minutes 1956 (volume 65) 14 September 1956. The minutes record that the income of the cemetery was £2,450 against operating costs of £2,700.

59 Manchester Corporation, Parks and Cemeteries Committee minutes 1956 (volume 65) 12 April 1957.

60 Manchester Guardian, 18 June 1958.

61 The Victorian Celebration of Death, James Stevens Curl, 2000.

62 Manchester Guardian, 1 November 1958.

63 The Weaver of Wellbrook. The full music and lyrics of this song, as well as a large collection of Ben Brierley's writings can be found on the remarkable Gerald Massey web site: http://gerald-massey.org.uk/brierley/

64 Manchester Courier & Lancashire General Advertiser, Monday 23 September 1867.

65 Manchester Courier & Lancashire General Advertiser, Thursday 23 January 1902.

66 Manchester Times, Saturday 20 May 1876. There is no mention of his funeral receiving military honours.

67 Ardwick Cemetery Annual General Meeting minutes 21 May 1837. GMCRO GB127.M74/5/11-1.

68 Deed of Settlement, GMCRO GB127.M74/5/10-1.

69 Manchester Guardian 30 April 1836.

70 Manchester Guardian 23 June 1838.

71 Ardwick Cemetery Annual General Meeting minutes 8 March 1839. GMCRO GB127.M74/5/11-1.

72 The Times, 23 May 1843 and 11 August 1848 respectively. Prices for Ardwick Cemetery shares were published infrequently up to 1848 and seldom after this time.

73 Manchester Courier & Lancashire General Advertiser, Saturday 3 August 1844.

74 Manchester Guardian 3 August 1844.

75 Manchester Courier & Lancashire General Advertiser, Saturday 17 August 1844.

76 Manchester Guardian, 20 August 1960.

77 John Dalton's Manchester, Centre for the Study of Science, Technology and Medicine, James Sumner, 2009.

78 Manchester Guardian 10 March 1850.

79 Manchester Guardian 11 December 1852.

80 London Gazette, 18 April 1854.

81 London Gazette, 30 October 1860.

82 Ardwick Cemetery Annual General Meeting minutes 13 March 1857. GMCRO GB127.M74/5/11-1.

83 Ardwick Cemetery Directors' Minute book 2 September 1852. GMCRO GB127.M74/5/12/1.

84 Letter dated 7 December 1871 from the directors to P. H. Holland recorded in the direc-

tors' minute book GMCRO GB127.M74/5/12/1.

85 Ardwick Cemetery Directors' Minutes GB127.M74/5/12/1. The minutes contain transcripts of the correspondence relating to this matter from 7 December 1871 onwards.

86 Ardwick Cemetery Directors' Minute book 6 December 1888. GMCRO GB127.M74/5/12/1.

87 Manchester Guardian 11 March 1892.

88 The cemetery's copy of the order is preserved at GMCRO GB127.M273/1/22/4-5

89 Manchester 'Blitz' Maps GMCRO GB127.MISC/1192/1 104 Pt. 11. These fascinating maps show the location where each bomb fell and indicate which buildings were damaged.

90 Manchester Guardian, 6 December 1957.

91 Manchester Corporation Bill 1958, Hansard HC Deb 09 July 1958 vol 591 cc475-537 .

92 Ardwick Cemetery Company Correspondence 1947-1955, GMCRO GB127.M74/5/23.

93 The case is well summarised in The Guardian, 3 December 1959, the award of damages on 11 December 1959 and the subsequent increase on 9 February 1961.

94 The Guardian, 27 October 1966.

Lines on a Tomb, the Inscription on which was Effaced by Time

O house of death! thou mouldering tomb,
Thou marble palace of the dead,
Whom hast thou shut up in thy womb,
Thou monument of grandeur fled?
Vain was his hope who put his trust
In thee for lasting fame;
For thou art hast'ning to the dust,
Like him whose titled name
Was once emblazon'd on thy side,
Who on thee trusted, when he died,
To tell posterity his fame.
The lines have faded from thy brow,
He thought would tell his worth;
His pride and power, where is it now?
Gone to its parent— earth!
On thee let pomp and wealth now gaze,
And tell them this their lot —
To live awhile in hireling praise,
Then die, for aye forgot.
And thou, that still dost seem to say
Thou holdest more than common clay,
Thou too wilt quickly meet thy doom,
Thou relic of a once-proud tomb;
Crumbled to dust thou soon wilt lie,
No more wilt fix th' observing eye,
And the inquiring gaze will pass
O'er thee, as o'er a worthless mass.

John Bolton Rogerson (1809-1859)

166

Municipal Cemeteries

Municipal Cemeteries

Before 1854 municipal authorities had no general powers to purchase land for the purpose of establishing and operating cemeteries. It was, however, possible for a corporation to obtain an Act of Parliament specific to that purpose. Leeds, like Manchester, was a rapidly growing industrial city and faced very similar problems with overcrowded and unsanitary urban graveyards. In 1842 the Leeds Corporation sought and obtained an Act of Parliament to grant them the necessary powers and to levy a rate to recover the costs involved in setting up cemeteries. The Leeds Burial Act received Royal assent on 16 July 1842 and Leeds Corporation subsequently opened cemeteries in 1845 in Burmantofts and Hunslet.

Similar Acts were obtained by Southampton Corporation in 1843 and by Coventry in 1844. However, most city corporations, including Manchester, chose not to become involved in establishing cemeteries. Burial in most cities therefore remained in the hands of the church and of an increasing number of private cemeteries. It was to be another decade before a coherent long-term solution was found. This took the form of the 'Burials (Beyond the Metropolis) Act' of 1853.

The 1853 Act established a new framework for how cemeteries were to be set up and operated but it left the matter in the hands of parish vestries. The Act enabled parishes to combine to set up burial boards and provided access to low-cost government funding to assist them in this purpose. The Act did not, though, provide any basis for borough corporations to open cemeteries.

In some cities it was not easy for the parishes to meet the requirements of the 1853 Act and so the following year a short statute, the 'Burials (Beyond the Metropolis) Amendment Act' was passed. This extended the provisions of the earlier Act and authorised borough corporations to form burial boards in the same way as parish vestries had been authorised under the 1853 Act.

Manchester Corporation's response to the opportunity afforded by the 1854 Act was far from immediate. Across the Irwell in Salford, the Corporation had quickly seized the new opportunity and in 1857 opened the large Weaste Cemetery. In contrast, Manchester Corporation waited twelve years to open their first burial ground.

There are probably two main reasons for the Corporation's slowness to act, aside from the inevitable problem of finding a suitable piece of land. Firstly, the churchwardens were still sitting on the substantial proceeds from the sale of Walkers Croft and looking actively into establishing a new parish burial ground. As we have seen, by 1854 these efforts had descended into fiasco and within a year or two it was clear that a new parish burial ground was unlikely to be established.

The second reason was that the contractual arrangement between the churchwardens and Manchester General Cemetery provided the city with access to a substantial out-of-town burial ground, albeit a private one. The contractual terms of this arrangement appear to have been quite reasonable. There were also several graveyards in which it was still permitted to undertake burials subject to a variety of conditions. It was possibly also the case that the Weaste Cemetery provided some further capacity by attracting business from its neighbour. Overall, the question of providing sufficient burial space did not seem to have great urgency.

Manchester Corporation eventually opened its first cemetery at Philips Park in 1866. This immediately became the principal cemetery for Manchester. Philips Park was not, however, a particularly convenient cemetery for families who lived on the south side of the city, which was developing rapidly as a desirable residential area, and so Philips Park was followed in 1879 by

Manchester Southern Cemetery, then and still the largest municipal cemetery outside London.

The new municipal cemeteries were a world apart from those which had gone before. The Burial Acts required new cemeteries to be at least two miles beyond the borough boundary and both were consequently located well outside the developed area of the city. This was not to last long, however, as the rapid growth of industry to the north and housing to the south soon swept past their gates. Fortunately, the Burial Acts had anticipated this situation and imposed a restriction on the building of any dwelling within 200 yards of a cemetery boundary.

The new cemeteries were also large. Each was several times larger than even the ten acre Manchester General Cemetery — itself five times as large as the largest of the previous parish burial grounds. This increase in size was the direct result of much more stringent requirements concerning the space which was to be allocated to each grave (see panel below).

The municipal cemeteries established a model which has now lasted a century and a half and worked successfully with little modification. Were it not for the trend in the 20th century away from burial and towards cremation, it is probable that even the vast Southern Cemetery would by now be full and Manchester would once again be looking for a new burial ground. However, Southern Cemetery remains the city's main burial ground.

Overcrowding

A major concern of those drafting the Burial Acts was that bodies were being packed so close together that the process of decomposition was considerably slowed down, creating possible dangers to health. This had been a failing in even the best-managed cemeteries and a scandal in the worst.

Published alongside the Burial Acts was a Home Office document entitled 'Instructions for Burial Boards in Providing Cemeteries and Making Arrangements for Interments'. The 54 clauses of this document set out in precise detail the business of establishing and operating a cemetery. In particular, the instructions specified minimum sizes for burial plots. An area of nine feet by four (36 square feet) was to be assumed for an adult's grave, seven feet by three (21 square feet) for a young person and five feet nine inches by two feet nine inches (about 16 square feet) for a child.

Using these figures and allowing for the area used for pathways and buildings, it was suggested that around 1200 graves could be accommodated in each acre. If each grave was used for an average of four burials then each acre might ultimately accommodate approaching 5000 burials.

It is instructive to compare this to the density of burials in the New Burial Ground at Angel Meadow and at Walkers Croft. Each of these burial grounds accommodated in excess of 30,000 burials in an area of around two acres, not allowing for paths, buildings and unusable areas. This amounts to a density of some 15,000 burials per acre, about three times the density suggested for the new cemeteries.

Even these were not the worst examples in Manchester's history. The 700 square yards (0.14 acres) of the Apple Market burial ground somehow found space for 6,383 bodies giving a density of about 44,000 burials to the acre. Outside Manchester there were apparently worse cases. The Home Office instructions refer to an (unidentified) burial ground in which the density exceeded 80,000 burials per acre, an almost unimaginable number. After the Burial Acts such densely packed graveyards were never to be seen again.

Philips Park Cemetery

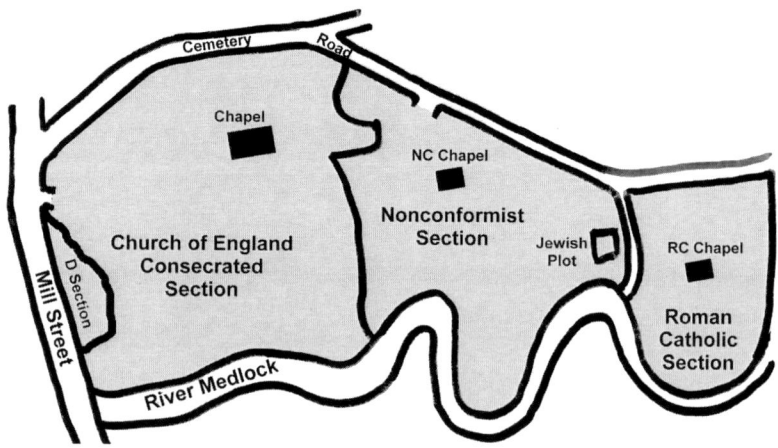

Philips Park Cemetery

A proposal that Manchester Corporation should open a new municipal cemetery finally emerged in the early 1860s. In 1863 the Corporation bought the '*Grange Estate*', a forty-six acre plot on the northern bank of the River Medlock and part of the estate of Lady Houghton. The price paid was about £14,000.[1] The land was directly across the river from Philips Park, Manchester's first public park, which had opened in 1846. A description of the cemetery shortly after it opened described it lyrically: '*The surface is undulating and slopes towards the river so that the cemetery, when laid out in ornamental walks &c. will appear as a part and continuation of the park itself.*'[2]

A design competition was held and the winning proposal was submitted by the architects Henry John Paull and Oliver Aycliffe of Manchester assisted Mr. William Gay of Yorkshire. Gay had previously designed Bradford's impressive Undercliffe private cemetery[3]. Their plan divided the cemetery into three areas. About half of the cemetery was to be consecrated by the Church of England, a further twelve acres set aside for dissenters and the remaining eight and a half acres were to be consecrated for Roman Catholic burials. Each of the areas would have its own chapel, each built to a different design, but all within an overall Gothic style. The Anglican chapel was designed to seat around 200 and each of the others about half this number.[4] One is left to wonder whether the architects expected that Catholic and dissenter funerals would attract half the number of mourners as those of the Established Church. A thirty foot wide carriageway ran across the cemetery linking the he main gate at the western end to the three chapels. From this artery numerous small pathways extended to the north and south dividing the whole into a large number of small burial sections. Extensive planting of trees and shrubs softened the overall appearance.

Setting out the cemetery and constructing the three chapels, the lodge and the office buildings commenced without great delay. The project was timely. Unemployment at the time was high and the creation of the cemetery was used as part of a public works programme to create employment. As many as 200 unemployed factory workers were found work on the project as part of a workforce which at times reached 400. The works undertaken were impressive, particularly given the limited earth-moving machinery available. Mounds of earth as high as thirty feet high were removed and used to fill in pools and ravines. A land drainage system was created which involved installing drain pipes twenty feet deep feeding into a culvert which in places lay thirty feet below the surface. The boundary wall on the western, northern and eastern sides of the cemetery was well over a mile long, built of stone and topped with wrought iron railings. The purchase of the land and the work to construct the boundary walls and buildings and to set out the cemetery cost the Corporation around £60,000 in total.

Philips Park Cemetery opened in stages. The Roman Catholic section was the first to open for interments on 24 August 1866.[5] The unconsecrated section followed on 1 May 1867.[6] The Church of England section was completed last and was consecrated on 2 August the same year by the Bishop of Manchester in the presence of the Lord Mayor, the Town Clerk and about 150 local residents. It opened for interments the following week.[7]

NOT THE IDEAL LOCATION

The riverside location was aesthetically attractive but looks are not everything. The surrounding area was becoming increasingly industrialised and while the Manchester Guardian's reporter had praised the look of the cemetery, he was scathing about the air quality, writing:

'When the wind is in the north west, there is blown across the cemetery all the offensive smells of manure manufacturers, chemical works and knackers yards, together with clouds of smoke from the various iron works and factories which are now springing up in that neighbourhood.'[8]

Nearly a decade later, when debating the effects of building of a Corporation gas works in the vicinity, Councillor Smith commented: *'the*

*The Church of England
Mortuary Chapel
(Photo courtesy of A. M. Berrell)*

atmosphere in the locality could not be worse than it is'.[9]

Air quality aside, the land was a questionable choice for a cemetery. The Home Office instructions to burial boards providing cemeteries were quite specific:

'VII Ground which is subject to periodical flooding or which contains water springs should be avoided as should also all ground the subsoil of which is apt to be charged with water by infiltration from rivers, streams &c. Generally wet soils

172

which do not admit of drainage should be rejected.'[10]

As we shall see, the lowest-lying part of the site was subject both to flooding from the adjacent river and apparently also to a troublesome level of ground water. The former problem should have been obvious and the latter could have easily been established by test bores. The River Medlock furthermore had a long history of floods and had broken its banks in both 1851 and 1860. Concerns had been expressed from the outset that the Roman Catholic section, part of which occupied the lowest part of the cemetery next to the river, appeared to be particularly exposed to this risk. It was not long before these fears were realised since in both 1866 and 1867 floods inundated this part of the cemetery and in the latter year several coffins were washed out of the ground[11]. To protect against flooding, a further 35 acres of land upstream was procured and works

undertaken to reinforce the river banks. These works consisted of the application of a layer of 'puddled clay' which was designed to stabilise the loose earth and prevent erosion when water levels were high. The flooding problem was, however, not so easily solved and would return with a vengeance some years later.

OLD HABITS DIE HARD

Philips Park was intended to make a clean break with the past history of cemetery mismanagement and abuses. It was to be operated by the Corporation under much stricter rules concerning burials than had been the case before the Burial Acts. While it is beyond argument that it offered a dramatic improvement on what had gone before, in its early years of operation it was not without some justifiable criticism.

In 1869 a letter dated 7 September was printed in the Manchester Times and Examiner. It was written by James Taylor of 54 Oldham Road and contained three specific accusations against the cemetery management. Taylor firstly claimed that *'as many as sixty bodies has been thrown into one hole'*. His second claim was that three feet or more of standing water in the bottom of graves had been concealed by inserting a 'false bottom' of wooden boards and that after the service was finished and the mourners had left these had been removed and the coffins pitched into the water before the grave was filled. His final accusation was that following burial services and after the mourners had departed bodies had been removed from the grave in which the mourners believed they were to be buried and buried elsewhere in the cemetery. Taylor's accusations led to an investigation by Mr. Philip Holland, the Government's Inspector of Burial Grounds.[12]

It emerged that three months previously the Corporation had received a letter from a Mr. N. Hobson which gave the names of several workers at the cemetery who had witnessed the removal of bodies from public graves to pits containing up to sixty bodies. The Corporation claimed that it had taken steps to prevent such abuses, though evidence given to the enquiry showed that the practice of multiple burials had continued as before. Holland's enquiry concluded that the accusations were founded in fact but nobody appears to have been officially censured as a result, despite calls by Mr. Taylor, the original complainant, that the Superintendent Registrar should be dismissed.

The Corporation position appears to have been that the Superintendent Registrar was unaware of the abuses and that these arose from the ignorance of subordinates. On the question of multiple burials they took the view that he was simply continuing the practices of his predecessor and that his motives were to limit the rate at which the limited space was used up. Joseph Heron, the Town Clerk, was supportive in this and remarked:

> 'You know what space we have got and the extent to which the ground is being occupied. I can understand why there has been this excess of zeal on the part of our servants. It is very unfortunate that it has taken place. But they saw that the ground was being rapidly absorbed and to prevent it being used up they were led into the error they have committed. Whatever is right and necessary we must comply with'.

Remarkably, Holland confirmed that the practice of interring several coffins in one grave was not prohibited but made it clear that he would take immediate steps to advise the Secretary of State to outlaw the practice.

During Mr. Holland's hearing the matter of flooding was raised by the Reverend J. Gornall, one of the Catholic chaplains at the cemetery. Mr. Holland responded that that the suitability of the land for use as a cemetery was not the business of the present enquiry. Councillor Greenwood assured Mr. Holland that the corporation had purchased a piece of land further up the river and undertaken works to reinforce the river bank. They had also deepened the river so that '...it was

174

impossible that any flood should rise as high as the one in 1867'. Three years later, Greenwood's confidence was shown to be disastrously misplaced.

THE GREAT FLOOD

On 13 July 1872 the river rose considerably. It had rained heavily the previous week and a month's rainfall was recorded on the 12th and 13th alone. The river rose rapidly and at noon on the 13th it broke through the boundary wall and swept across two acres of the Catholic section of the cemetery. The waters swept away headstones and washed away the loose sandy soil on the sloping portion of the river bank. Coffins were washed out of the ground and down the river, where many broke apart on a nearby weir. The bodies were then carried downstream. Some were deposited in the gardens and cellars of nearby dwellings but others were carried further, with a report that nineteen bodies had been counted floating past Knott Mill on the other side of Manchester. After the flood had subsided, some fifty to sixty bodies were recovered from various locations.[13] The total number of bodies disinterred was officially said to be 76 but there were claims that the number was considerably greater. The true total will almost certainly never be known.

There was an enquiry into the circumstances of the flood on 24 July. At the insistence of the Roman Catholic representatives, this was held in the Catholic chapel at the cemetery. Mr. Holland, the Government Inspector, was once more in attendance and Reverend Gornall wasted no time in pointing out that the works to prevent flooding, which had been reported by Councillor Greenwood at the hearing in 1869, had proved wholly inadequate. Holland was evasive and rejected having any responsibility for the inadequacy of the action taken to reduce the flood risk. The Cemetery Superintendent and Town Clerk did their best to paint Gornall, who had resigned as chaplain two years earlier, as a disgruntled trouble-maker.

The severity of the flood was put down to an estimated 30,000 pieces of calico which had been washed down the river from Messrs. Wood and Wright's printworks and had blocked the weir. This had caused the river to rise even higher and ultimately to find an alternative outlet through the cemetery. These circumstances were seen as exceptional and the rise in the water level was considerably greater than anything which might have been reasonably expected.

Despite the Corporation's denial of responsibility and protestations of the adequacy of the existing flood defences, they shortly afterwards commissioned substantial works to remove the flood risk for good. This involved constructing 1,400 yards of stone retaining wall at a total cost of £6,400. These works were finally completed in 1876 and proved effective, though the scouring effects of the river constantly undermined the wall, which required frequent underpinning and repair. Finally, in 1913, a more extensive programme of works was completed to provide a more effective solution. This included a major re-shaping of the river bed to reduce the erosion of the wall's foundations. There was, happily, no recurrence of the dreadful events of 1872.

The 1872 flood left a deep impression on Manchester's people and was remembered for decades after. The disaster was even commemorated in a song, the greater part of which deals with the dreadful events at the cemetery. In respect of the inundation of the cemetery the song relates:

Still on the mighty water came
Where lay the silent dead,
And soon, alas! The coffins were
Uplifted from their bed

And ghastly forms were now beheld
Hurrying quickly by;
Brave men stood awe-struck at the sight
And women raised a cry.

Soon every effort was put forth
To stop them in their course;
Men drew the bodies to the bank,
And then the scene was worse.

Ghastly forms of old and young
Lay open to our view;
God grant that such appalling sights
May ne'er be seen by you!

Of all the bodies washed away
Some sixty have been found;
And now each one has been re-laid
Beneath the sacred ground.

Long as we live we'll ne'er forget
That awful Saturday,
When from the ground near Philips Park
Were bodies washed away.[14]

MILITARY FUNERALS

Philips Park was the location of several noteworthy military funerals. Richard Brown was one of a select few. The inscription on his gravestone read *'In memory of Sgt. Richard Brown (late 11th*

Hussars) died August 20, 1890 aged 68 years. One of the 600 who made the memorable charge at the Battle of Balaclava'.[15] A new memorial (shown in the illustration) has more recently been added over the original inscription. Although, like many other former soldiers, Brown had died in Withington Workhouse, he had only been admitted three days before his death owing to his medical condition and not for reasons of poverty.[16]

In 1902 Patrick Croffigan, aged 64, was buried with military honours. Croffigan had enlisted with the 68th Regiment (Durham Light Infantry) in 1854 and seen service in the Crimea, participating in the battles of Alma, Balaclava, Inkerman and Sebastopol. He had later seen action in the New Zealand (Maori) wars. The last seven months of his life had been spent in a home run by the Little Sisters of the Poor and was spared the ignominy of a pauper funeral through the generosity of a Mr. Wood of Great Ancoats Street who paid for the funeral.[17]

Another Crimea veteran was John Berry. Berry was buried in 1907. Although he died in extreme poverty, he was spared a pauper grave by the Crimea and Indian Mutiny Veterans' Association who paid for his funeral.[18]

The most famous and honoured former soldier to be buried at Philips Park was undoubtedly Private William Jones VC. Jones was a veteran of the Zulu Wars and had received the Victoria Cross for his part in the defence of Rorke's Drift in 1879. Defending the post hospital to the last, he and Robert Jones managed to remove six men to safety, the seventh man being killed. After leaving the army the following year, he had had a variety of occupations — at one time joining Buffalo Bill's Wild West Show — before finally settling in Rutland Street, Chorlton-on-Medlock. Falling on hard times, he pawned his VC in 1910, though this has since found its way to the South Wales Borderers Museum. He was eventually admitted to the Bridge Street Workhouse where he died on 15 April 1913. He was buried at Philips Park on 21 April.

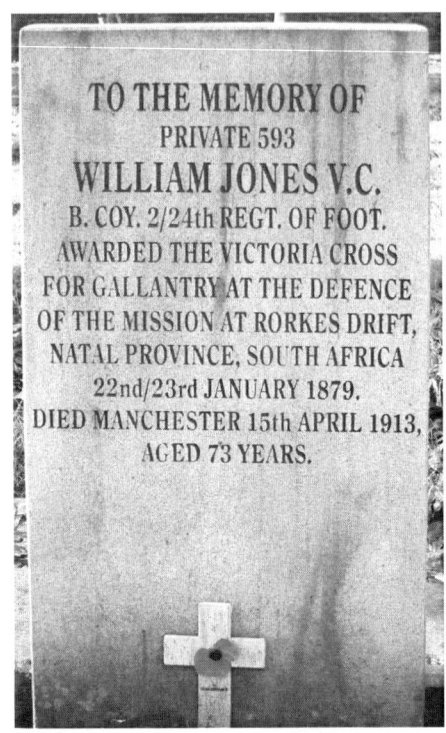

Although Jones was buried in a common grave, which he would ultimately share with nine other unfortunates, there was nothing simple about his funeral. His body was borne to the grave by six members of the South Wales Borderers and three volleys were fired over the grave by twelve men of the Army Service Corps. A bugler sounded the last post while several hundred people watched the proceedings from a respectable distance.[19]

Jones and the other nine occupants of the grave were remembered on a simple headstone which recorded their names and dates of birth and death. A plaque has more recently been installed (originally on the Anglican chapel but now moved to a position by the entrance) to commemorate this remarkable man.

Jones was not the only holder of the Victoria Cross to be laid to rest at Philips Park. George Stringer of Newton Heath served with the 1st Battalion, Manchester Regiment in Mesopotamia. He received the award on 8 March 1916 for single-handedly holding back the enemy while his Battalion withdrew. Remarkably he survived, and two days later saved the lives of two officers for which he was mentioned in dispatches. He was invalided out in 1917 and subsequently worked as a doorman for the Manchester Assistance Board. He died in 1957 at the age of 68. He is also commemorated by a memorial plaque.

THE CHEETHAM TRAGEDY

One of the saddest funerals took place in n 1905. David Taylor, his wife Mary and two sons, aged fourteen and ten, had lived in Manchester for about eighteen months, having moved there from their native Aberdeen. David, who worked as a clerk for the Edison-Bell Phonographic Company was in some financial difficulty. The reason for this is unclear, as he was not badly paid, but may be connected with suggestions that his wife drank to excess. Some irregularity had been found in the company's accounts and David feared that he would be dismissed from his post as a result. On the morning of 18 April their live-in servant, Mary Warburton, found David and Mary and their two sons dead in their beds. Each had been shot in the head, David apparently by his own hand. What is more, 'Her Majesty', the family's pet Irish terrier had also been shot dead and their pet cat 'Kitty' killed with chloroform. David had left ten letters, written during the night before the killings and a short pencilled note written before he turned his revolver on himself. His final words were 'Poor Mary never moved. None of them knew anything, I think, and the servant seems to have heard nothing, I was afraid she might wake'.[20]

An inquest the following day concluded that David had murdered his wife and sons and had himself committed suicide.[21] The family were buried at Philips Park on 22 April. Although it had been indicated that the funeral would be at 10am, the bodies were brought to the cemetery at 6am and buried within the hour "in order to avoid any unseemly scene at the interment". By 10am, when about a hundred people turned up, the grave had been filled and covered with wreaths

from the staff of Edison-Bell, neighbours and friends. There was also a wreath from the boys of the Cheetham Higher Grade School, which presumably one or both of his sons had attended.[22]

PHILIPS PARK IN THE TWENTIETH CENTURY

There was a proposal in 1904 to purchase a fourteen acre plot of land between the northern side of the cemetery, adjacent to the Roman Catholic section, and the Lancashire and Yorkshire Railway line. The land was owned by the Dean and canons of the Cathedral and the asking price was £7,500.[23] This piece of land would allow the cemetery to be extended to the north by about a third of its existing area. Although the Parks and Cemeteries Committee were warm to the proposal, negotiations were not concluded until the end of 1906. The land was never, however, used to extend the cemetery.

Four years later there was a spike in unemployment and the Corporation considered a programme of public works to create work for the unemployed. The construction of a new cemetery was suggested as a possibility and this was justified by a statement that Philips Park would only meet the need of Manchester 'for six or seven years more'.[24] This is an incredible statement since at this time, while there had been something over 91,000 burials at Philips Park over 42 years, this was not even one third of the total which would ultimately be accommodated. Common sense seems to have prevailed and the proposal went no further.

In an echo of the 19th century cholera epidemics, deaths in Manchester surged between June 1918 and May 1919 as Spanish influenza swept through the city, eventually claiming over 7000 lives.[25] In the last week of November 1918, around the peak of the epidemic, there were 374 reported deaths and this put the cemeteries under some pressure.[26] To cope with this spike in demand, temporary staff were taken on at Philips Park with the number of staff employed rising to over one hundred.

DECLINE AND CLOSURE

Philips Park, managed by the Corporation, did not suffer the neglect which characterised Manchester's private cemeteries. The memorials remain in place and vandalism does not seem to have been a substantial problem. It is the buildings which have suffered most from the ravages of time.

The Catholic and Dissenters' chapels were demolished in 1971. The location of the former is now a garden and there is a memorial plaque to record that the chapel once stood on the spot. The Anglican chapel remains intact but it is now unused and boarded up, the roof slates mostly gone and the elements gradually taking their toll. It seems only to be a matter of time before it is lost completely.

There has also been a small boundary change. In 1992 the former Mill Street was widened and became today's Alan Turing Way. This work required a narrow strip of land to be taken from the western edge of the cemetery and human remains to be removed from 30 plots (D8-D16 and D30-D42). They were re-buried in another part of the consecrated section.

Philips Park Cemetery ceased the provision of new graves in 1987, though additional burials in family graves are still permitted and occasionally take place. Since the cemetery opened the registers record a total in excess of 315,000 burials.

Aside from the uncertainty surrounding the Anglican chapel, the cemetery would seem to have a bright future. The Friends of Philips Park Cemetery are working to create a safe and welcoming cemetery where visitors can enjoy pleasant surroundings and peaceful gardens.

Philips Park Lodge

Southern Cemetery

While Manchester had been expanding rapidly to the south of the city, the majority of burial provision was to the north and east This was recognised by the City Council when in June of 1871 it instructed the Parks and Cemeteries Committee to submit a proposal to meet the need for burial space on the south side of the city. The committee found it difficult to locate a piece of land which would be suitable for the purpose and which the owner was prepared to sell for such a use. Nevertheless, in May 1872 they identified 80 acres of suitable land which they purchased from a Colonel Fielding for a price of £31,500. A second, smaller, adjoining plot was purchased shortly afterwards, bringing the total to 97 acres.

The cost of the land met with some criticism. Speaking ahead of the 1875 municipal elections, Edward Henry Downs, the Conservative candidate for Exchange ward, claimed that the 80 acre plot had been on the market for £20,000 shortly before the purchase and that the Corporation had acted prejudicially to the interests of the ratepayers in paying a higher price[27]. Downs, however, failed to be elected and no more was heard of his claim.

At the time, the location was seen as a long way from the population which it was intended to serve but it was recognised that this would not be a permanent situation and that the city would in time expand up to and beyond the new cemetery.

In 1873 the corporation invited submissions to design a cemetery to cover 47 acres of the plot, the remainder to be reserved for future expansion. The competition, and an award of £100, was won by Henry John Paull who had previously designed Philips Park Cemetery. Unlike Philips Park, the site was neither irregular in shape nor sloping down to a winding river but broadly

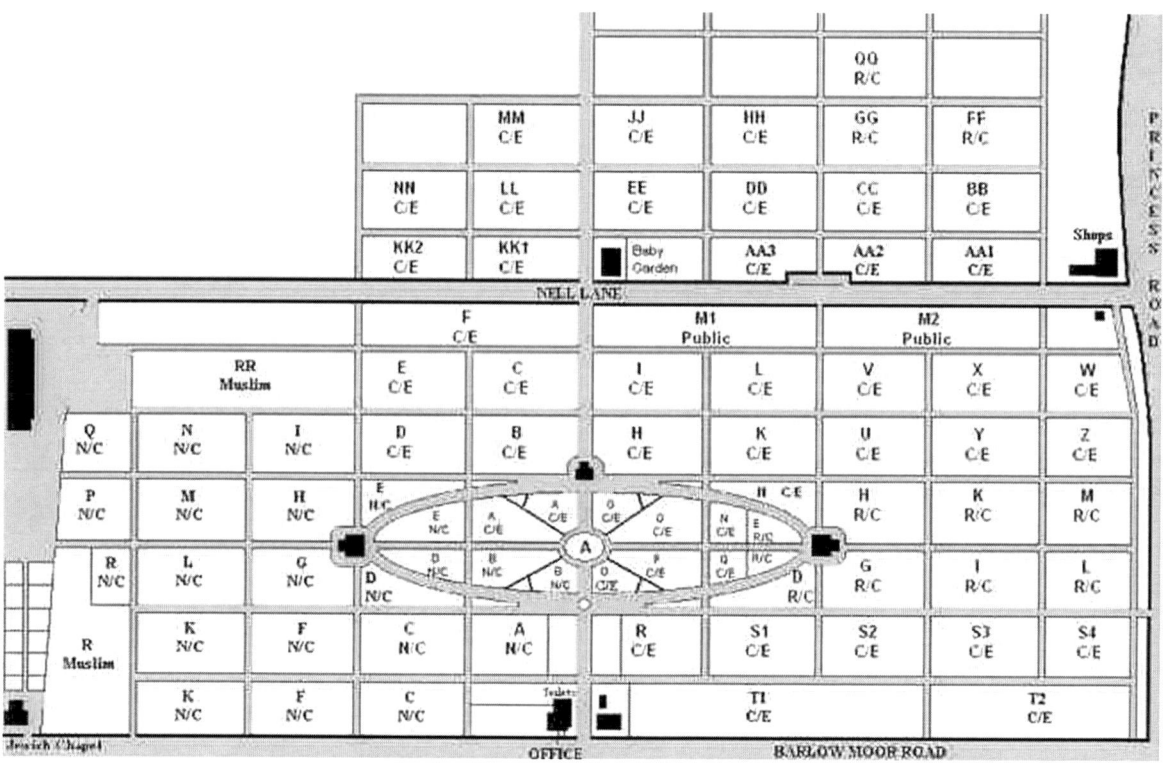

rectangular, bounded by straight roads and pretty much level from end to end. The 'informal' layout which Paull had adopted for Philips Park was not really appropriate to such a site and he laid out the burial plots in a 'grid' pattern.

As at Philips Park, the cemetery was to be divided into Anglican, Roman Catholic and Nonconformist sections, each with its own mortuary chapel. Paull placed each chapel alongside its respective burial section, on the periphery of a central elliptical carriageway, which provided an easy and direct route for funeral carriages to enter and depart the cemetery. Paull's design occupied the central part of the plot between Barlow Moor Road and Nell Lane, leaving wide strips at either side for future expansion.

Once contractors started work, it became clear that drainage was to be a major problem; ground water being found as little as three feet below the surface. The drainage works, which cost in excess of £20,000, included the construction of a two mile long outfall sewer which discharged into the River Mersey. It was therefore not until May 1877 that Messrs. Neill and Son were contracted to erect the chapels and lodge buildings, which included houses for the sexton and registrar. Not the least of the works was the three-quarter mile long boundary wall with its cast iron palisading which cost £4,300. The cost of the cemetery, including the land, was £98,000. This included the substantial sum of £14,000 spent on planting trees and shrubs.

THE OPENING

The Church of England section, which covered some twenty acres, was consecrated by the Bishop of Manchester on 26 September 1879. The weather was particularly bad and the formalities had to be conducted inside the Anglican chapel.[28] The consecration of the Roman Catholic section three days later by Canon Wrenall enjoyed better weather and he and Father Hill were able to walk the boundary while reciting the Latin service.[29]

The cemetery was opened on 9 October 1879 by the Mayor of Manchester, Alderman Charles Grundy. In his address to the assembled dignitaries he made it clear that this was not a commercial undertaking. He summarised the position clearly:

> 'In a commercial sense the cemetery will not be likely to repay the cost, but will involve a charge upon the city fund, but the enterprise is one of social necessity and precludes the consideration of pecuniary gain or loss'.

The opening ceremony was followed by a luncheon at the Town Hall attended by members of the council, the architect, Mr. Paull, the Bishop of Manchester, James Fraser, and several of the city's dissenting ministers. Proceedings concluded with the Mayor proposing a toast "to the Parks and Cemeteries Committee".[30]

Southern Cemetery: Main Entrance Gates

*The Nonconformist Chapel
(Now disused)*

The first funeral took place five days later. The deceased was Eliza Ann Hughes of Grove House, Greenheys, who had died at the early age of 32 from heart disease. Eliza was the widow of packing case maker James Hughes who, also aged 32, had died the previous year from an unspecified liver complaint. Her father was Joseph Taylor, a brewer and at the time the owner of the Eagle Brewery in Greenheys. Joseph would be interred in the same vault, alongside his daughter, in 1901.

BURIAL FEES

Southern Cemetery catered for all requirements from the simplest burial in a public common grave up to private family vaults and mausolea.

Burials in public graves were priced at thirteen shillings for persons over ten years old and eight shillings for those below this age. A stillborn child would be buried for two shillings and sixpence.

Private graves could be purchased at prices of two, three, four, five and six Guineas. The price was determined not by the nature of the grave itself but by its location in the cemetery. These prices included the first burial and all related fees. Subsequent burials were charged at either fifteen shillings, one Guinea or thirty shillings, again according to location but exclusive of the minister's fees for the burial service. Further charges were made for the right to erect headstones or memorials and for other services such as maintaining grass or floral planting over the grave. For those wishing to purchase vaults or erect mausolea prices were available 'on request'.

One aspect of the burial fees which was to cause considerable friction was the imposition of a surcharge on the funerals of those who did not live in the Borough of Manchester. This surcharge amounted to about 80% on the purchase price of a family grave and about 50% on interment in a public grave. Whilst it is understandable that the ratepayers of Manchester were funding the purchase of the cemetery through their rates and so might reasonably expect a discount, the level of the surcharge on non-ratepayers seems greatly excessive.

THE OAK HOUSE HOTEL

The Corporation were involved in a somewhat badly handled action in 1886. Across Barlow Moor Road from the south east corner of Southern Cemetery stood a large house, originally a private residence, called York House. In 1881 the property had been renamed Oak House in anticipation of it becoming a hotel but successive attempts to secure a licence to sell intoxicating liquors had been rejected owing to objections by the cemetery's registrar and chaplain. On 24 August 1886 Walter Stott was finally granted a provisional licence, the Parks and Cemeteries Committee having agreed the day before not to oppose the application. The idea of licensed premises close to the cemetery was clearly felt inappropriate by several members of the Corporation, who after discussing the matter at a meeting on 1 September, directed that a letter be sent to the magistrates demanding that a full licence should be refused. When the matter came before the licensing magistrates in October, the Corporation appears to have sent a Mr. T. Hudson to the hearing. The hapless Hudson seems to have been somewhat unsure of the reason for his attendance. When the magistrates asked whether there was any objection to the application, Hudson attempted to draw the magistrates' attention to the Corporation's letter. Three times the Chairman asked Hudson whether he was there to oppose the application. At first Hudson replied that '*I do not know whether I appear to oppose, but I desire to draw your worship's attention to a memorial from the Manchester Corporation*'. Asked a second time, he tried a different tack '*The Corporation are opposed to the confirmation of the licence*'. After a third time of asking, Hudson remained silent. The Chairman of the Licensing Committee was contemptuous and remarked that '*he knew nothing about this or any other licence except what he heard in that court. He had had papers sent to him which he did not read but which he put into the waste paper basket.*' The licence was duly granted.[31]

THE JEWISH SECTION

At the time of its opening, Southern Cemetery had no provision, other than the unconsecrated (dissenter) section, for the burial of Jews. Manchester's Jewish community dated from the eighteenth century and they had established several synagogues. Each congregation was substantially independent and attracted a particular segment of Judaism. Some were of an orthodox character, others reflected reformed practice. Some had Sephardi (Spanish and Portuguese) congregations, others Ashkenazi (mostly from Germany and Eastern Europe) and there was no person or body which represented the community as a whole. A number of Jewish

cemeteries had been established by different congregations on the outskirts of Manchester, the earliest in Pendleton in 1794.[32]

One of the congregations, it is unclear which, made an initial approach to the Parks and Cemeteries Committee in January 1890 for space to be allocated in Southern Cemetery for burial of their members. The approach was rebuffed when the committee ruled that they could only sanction a dedicated area if it was open to all Jews and not simply to those of a particular congregation. Their concern was that if other churches sought exclusive sections, this would lead to an unacceptable level of sub-division.[33] A fresh approach was made the following September by a deputation representing the community as a whole and agreement was quickly reached. A 1,247 square yard plot was set aside to accommodate a small chapel and 267 graves. The total cost of the building and setting out the area was estimated to be £600.[34]

THE BEST OF NEIGHBOURS?

When Southern Cemetery was opened, it was in the township of Withington and outside the Manchester boundary. It remained so until Withington was incorporated into the borough of Manchester in 1904. It might have been expected that putting a 97 acre cemetery in the middle of their district would not have been very well received by the Withington Local Board of Health (which in 1894 became Withington Urban District Council) but it was particularly galling for them that Withington residents were charged considerably higher fees for burials than those paid by Manchester ratepayers. This anomaly was accepted until 1890 when the Withington Local Board successfully approached Manchester Corporation to negotiate a reduction in the premium on burial fees from 75% to 50%. In August 1892 the churchwardens of St. Paul's Church, Withington petitioned the Local Board. They complained that although they welcomed the reduction, the fees were still well in excess of what could be afforded by their working class parishioners. They also pointed out that the burial ground at St. Paul's was now almost full and, in the absence of alternative provision, parishioners would be forced to use Southern Cemetery at these inflated rates. Their petition asked the Local Board to obtain a plot of land for use as a cemetery for the township[35]. At a special meeting on 12 October the council agreed to pursue the matter and added that Lord Egerton of Tatton was offering a suitable plot of land to the north side of Barlow Moor Road, adjacent to the new Crematorium.[36]

Having purchased eleven acres of land, nine for the cemetery and a further two for a proposed refuse incinerator at a cost of £4,413, the proposal stalled. In 1895 it was reported that the land was sown with oats[37] and it remained under cultivation until 1900 when Manchester Corporation offered to buy the land from the recently formed Withington Urban District Council, offering a price of £500 per acre. Their offer also included a guarantee that Withington ratepayers would be given access to the same burial fees at Southern Cemetery as enjoyed by Manchester ratepayers.[38] The Council rejected this approach by a substantial majority.[39] It is clear that the matter was no longer an economic issue but was driven more by resentment of Withington's increasing dependence on Manchester for burial and other services.

Following the rejection of Manchester's offer, it looked like the Council intended to press ahead with the cemetery. Another year passed and in August 1901, following a public competition, a design was agreed by the Council at its meeting in January 1902. It was estimated that a further £8,000 to £9,000 would be required to erect buildings and carry out ground works.[40]

The spring of 1902 saw a flurry of letters published in the Manchester Evening News. These all complained about the high level of Withington's rates and many specifically identified the proposed cemetery as a waste of money[41]. While the Council did not drop the proposal, nothing was done to advance it.

By 1903 the prospect of the amalgamation of Withington into Manchester was being actively debated. The Secretary of the Withington Amalgamation League wrote to the Manchester Courier in May to point out, amongst other issues, that the premium on burial charges at Southern Cemetery, by now further reduced to one third, resulted in total annual costs of £140 to the local residents. To save this sum, he claimed, the Council would incur an annual cost of £1,200 to fund its own cemetery.[42]

The following year the amalgamation was completed and no more was heard of the proposed new cemetery. Through the amalgamation Withington residents automatically became eligible for the same burial fees as other Manchester ratepayers. Part of the land was later sold to the Manchester Crematorium Company to extend its columbarium and memorial garden. The remainder was developed for housing.

BURIAL FEES (AGAIN!)

Although the amalgamation of Withington into Manchester removed the differential in fees which had caused such annoyance to Withington residents, the issue did not disappear. Those living outside the expanded Manchester boundary still on occasion appealed to Manchester Corporation for rebates.

Some, like Elizabeth Newton, argued that they had originally bought a grave when living outside Manchester but now lived in the city and so should be rebated the difference in fees. Elizabeth was successful and received a rebate of £3-10-6. Others, whose circumstances had changed similarly, were also successful in their appeals.

Perhaps the most hopeful claim came from Herbert Wilson. His estranged wife had died in 1938 while she was residing at Sale, Brooklands. Herbert had paid for her burial at Southern Cemetery but had been charged a premium of four Guineas. Herbert, who lived in Manchester, claimed that the premium should be refunded. His argument was that while he and his wife were admittedly living separately, there had been a reconciliation before her death and that '...*my wife was my legal property as their (sic) was no divorce*'. On this basis, he claimed, she should be regarded as having been resident in Manchester and entitled to burial at the reduced fee. His creative appeal was rejected.[43]

EXPANSION

Although the cemetery still had a lot of unused space, it was clear that this would not last for ever and in 1926 the Corporation purchased a further 90 acres across Nell Lane to the north of the cemetery at a cost of £39,035. The proposal to spend this sum met with some opposition. Councillor Johnson argued that it was over-priced, since the rateable value was small, and suggested that £5,500 was a more appropriate price. Councillor Simon argued that it was a waste of money to purchase further land for a cemetery when it would be more cost-effective for the Corporation to build a crematorium and encourage cremation. Neither of these arguments found significant support and the proposed purchase was agreed.[44]

It was not, however, until 1943 that this area was brought into use. Not all of the land was used by the cemetery. About 42 acres to the northwest of the plot was set aside for housing development. The remaining area was used to expand the Church of England consecrated section.

EMBEZZLEMENT

Henry Hurst had been appointed Cemetery Registrar and Superintendent in 1916. He had started working for the Corporation as a boy and this was a good appointment to secure. His salary of £200 per annum was not excessively generous, but the post included a free house, gas and coal, so he and his growing family should have enjoyed a comfortable lifestyle. By 1929 his family had grown to nine children and his salary

to £360 but this seems to have been insufficient for his needs, or possibly his desires.

On 22 March 1929 the 55 year old Hurst appeared in the police court charged with embezzling £150-2s from his employer. He was remanded on bail. On 11 April he appeared again but by this time it seems that the financial records of the cemetery had been more closely examined by the City Treasurer and the charge was now that he had, between September 1923 and August 1928, embezzled no less than £8,011. He was committed for trial at the Assizes. Hurst's *modus operandi* was to deposit cheques received for fees into his personal account and to replace these with lesser sums in cash, falsifying the records accordingly.

There is no record of Hurst's reasons for embezzling such large sums, no suggestion of an extravagant lifestyle, gambling addiction or other reason why he would need to steal around five times his annual salary each year. Neither is there a record of whether any of the money was recovered.

In his defence, Hurst cited ill-health. He had, he claimed, been a sick man for eighteen years. He had had a breakdown and suffered from neuritis and cardiac debility. Doctors doubted whether he would live much longer. If this was true, perhaps the thefts were an ill-judged attempt to provide for his family when he was gone.

Hurst was sentenced to penal servitude for three years. This was perhaps the lesser of his punishments. Not only did he lose a comfortable job, but also the promise of retirement (should he live to enjoy it) in ten years time on two-thirds salary. If one feels any sympathy though, it must be for his wife and children who would have been left destitute.

WORLD WAR II

Shortly after war was declared Manchester Corporation turned its attention to making Corporation owned land available for cultivation. The unused land at Southern Cemetery, presumably the plot to the far side of Nell Lane, was identified as one of several possible sites. Whether it was actually used is unclear.

The Christmas blitz of 22/23 December 1940 resulted in many casualties and many of the victims were buried at Southern Cemetery. The largest single funeral was on 28 December 1940 when seventy-two victims were buried, eight of them unidentified.[45] A special plot (plot Q) was set aside for raid victims for whom alternative burial arrangements had not been made. In total 136 people were buried in this plot. For some years afterwards, the mayor would lay a wreath on the plot on the anniversary of the raids.

Seventeen firemen were killed during these raids of whom seven were amongst those buried in plot Q on 31 December.[46] One of these was Alexander Paul, a Jewish auxiliary fireman. Paul's body was re-buried in the Jewish section of the cemetery on 17 February 1948. The difficulties in obtaining stone for memorials during the war meant that many graves of those buried at this time were either unmarked or were marked by a wooden cross. Many of these survived long after the war until the Parks and Cemeteries Committee ordered their removal in 1958.[47]

NOTABLE BURIALS: TWO VICTORIA CROSSES

Southern Cemetery has seen many burials of former soldiers but two of those buried are distinguished through receiving the highest award for gallantry, the Victoria Cross.

The burial of 63 year old Colour Sergeant John Prettyjohns in 1887 seems not to have been marked by military honours. Prettyjohns has the distinction of being the first member of the Royal Marines to be awarded the Victoria Cross. He received the award for his part in the battle of Inkerman in the Crimea campaign in 1854. His Royal Marines Light Infantry unit had been given the task of clearing caves of snipers but was trapped in one of the caves by a large number of advancing Russian troops. Running low on ammunition, Prettyjohns had his men pile up stones and when the first Russian reached the

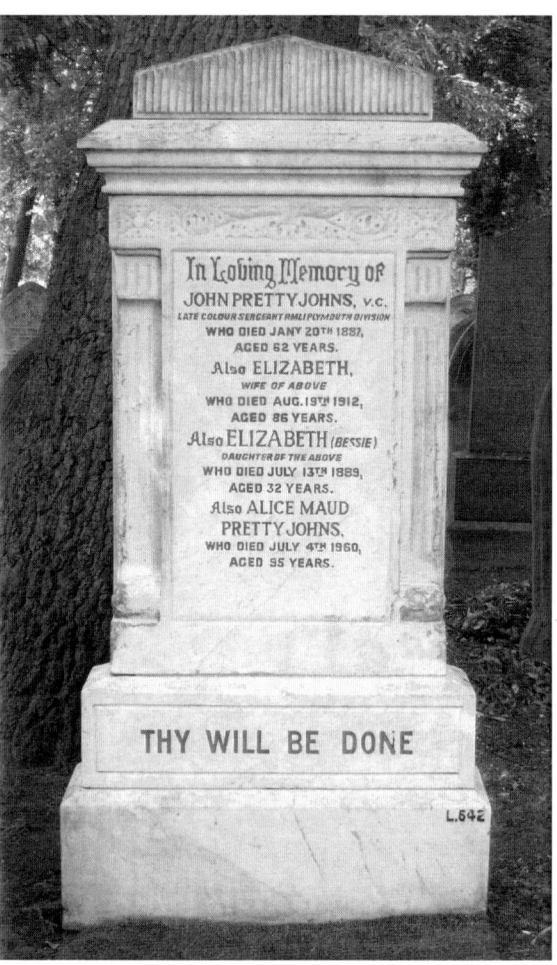

The John Prettyjohns Memorial

cave entrance he seized him and threw him bodily back down the steep incline. He and the other marines then hurled a volley of stones at the rest of the attackers, causing them to retreat in some disorder.

Although Prettyjohns' death was reported in the Manchester newspapers[48], there are no accounts of his funeral, which suggests that it was probably a modest affair.

Major Henry Kelly was born just six months after the death of John Prettyjohns. Kelly was awarded the Victoria Cross in 1916 while a Second Lieutenant in the Duke of Wellington's Regiment. His award was for:

'...most conspicuous bravery in an attack. He twice rallied his company under the heaviest fire, and finally led the only three available men into the enemy trench, and there remained bombing until two of them had become casualties and enemy reinforcements had arrived. He then carried his Company Sergeant Major, who had been wounded, back to our trenches, a distance of 70 yards, and subsequently three other soldiers. He set a fine example of gallantry and endurance.'

Kelly went on to win the Military Cross in 1918 to which shortly afterwards he added a bar. He was promoted temporary Major before being discharged in 1920. He subsequently served with the International Brigade in Spain in 1936. At the outbreak of World War II he reenlisted in the Cheshire Regiment, in which he served on the home front until court martialled in 1944 for making a false claim for £2 10s in travelling expenses. Following this he resigned his commission in a very sad ending to an otherwise exemplary military career. He lived out his final years in Wythenshawe but died in Prestwich Hospital. He was buried in the Roman Catholic section of Southern Cemetery on 22 January 1960.

MORE NOTABLE BURIALS: JOHN RYLANDS

The cotton manufacturer and millionaire philanthropist John Rylands was buried in 1888. His was one of the largest funerals to have taken place at Southern, or indeed any other Manchester Cemetery. The funeral cortège included some 200 carriages and it was estimated that about half of his 11,600 employees attended. There were, in addition, large numbers of Mancunians who had come to pay their last respects to this much admired man.[49] Rylands' last resting place was in a vault lined with white tiles. Before his death he had purchased no fewer than eighteen contiguous vault plots to accommodate his vault and its associated memorial.

His wife Enriqueta died in 1908. Her body was cremated at the adjacent Manchester Crematorium and an urn containing her ashes was interred in the same vault. Rylands had been married three times. His first two wives and three of his children had been interred in a family vault at the Rusholme Road Cemetery but by this time it was clear that Rusholme Road was becoming derelict and run down and this doubtless influenced his decision to establish a new vault at Southern Cemetery.

The Rylands memorial is one of the most impressive in the cemetery but what you see today is only a small part of the grand memorial designed by architect C. R. Heathcote and completed in 1890. The surviving red granite memorial and its plinth were surmounted by a twenty-eight foot high white Sicilian marble structure not dissimilar to the Albert Memorial. This

The John Rylands Memorial

consisted of six pillars supporting an ornate domed canopy. There were six marble angels on the lower level of the canopy and six more on a level above them. An ornate bronze railing surrounded the whole memorial.[50] Unfortunately, the marble structure was attacked by vandals and was removed in 1927. Then in 1967 the bronze railings were stolen, leaving the memorial as we see it today.[51]

A Famous Aviator...

The name of Sir John William Alcock is more immediately familiar when set alongside that of his co-aviator Sir Arthur Whitten Brown. Alcock and Brown achieved fame with the first non-stop flight across the Atlantic, departing from from Newfoundland on 14 June 1919 and landing in Ireland the following day.

John Alcock was born at Seymour Grove, Old Trafford in 1892 and it was therefore fitting that a month later on 19 July he and Brown were both knighted by King George V. Four days after their triumph they were honoured with a civic reception at Manchester Town Hall. Alcock did not enjoy his fame for long. On 18 December of the same year, he was killed when his aircraft crashed in France. His body was returned to England and he was buried at Southern Cemetery on 27 December 1919.

...and a Famous Artist

The artist L. S. (Laurence Stephen) Lowry was born in Stretford but lived much of his life in Pendlebury. In his later years he lived in Mottram-in-Longendale where he died in 1976. He was buried at Southern Cemetery next to his parents Robert and Elizabeth. Lowry is most commonly associated with Salford, where a substantial body of his work is displayed in the gallery of The Lowry Arts Centre. Standing in front of Lowry's headstone is a jar containing several used artist's brushes.

The Star of Have a Go

The character actor and broadcaster Wilfred Pickles was best known for his radio series '*Have a Go*', which ran from 1946 until 1967 and was built around interviews with ordinary people and light-hearted quizzes for small prizes ('*What's on the table, Mabel?*'). He was buried, following his death in 1978, at Southern Cemetery. He was joined eleven years later by his widow, the popular 'Mabel' who worked with him on the show. There is perhaps some irony that Pickles, who might have been described as a '*professional Yorkshireman*' was buried on the '*wrong*' side of the Pennines.

Sir Ernest Marples

Readers of a certain age will remember former Transport Minister Sir (Alfred) Ernest Marples and the slogan '*Marples must go!*' which reflected the unpopularity he aroused, not least through his implementing the Beeching proposals to reduce the size of the railway network. Marples was a local man, born in Levenshulme in 1907. He had lived his last three years in Monaco where he had moved in 1975 to escape a UK tax claim and where he died in 1978. He was cremated at Manchester Crematorium and his ashes were interred at Southern Cemetery.

The John Alcock Memorial

Sir Matt Busby's Grave

SIR MATT

The most famous manager of a Manchester football club was almost certainly Sir Matt Busby. Busby's remarkably long tenure at Old Trafford from 1945 to 1969 has only recently been overtaken by the most recent former manager, and fellow Scot, Sir Alex Ferguson. Possibly his greatest achievement was his successful rebuilding of the team after the Munich air disaster in 1958. Busby was buried at Southern Cemetery on 27 January 1994. His memorial at Southern Cemetery is modest in comparison to his statue which stands outside the Old Trafford ground on the former Warwick Road North, which had been renamed Sir Matt Busby Way in 1993, less than a year before his death.

...AND A FEW MORE

Also among those buried at Southern Cemetery can be found Daniel Adamson (1820-1890) the driving force behind the Manchester Ship Canal; Jerome Caminada (1844-1919), Manchester's first CID Superintendent and known as Manchester's Sherlock Holmes and Lesley Ann Downey (1954-1964), one of the victims of 'Moors Murderers' Ian Brady and Myra Hindley. An unusual hero is Philip Baybutt (1844-1907) who was awarded the Congressional Medal of Honour for the capture of a Confederate flag in the American Civil War in 1864. Baybutt was a former Old Trafford resident who, while visiting his brother in the USA in 1864, joined the 2nd Massachusetts Cavalry to fight for the Union army. After the war he returned to Manchester where he worked as a shipping clerk.[52]

SOUTHERN CEMETERY TODAY

Southern Cemetery remains Manchester's principal cemetery to the present day. Only the Anglican chapel is still in use, though the Nonconformist and Catholic chapels remain in reasonable repair. An active 'friends' group works to help keep it in good order and to improve amenities for visitors. There have been over 350,000 burials to date but there is still substantial space left for future burials. This fortunate situation might not have been the case had there not been a major change in ideas about how to dispose of the dead.

Around the same time as Southern Cemetery was planned, the Cremation Society of Great Britain was formed and serious thought was being given to the idea that cremation of the dead should be adopted in preference to burial. These new ideas did not have an immediate impact. By 1900 barely a thousand cremations had taken place in England. However, by the end of the 20th century cremation was to account for around 70% of funerals in England. This change in public sentiment would dramatically reduce the pressure on cemeteries. It was a development in which Manchester was well to the fore.

Notes for Municipal Cemeteries

1 Manchester Guardian, 7 May 1863.
2 Manchester Guardian, 20 September 1866. This article provides one of the best contemporary descriptions of the cemetery.
3 William Gay had also designed Liverpool's Toxteth Park Cemetery (1856), though Undercliffe is widely acknowledged to be his finest work.
4 Manchester Times 27 February 1864.
5 Manchester Courier & Lancashire General Advertiser, Tuesday 23 August 1866.
6 Manchester Courier & Lancashire General Advertiser, Saturday 27 April 1867.
7 Manchester Courier & Lancashire General Advertiser, Saturday 10 August 1867.
8 Manchester Guardian, 20 September 1866.
9 Manchester Guardian, 18 February 1875.
10 Home Office Instructions for Burial Boards in Providing Cemeteries and Making Arrangements for Interments, 1854.
11 Manchester Times, Saturday 13 July 1867.
12 Manchester Times, 23 October 1869.
13 Phillips Park Cemetery, Joan Gill, Manchester Genealogist Vol. 37 No. 4, 2001.
14 The complete lyrics for the song can be found on the Medlock Valley web site www.philipspark.org.uk/Sites/MedlockValley/Objects/PDFs/The_Great_Flood.pdf
15 Manchester Guardian, 28 December 1967. A short notice of Brown's funeral appeared in the Manchester Courier & Lancashire General Advertiser of Monday 25 August 1890.
16 Manchester Courier & Lancashire general Advertiser, Saturday 30 August 1890.
17 Manchester Evening News, Wednesday 16 July 1902.
18 Manchester Courier & Lancashire General Advertiser, Friday 12 July 1907.
19 Manchester Courier & Lancashire General Advertiser, Tuesday 22 April 1913.
20 Manchester Guardian, 19 April 1905.
21 Manchester Guardian, 20 April 1905.
22 The Observer, 23 April 1905.
23 Manchester Courier & Lancashire General Advertiser, Thursday 7 July 1904.
24 Manchester Courier & Lancashire General Advertiser, Thursday 3 September 1908.
25 Report on the Epidemic of Influenza in Manchester, 1918-19, James Niven, M.A., M.B., LL.D., Medical Officer of Health for Manchester.
26 Manchester Guardian, 9 December 1918.
27 Manchester Evening News, 23 October 1875.
28 Manchester Courier & Lancashire General Advertiser, Saturday 27 September 1879.
29 Manchester Evening News, Monday 29 September 1879.
30 Manchester Times, 11 October 1879.
31 Manchester Courier & Lancashire General Advertiser, Wednesday 6 October 1888.
32 Manchester Evening News, Tuesday, 27 January 1903. The date appears in one of a series of articles on the history of Manchester's Jewish Community.
33 Manchester Courier & Lancashire General Advertiser, Wednesday 5 February 1890.
34 Manchester Evening News, Wednesday 29 October 1890.
35 Manchester Courier & Lancashire General Advertiser, Friday 19 August 1892.
36 Manchester Evening News, Wednesday, 22 November 1893.
37 Manchester Courier & Lancashire General Advertiser, Friday 10 May 1895.
38 Manchester Courier & Lancashire General Advertiser, Friday 9 November 1900.
39 Manchester Courier & Lancashire General Advertiser, Friday 9 November 1900.
40 Manchester Courier & Lancashire General Advertiser, Friday 17 January 1902.
41 Manchester Evening News. Tuesday 29 April 1902. The letter from the pseudonymous 'Ripe for Amalgamation' is typical and highlights 'an expensive cemetery scheme which will further increase the rates'. He calls for the resignation of the Council and for Withington to be amalgamated into Manchester.
42 Manchester Courier & Lancashire General Advertiser, Monday 30 May 1903.
43 Manchester Corporation Parks and Cemeteries Committee minutes 1938 (volume 51). What the Parks and Cemeteries Committee thought of Herbert Wilson's chauvinist attitude is not recorded.
44 Manchester Guardian, 2 December 1926.
45 Manchester Guardian, 29 and 30 December 1940.
46 Manchester Guardian, 1 January 1941. The exhumation and re-burial of Alexander Paul

is recorded in the register for Southern Cemetery against his original burial.

47 Manchester Corporation, Parks and Cemeteries Committee minutes 1957 (volume 66)

48 Manchester Courier, Saturday 29 January 1887. An excellent biography of John Prettyjohns can be found on the internet at www.royalengineers.ca/prettyjohns.html

49 Manchester Courier & Lancashire General Advertiser, Monday 17 December 1888.

50 Manchester Times, Friday 1 August 1890.

51 John Rylands, D. A. Farnie, John Rylands University Library, 1993. The book includes a photograph of the memorial but incorrectly dates its completion to 16 May 1889, when it was actually completed the following year.

52 The American Civil War Society (UK) website http://acws.co.uk/archives/index.php?page=englishmen&dir=history has a short but useful biography of Philip Baybutt.

The Rise of Cremation

A Brief History of Cremation

Cremation of the dead was common practice in the bronze age but was replaced by burial during the Roman occupation and subsequent Christianisation of Britain. Cremation acquired a wholly negative image within the Christian church, perhaps because it was seen as a pagan practice. It increasingly became associated with practices such as the burning of witches and heretics and would not be seriously considered as a method of disposing of the dead until the nineteenth century.

There was a brief flowering of interest in the 1850s, when cremation was seen by a few far-sighted people as a practical answer to the problems of overflowing and insanitary graveyards but the idea failed to attract significant support. With the improvements to burial grounds following the Burial Acts, the problems were reduced and interest lapsed once again.

By the 1870s cremation was turning from theory into reality on the continent, particularly in Italy and Germany, and interest was stirring in England. The Cremation Society of Great Britain was created in 1874, substantially through the efforts of Sir Henry Thompson, the surgeon to Queen Victoria. Funds were raised and the Society constructed England's first crematorium at Woking. Its effectiveness was demonstrated by the cremation of a number of animal carcases. Cremating a human corpse was, however, a different matter.

The legality of cremation was open to serious question and a stand-off developed in which the Home Office made it clear that should the Society attempt to cremate a human body they would bring a prosecution to test the law. The Society was not disposed to follow this confrontational route, since an adverse decision would have been a major setback to their cause and the publicity surrounding even a favourable outcome might have proved negative overall.

The stalemate was finally broken in 1884, though not by any action on the part of either of the interested parties. William Price, an eccentric Welshman, a doctor, a former Chartist and a self-styled druid was 84 years old in 1883 when he fathered a son with his 24 year old housekeeper. The child, which he had named Jesu Grist (Jesus Christ) Price, died aged only five months the following January. Price was a believer in cremation and so attempted to burn the child's body.

This act, which he undertook quite publicly, outraged the local population, who intervened to stop the cremation and inform the authorities. Four weeks later Price was brought before Sir James Fitzjames Steven at Cardiff Assizes on a charge of attempting to burn the child's body rather than bury it and by doing so prevent an inquest from taking place.

To Steven the legal position was not in doubt. He made it clear in his directions to the Grand Jury that since there was no law which specifically prohibited cremation, no offence had been committed. He also pointed out that a Coroner did not have any right to conduct an inquest without due cause and that there was no such cause in this case.

The matter was, however, less than clear to the jury, which failed to agree upon a verdict and so was discharged. A second jury was arraigned and the case re-heard. The new jury accepted Steven's argument and found that Price had no charge to answer. He was therefore acquitted. Price successfully cremated his deceased child without further incident or legal challenge two months later.

The outcome of the Price case was to provide the legal clarity which the Cremation Society had been seeking. In light of the judgement it was unlikely that any case would be brought against them for performing cremations and the following year the first cremation was carried out at Woking.

Even if the Woking Crematorium was now a reality, the public was in no hurry to turn its back on burial and the number of cremations at Woking rose painfully slowly. There were only two more in 1885 and a further ten in 1886. It was not until 1892 that the annual total exceeded 100. Cremation was also something which attracted a substantially middle class clientele. This was undoubtedly in part because of the higher cost involved but possibly also because the middle classes were more open to such a radical idea.

The limited public enthusiasm for cremation probably explains why, unlike private cemeteries, there was no flood of 'get-rich-quick' joint stock proposals. It was cremation societies which would move cremation forward into the twentieth century and municipal authorities which would take up the baton after a proper legal framework for cremation was established in 1902.[1]

More crematoria were built and the number of cremations steadily increased up to the time of the Great War but numbers remained insignificant when compared to burials. The war was, however, to bring about a significant change. Many people's reservations towards cremation related to the idea of corporeal resurrection, that is that a complete body was required for resurrection on the Day of Judgement. In the war the bodies of many gallant men had been completely destroyed by shellfire or mines laid under their trenches. It was inconceivable that these men would be denied resurrection and so by implication neither would those whose bodies were cremated. Bishop James Fraser had summarised this argument eloquently in 1874 when he expressed the view that:

'the omnipotence of God is not limited and he would raise the dead whether he has to raise our bodies out of churchyards or whether he has to call our remains like the remains of some ancient Roman out of the urn in which they were deposited 2000 years ago'.

Although opinions did not change overnight, the number of cremations picked up between the wars so that by the end of the Second World War cremation accounted for about ten percent of all funerals in England. The next two decades were a period of strong growth and in 1968 the number of cremations finally and permanently overtook the number of burials.

Today the percentage of funerals involving cremation has levelled out at slightly over seventy percent and is possibly as high as it will rise. A significant reason is immigration. There has been a substantial increase in the Muslim population and to Muslims cremation is not acceptable. More recently, large scale immigration from Eastern Europe has increased the Roman Catholic population. Roman Catholics were prohibited from cremating their dead under threat of excommunication. This threat was only removed as recently as 1963. While now permissible, cremation has not yet been widely accepted by Catholics and possibly never will be.

Another factor which might limit the extent to which cremation is practiced is the growth of natural or 'woodland' burial. There are now 270 natural burial grounds in the UK, predominantly in England.[2] The numbers buried in this way are small, but increasing, so perhaps this will be a more significant practice in the future.

Cremation was a radical change and Manchester was to be in the vanguard. Within ten years of the first cremation at Woking, Manchester had formed its own Cremation Society and opened the second crematorium in the country.

Manchester Crematorium

The Manchester Cremation Society was formed in 1888 and two years later established the Manchester Cremation Company, which soon raised capital of £6,000 by issue of shares towards the construction of a crematorium. The list of subscribers was headed by the Dukes of Westminster and Sutherland and included that most vocal proponent of cremation in England, Sir Henry Thompson.[3] The list included representatives of many prominent Manchester families including the mercantile family of Behrens and the solicitor Richard Marsden Pankhurst, husband of the more famous Emmeline. [4]

The main instigator of the Manchester Cremation Society was Henry Simon. Simon had been born in Silesia (now part of Germany) but had come to England where he had built a successful engineering business. It is noticeable that the list of shareholders contains a substantial number of local businessmen who had been born in states which in 1870 became part of the unified Germany. This may reflect both Simon's influence among his fellow countrymen and perhaps their greater openness towards cremation; a crematorium had already been established at Gotha in Thuringia (now part of Germany) in 1878.

The company originally hoped that their crematorium could be constructed on unused land at Southern Cemetery and approached the Municipal Parks and Cemeteries Committee at the beginning of 1890.[5] The Committee rejected their approach. They rightly pointed out that municipal corporations did not have the authority to establish crematoria but they were also perhaps reluctant to get involved in what might become a controversial development.[6] This rejection did not delay the company's plans for long, since within two months they were reported to be in negotiation to purchase a three acre plot from Lord Egerton.[7] The company eventually purchased 6.75 acres of land on Barlow Moor

Manchester Crematorium

Road from the Egerton Estate for the very reasonable price of £750. This plot directly adjoined the western boundary of Southern Cemetery (which to this day leads many people to believe that the crematorium is a part of Southern Cemetery). At a further cost of £6,560-19s-8d the company built its crematorium. The building was designed in the Romanesque style by local architect Alfred E. Steinthal (1859-1928) of the Steinthal and Salomons partnership.

The new crematorium was successfully tested at the beginning of August 1892[8] and was officially opened on 2 October by the Duke of Westminster, one of its leading subscribers and a prominent campaigner for cremation who would himself be cremated at Woking in 1899. By the time of the official opening, however, two cremations had already been carried out.

THE FIRST CREMATION

The first person to be cremated in Manchester was Thomas Morgan Brown. Mr. Brown was not a Mancunian; at the time of his death he resided at Carlisle. Brown had requested in his will that his body should be cremated and on 22 August

1892 the hearse, carrying Mr. Brown's body in a plain spruce coffin, arrived at the crematorium accompanied by a single coach carrying one of his executors. There was, at Mr. Brown's wish, no religious service. The local press attended this first cremation and reported on proceedings the following day:

> 'Mr. Henry Simon, whose company had supplied the cremation apparatus, set the process in motion and the doors opened, the coffin ran on the level into the furnace. In about an hour all that remained of the body was a handful of calcined dust which was placed in an urn and handed to Mr. Brown's executor'.

Despite the lack of ceremony, the report in the Manchester City News was complimentary and continued:

> 'The supporters of the cremation movement are to be congratulated upon the handsome appearance of the building, the completeness of the arrangements for cremation and the simple and reverent manner in which they have arranged for the same to be carried out'.[9]

WHAT TO DO WITH THE ASHES?

With no historical model to which to refer, the proprietors of the first crematoria had to come up with a suitable way to deal with the cremated remains. Manchester followed the practice which had been established at Woking. The chapel building was flanked on both sides by arcades which served as columbaria[10]. The walls on either side were lined with small compartments into which urns containing the ashes could be placed and sealed behind a memorial tablet.

There was also, for those who preferred something more in line with tradition, a burial ground in which the urn could be buried and a conventional (though small) 'headstone' erected over the burial place as a memorial. Many families simply chose to bury the urn in a family grave

or vault in one of the private or municipal cemeteries.

In later years, further columbaria were added but, as space became short, no more could be accommodated and it became the practice for ashes to be scattered in the memorial garden. The deceased could be commemorated on a small memorial plaque or in a Book of Remembrance.

SLOW GROWTH

Manchester Crematorium did not struggle quite so hard as Woking to attract business but nevertheless was far from a runaway commercial success. While only two further cremations followed in 1892, the following year saw thirty and numbers rose almost to ninety by 1899. At this point numbers hit a plateau and it was not until 1908 that they reached(and thereafter maintained) over one hundred cremations each year.

By the end of 1900 over 400 cremations had taken place. Business was growing, but still only slowly. Aside from religious reservations, price was a major issue. The price of burial in a private grave at this time was somewhat lower than the cost of cremation. Southern Cemetery could offer a private grave for as little as two Guineas, including the first interment, and for a subsequent interment the charge was as little as fifteen shillings. By comparison, each individual cremation cost five Guineas. The company was not unaware of the high cost and offered a reduced price of two Guineas 'for the working classes or those of limited means', though how eligibility was judged is unclear. Another part of their attempt to attract less affluent clients was to construct a vault for 2,000 urns where the ashes of those who could not afford a niche would be deposited free of charge.[11] Despite these efforts, it is probably safe to assume that very few of the working class were cremated during the first three decades[12].

A significant reason for the high cost was the low volume of business, which loaded a substantial burden of fixed costs onto each cremation. In addition was the cost of fuel. The cremators were fuelled using coke and significant quantities were needed to achieve a working temperature. If the cremator was heated for only a single cremation, the cost of fuel alone was around ten shillings per cremation. The considerable increase in volumes and a change to gas in the 1930s dramatically reduced the fuel cost to an estimated 6d per cremation by 1948.

Cremation continued to be controversial. While the Church of England did not oppose it, individual ministers often had their reservations. The Roman Catholic Church was vehemently opposed. The Roman Catholic Bishop of Salford, Dr. Bilsborrow, when consecrating an extension to Bury Cemetery in 1900, said that: *'Christians should shrink with horror from cremation...'*[13]. Pope Leo XIII, who branded cremation *'a detestable abuse'*, banned the cremation of Catholics in 1886.[14] Those who assisted in the cremation of a Catholic were to be excommunicated. The Catholic Church would remain opposed to cremation until the ban was lifted by Pope Paul VI in 1963.

Business was increasing slowly but interest (or curiosity) was growing rapidly and the management produced useful income by charging visitors threepence for admission. In 1909 the 1,130 visitors generated a quarter of the profit for that year. Over 5,000 more visited over the following three years. Possibly these visits helped the gradual change of attitudes to cremation. From 1909 onwards, profit increased steadily and by 1912 had reached £428-3s-0d. The crematorium began 1913 with operating reserves exceeding £1,000.

By 1900 there were still only four crematoria in Great Britain: Woking, Manchester, Liverpool and Glasgow, so those wishing to cremate deceased family members had to be prepared to travel. While the considerable majority (259) of the 412 cremations which had taken place up to 1900 came from Lancashire addresses (with Manchester and it suburbs predominating) and a further 57 from Cheshire addresses. Many came

from further afield; a total of 23 came from various towns in Yorkshire and a further 11 from Warwickshire. Other counties with significant numbers were Leicester (8), and Nottingham and Durham (7 each). Eight came from various Welsh towns and two individuals from as far afield as Devon and Essex. The addresses given for two ladies are respectively Berlin and Wiesbaden in Germany and it seems likely that they were either visiting German families resident in Manchester or the wives of visiting businessmen. One of these ladies, 63 year old Louise Merttens, may possibly have been the mother of the merchant Frederick Merttens, one of the Crematorium Company's original subscribers.

BUSINESS STARTS TO BOOM

The Great War seems to have brought about a change in attitudes to cremation and following the armistice, the number of cremations increased noticeably. By 1925 the directors felt sufficiently confident to build a new columbarium with space for 600 urns and to provide a garden of remembrance at a cost of £3,130.[15] Additional land was purchased to accommodate this extension. This was possibly a part of the plot acquired by Withington Local Board in 1892 as part of their abortive proposal to establish a cemetery but which had passed unused into the hands of Manchester Corporation following the incorporation of Withington into Manchester in 1904.

The improved business also finally rewarded the remarkably patient shareholders. For nearly thirty years they had received no dividend on their investment but in 1920 a dividend of five percent was declared. This was maintained until 1931, when it was increased to ten percent. The ten percent dividend was maintained for another twenty years until in 1951 it increased once more to twenty-five percent.

As another sign of their improved situation in 1936 the directors approached the Corporation Parks and Cemeteries Committee with a request to purchase a further seven acre plot of land adjoining the north of the site which they proposed to develop as an extended garden of remembrance and permanent open space.[16] This had also formerly been part of the proposed Withington cemetery. The Corporation did not, however, sell and the land was used for housing.

The failure of the land purchase may have been connected with Manchester Corporation's plans, which were also formulated around this time, to build its own crematorium on the Southern Cemetery site.[17] The proposed municipal crematorium would have been sited on the corner of Princess Road and Nell Lane at an estimated cost of up to £32,744.[18] Had this proposal gone forward, it could have had a catastrophic effect on Manchester Crematorium but no concrete proposal had emerged by 1939 and following the outbreak of war no more was heard of it. By this time the number of cremations had reached an annual total of around 2,000. This rapid growth continued both during and after the war so that by 1952 the annual number of cremations exceeded 5,000.

It was not only the Corporation's plans which were frustrated by the war. The company were planning to build second chapel and cremator in the 1930s but this also had to be set aside. Work was resumed after the war, though it was delayed as a result of of post-war austerity. The new chapel was finally dedicated on 24 July 1954.[19]

THE IMPACT OF MUNICIPAL CREMATORIA

By this time, business had reached its zenith and was now beginning to decline from its 1952 peak. The reduced number of cremations did not signify a reduction in the popularity of cremation — quite the contrary, cremation would continue to grow in popularity, with the total number of cremations in England overtaking that of burials in 1968 — but because the number of crematoria was increasing and many who might previously have had to travel some distance to Manchester now had a crematorium closer to home. Manchester Crematorium no longer had the local monopoly which it had enjoyed for over sixty years.

New municipal crematoria were established around Manchester: at Middleton in 1952, Oldham and Dukinfield in 1953, Bolton in 1954, Eccles in 1955 and Salford (Weaste) in 1957. As a consequence, business declined from about 5,000 in 1952 to around 4,000 in 1958. Manchester Corporation eventually did open its own crematorium in 1959, but fortunately for Manchester Crematorium they chose to build it at Blackley on the far side of the city, so the effect on business was limited. It was perhaps a smaller impact than that from Altrincham Crematorium, which opened around the same time[20].

At the start of the 1960s numbers had fallen back to around 3,500 per annum. There has been some further reduction in the number of cremations, which has now stabilised at a little under 3,000 per annum.

LOST RECORDS

The documentary records of Manchester Crematorium were lost during the blitz of December 1940, when the Company's offices in York Street were hit by a German bomb. Unfortunately, all of the records were lost including both the cremation registers and the records of ownership of each of the niches in the columbaria. Through the efforts of volunteers from Manchester and Lancashire Family History Society, something over half of the names of those cremated before the end of 1940 have been recovered from the memorial plaques at the crematorium and from contemporary newspaper death announcements. These are now held in the Society's collection.

MANCHESTER CREMATORIUM TODAY

Unusually, Manchester Crematorium is still a private business. Despite the increased competition from municipal crematoria and the need to invest in environmental improvements, such as the removal of mercury (which arises from mercury amalgam dental fillings) from the flue gases, Manchester Crematorium remains a thriving business with a present day balance sheet in excess of £2 million.

Notes for The Rise of Cremation

1. For a comprehensive history of cremation in England there is no better source than Brian Parsons' 'Committed to the Cleansing Flame – The Development of Cremation in Nineteenth Century England' This excellent history does not, however, provide much information on the development of cremation beyond the history of the Woking Crematorium.

2. See www.naturaldeath.org.uk for a list of locations.

3. The list of subscribers and the amounts subscribed is reproduced in Chris Makepeace's concise anniversary history 'Manchester Crematorium 1890-1990'. This publication also includes a list of the names and occupations of the first 412 people cremated, including their ages and occupations. The occupations indicate clearly that the early adopters of cremation were predominantly the middle classes.

4. Despite his progressive beliefs and his financial support for Manchester Crematorium, Richard Pankhurst was buried at Brooklands Cemetery, Sale, in 1898.

5. Manchester Courier & Lancashire General Advertiser, Saturday, 4 January 1890.

6. Manchester Evening News, Saturday 25 January 1890.

7. Manchester Evening News, Saturday 8 March 1890.

8. Manchester Courier & Lancashire General Advertiser, Saturday 6 August 1892.

9. Manchester City News, 27 August 1892

10. The tern 'columbarium, derives from the Latin columba, meaning 'a dove'. The small square niches were considered as resembling dovecotes.

11. Manchester Courier & Lancashire General Advertiser, Friday 21 December 1900. Report of the Cremation Society AGM. The treasurer reported that the accounts showed a trading surplus of £93.

12. An article on the subject of 'Cremation of the Dead' was published in the weekly magazine The Woman's Signal of 21 April 1898. It commented *'At present the practice is confined to the educated and refined classes; the others neither know nor care anything about the sanitary or aesthetic grounds for preferring cremation to burial'.*

13. Manchester Courier & Lancashire General Advertiser, Monday 16 July 1900.

14. Purified by Fire, A History of Cremation in America, Stephen Prothero, University of California Press, 2001.

15. Manchester Guardian, 2 January 1926.

16. Manchester Corporation, Parks and Cemeteries Committee minutes 1936 volume 51. The proposal was discussed at the meeting on 18 September.

17. Manchester Corporation, Parks and Cemeteries Committee minutes 1936 volume 51. The proposal was made at the meeting on 17 April 1936 and agreed in principle on 18 December.

18. Manchester Guardian, 20 March 1937.

19. Manchester Guardian, 16 July 1954.

20. Manchester Guardian, 24 Jan 1958. At the 1958 AGM, the directors, increasing their total remuneration from £850 to £1,050, commented that in view of the competition coming from the new crematorium at Altrincham, they were not justified in taking out more in directors fees. They were still able to agree payment of a 20% dividend.

Epilogue

The history of burial in Manchester is one of a wheel coming almost full circle. The single burial ground which served the parish from time out of mind until the middle of the eighteenth century was, over the next hundred years, supplemented by a couple of dozen more as the town grew into a city. Even with this massive expansion demand constantly outstripped supply. In an environment which was completely unregulated massive over-crowding of graveyards was the inevitable result. The outcome in virtually every burial ground was conditions which offended both decency and public health. Despite this, there was little sign that either church or council was prepared to take any significant action to bring about improve-ment. It required action by government in the form of the 1854 Burial Act, to close the most offensive graveyards and to impose minimum sanitary requirements on the remainder. More importantly, the municipal authority was empow-ered to invest heavily in capacious out-of-town cemeteries. Manchester once more relies on a small number of well-regulated cemeteries and crematoria.

One cannot help but be struck by a paradox. The Victorian era was remarkable for the impor-tance which was given to the appearance of respectability. The Victorian funeral was an occa-sion on which the respectability of the deceased and family were prominently on display. Great attention was paid to correct forms of mourning both in dress and behaviour and the funeral itself could be a set piece performance with little expense spared on coffin, pall, hearse, mutes, invitations and in memoriam keepsakes. However, once the service was over, the reality of the burial was altogether different. The body would be placed in a grave which might have been cut through the remains of previous, some-times recent, burials — possibly those of other family members — and in the knowledge that it might not be long before the same fate was to befall the newly interred. Mourners cannot have been ignorant of the reality. Even if the remains of those disinterred were not immediately in evidence, the smell could not have been ignored.

Yet conditions which should have been the cause of public outrage seem by-and-large to have been accepted. It is almost as though people did not see what they did not want to see. Certainly, when a new burial ground was on offer, the better-off were quick to patronise it but there was no serious movement in Manchester to demand more decent and hygienic conditions. Aside from the occasional anonymous letter to the newspapers, business continued as usual. When change came, it was imposed from outside through the Metropolitan Burial Acts and even when new rules were introduced it was not only the graveyard owners who protested. There were many grave owners who complained that family vaults and graves, which had hitherto demon-strated an impressive capacity to contain great numbers of their family dead, were to be closed without compensation.

A century and a half after the Burial Acts it is difficult to believe that such conditions existed, let alone were tolerated. When you walk around Manchester today, you will seldom be far from one of the old burial grounds, yet of most there is little evidence that they ever existed. Many have disappeared completely but some still remain, mostly unmarked, their silent residents contin-uing their eternal slumber. When you wait for the Metrolink at Victoria Station or St. Peter's Square or take a rest in St. Mary's or St. John's Gardens, they are still close by. Take a moment to remember them — the people who helped to build this great city.

Appendices

Appendix 1: Notes on Terminology

Money

Where monetary values are stated, these are in pre-decimal currency. For those too young to remember Britain's old currency, some explanatory notes may be worthwhile.

The pound was the only unit of currency which did not change on D-Day (Decimalisation Day, 14 February 1971). The pre-decimalisation pound, however, was divided into 20 shillings and each shilling further divided into 12 pence. There were therefore 240 pence to in one pound. One old penny was worth about 0.4 new pence. The smallest coins were the halfpenny and the farthing (one quarter of a penny) the latter ceasing to be legal tender in 1960.

Monetary values were expressed in pounds, shillings and pence, using the format L – s – d , deriving from the Latin librae, solidi, denarii and written as (e.g.) £5 – 7s – 6d though the letters 's' and 'd' were frequently omitted (e.g. £5 – 7 – 6).

To confuse matters further professional charges were usually expressed in Guineas (one pound and one shilling - £1 – 1s – 0d), a terminology which today lives on chiefly in the world of horse racing.

Measurement

All measurements are given in Imperial measures. One inch is equal to about 25 millimetres, there are 12 inches to the foot (about 0.3 metres) and three feet to the yard (0.9 metres). 1,760 yards make up 1 mile (about 1,609 metres). Land areas are given in acres. One acre being 4,840 square yards, or just over 0.4 Hectares.

Collegiate Church and Cathedral

Manchester was a large parish extending about ten miles in each direction east-west and north-south. At the heart of the parish was the parish church. Up to the founding of the Diocese of Manchester in 1847 Manchester's parish church was better known as Christ's Church or the Collegiate Church (it having been established with a college of priests). When the diocese was created, the Collegiate Church became Manchester Cathedral. I have so far as is possible used the two terms to describe the church according to the time context.

Town and City

Manchester was for most of its history a large town whose civil administration was largely effected through manorial courts. It was incorporated as a borough in 1838, a status which it had previously held briefly from 1301 to 1359. It was granted city status in 1853. I have tried to use the appropriate description according to the time context.

Appendix 2: The Metropolitan Burial Acts

By the time Queen Victoria came to the throne the appalling state of urban burial grounds had become too visible to ignore. The issue was set before the public in disturbing detail by George Alfred Walker, a London doctor, in his 1839 book 'Gatherings from Grave Yards' which described the state of the capital's burial grounds. Walker described the Enon Chapel, just off Clement's Lane where a great number of bodies had been buried in a basement beneath the boarded chapel floor and over which there was virtually no covering of soil; the chapel in Portugal Street where bones lay on the surface; Whitechapel church where some coffins were within a foot and a half of the surface; and St. Clement's Church in the Strand, where 'the products of the decomposition of animal matter are so powerful that lighted candles, passed through the opening into the vaults, are completely extinguished'. The picture which Walker painted was of burial grounds which, although full to overflowing, still managed to find space for further burials.

Walker's work was not wasted. The sanitary reformer Edwin Chadwick, took up the issue and following on where Walker had left off, published two reports in 1842 and 1843 containing the results of a special inquiry into the practice of interment in towns. These shocking reports provided the platform to reform the laws applying to urban burial.

Government acted, albeit slowly, and passed the Metropolitan Interments Act in 1851. This was followed a year later by the Metropolitan Burial Act . These Acts were sweeping in their effect but were limited to the regulation of burials in the capital and had no force outside. However, even as the legislation affecting London was being drafted, the Board of Health was busy inspecting burial grounds up and down the country including, specifically, Manchester and Salford.[1] A further Act, the Burials (beyond the Metropolis) Act was passed in 1853 and extended the provi-

sions which the earlier Acts had applied in London to all towns and cities throughout England and Wales.

The 1853 Act was specifically addressed to parishes but it quickly became clear that in cities which contained several parishes the parish might not be the best body to implement the Act either effectively or efficiently. A further Act was therefore passed in 1854, the Burials (Beyond the Metropolis) Amendment Act. This short Act was designed to enable boroughs to assume responsibility for the provision and upkeep of burial grounds[2].

The Burial Acts contained a number of important powers. The most immediately beneficial power was that the Secretary of State was now empowered to order the immediate closure of any burial ground and to place restrictions on the opening and use of new graves in those which remained open. A second important provision was to impose minimum standards concerning the mode of burial. These included the area of ground to be allowed for each grave, the number of bodies which might be buried within each and the minimum depth of soil which should cover each coffin. The Acts also, perhaps more important in the longer term, gave metropolitan authorities the powers to acquire land and establish municipal cemeteries. An important provision was that these new cemeteries should not be established any closer than 200 yards from any dwelling house and that their location should take into account the anticipated expansion of the town or city. These provisions were underpinned by providing both parish burial boards and urban boroughs with access to finance at low interest rates.

Not everybody was supportive of the changes. In a lengthy diatribe against the Acts — or, at least, against those parts which required the closure of parochial burial grounds — the Archdeacon of London, William Hale Hale, protested loudly in 1855 that the state had usurped the ancient common law right of burial in the parish churchyard. His dismissal of the health hazards and nuisance created by overcrowded burial grounds in cities is quite breathtaking in its denial of reality. Hale seems to have had an over sentimental view but he was perhaps also mindful of the inevitable loss of burial fees involved.[3]

The Burial Acts granted general powers for the closure of burial grounds but the closure of specific graveyards was left to the Privy Council which would issue Orders in Council in respect of individual burial grounds, based upon information provided by Home Office inspectors. The Orders would typically contain a list of burial grounds to be closed with the dates upon which this was to be made effective and a list of burial grounds which could remain open but subject to restrictions. An Order in Council was issued on 21 March 1854 concerning the burial grounds in Manchester. The text of this is included below.

The Burial Acts represent the most important watershed in the history of burial turning a virtually unregulated industry into what would rapidly become a municipal undertaking. Many burial grounds were closed overnight whilst others were placed in a position where the number of burials was dramatically reduced. Most of the burial grounds in existence at the time of the Acts had either closed or become virtually inactive by the opening of the twentieth century. Only Manchester General Cemetery, located outside the city and still far from full, would continue to operate at much the same level as before.

THE EFFECTS OF THE ACTS

The implementation of the Burial Acts through the Order in Council of 15 April 1854 had immediate and dramatic results. The substantial majority of the city's burial grounds were closed with almost immediate effect. There was to be no compensation for the loss of burial fees or consideration that the proprietors might owe money against mortgages on the land concerned. On this latter point, it appears that only the burial ground at Every Street was affected (see page 98).

The dissenting chapels were, perhaps, the most severely affected. Every one of the nonconformist burial grounds was named for closure and some chapels would have incurred a noticeable loss of income. For the Protestant congregations the loss of denominational graveyards would have been disappointing but they were not to be deprived of a burial place since the Dissenters' Cemetery at Rusholme Road remained open, albeit with restrictions which increased burial charges. For Roman Catholics, the Acts were more problematic. Closure of the city burial grounds left Manchester with no burial ground consecrated according to the Catholic faith. The remaining options were burial in graveyards consecrated by the Church of England or in burial in unconsecrated ground at the Ardwick or Manchester General Cemeteries. Fortunately, the original closure orders were modified and burials were allowed to continue, subject to some restrictions, until 1858, when St. Mary's Roman Catholic church opened and since it was outside the city it was permitted to open a graveyard. This provided a consecrated burial place until Philips Park municipal cemetery opened in 1868 with a section consecrated for Roman Catholic burials.

For those burial grounds which were allowed to remain open, the problem was one of cost and capacity. Up to 1854 they had been able to pack as many burials into the available space as they desired. The Acts limited the number of burials in any grave by both requiring a minimum covering of earth both over and between coffins and by prohibiting the disturbance of earlier burials to make space for later ones.

The problems were particularly severe when it came to low cost burials which involved the burial of several (or indeed several dozen) unrelated bodies in a common grave or pit. The Acts initially demanded that each burial of unrelated persons should be in a separate grave. This made these most basic burials more costly to the proprietors than an interment in a family grave. This was something of an anomaly since the Burial Acts had no issue with burying several related persons in a family grave. The instructions were soon relaxed such that the two situations were treated identically, though it was no longer possible to inter several bodies in a common grave at the same time.

The chief impact of the Burial Acts, however, was to enable municipal corporations to establish cemeteries. Over the next fifty years these would effectively take over all of the burials in Manchester.

Notes for Appendix 2

[1] Manchester Guardian 10 March 1850
[2] Burials Acts 1852, 1853 and 1854, Explanatory Analytical Abstract, James J. Scott, 1855. This small book, designed to assist those charged with implementing the Acts, provides an explanation of their provisions.
[3] Intramural Burial in England not Injurious to the Public Health, its Abolition Injurious to Religion and Morals. A Charge, Addressed to the Clergy of the Archdeaconry of London, May 16, 1855. W.H. Hale, M.A. Archdeacon of London, 1855.

From the London Gazette, 18 April 1854

AT the Court at Windsor, the 15th day of April, 1854. PRESENT, The QUEEN's Most Excellent Majesty in Council WHEREAS the Right Honourable Viscount Palmerston, one of Her Majesty's Principal Secretaries of State, after giving to the Incumbents and the Churchwardens of the parishes hereinafter mentioned, ten days' previous notice of his intention to make such representation, has, under the provisions of an Act, passed in the last session of Parliament, instituted 'An Act to amend the laws concerning the burial of the dead in England beyond the limits of the metropolis' and to amend the Act concerning the burial of the dead in the metropolis, made a representation stating that, for the protection of the public health, no new burial-ground should be opened within the city of MANCHESTER, or within two miles of any part of the boundary of the city, without the previous approval of one of Her Majesty's Principal Secretaries of State, and that burials should be discontinued therein with the following modifications :—

Burials to be discontinued forthwith in the Cathedral and burial-ground, in St. Anne's Churchyard, St. Mary's Churchyard, St. John's Church and Churchyard, St. George's Church and Churchyard, St. Michael's Church and Churchyard, St. Matthew's Church, St. Peter's Church, St. James's Church and Churchyard, St. Luke's Churchyard Chorltonon-Medlock, St. Mark's Church Cheetham, St. Thomas's Church and Churchyard Ardwick, in the Independent Chapel Burial-ground Grosvenor-street, Great Bridgwater-street Chapel Burial-ground, Cross-street Unitarian Chapel and Burial-ground, St. Augustine's Roman Catholic Chapel and Burial-ground, Swedenborgian Chapel Burial-ground, All Saints Church Chorlton, St. Saviour's Church Chorlton, St. Luke's Church Cheetham, and St. Andrew's Church Ancoats.

Burials to be discontinued from and after the first of March, one thousand eight hundred and fifty-five, in St. Mark's Churchyard Cheetham, and the Quakers' Burial-ground Mount-street.

In all the undermentioned burial-grounds, no interment to take place in any grave without a covering of at least four and a half feet of earth, measuring from the upper surface of the coffin to the level of the ground :—

In the churchyard of All Saints Chorlton, with the exception of private vaults and graves, only one body to be buried in each grave, and burials wholly to cease from and after the first of March, one thousand eight hundred and fifty-six.

In St. Saviour's Churchyard Chorlton, burials (with the same exceptions) to be discontinued.

In St. George's Churchyard Hulme (with the same exceptions), only one body to be buried in each grave, and burials wholly to cease from and after the first of March, one thousand eight hundred and fifty-six.

In St. Luke's Churchyard Cheetham (with the same exceptions), only one body to be buried in each grave.

In St. Andrew's Churchyard Ancoats (with the same exceptions), only one body to be buried in each grave, and burials to be wholly discontinued from and after the first of March, one thousand eight hundred and fifty-five.

In the burial-ground of Upper Brook-street Unitarian Chapel (with the same exceptions), burials to be wholly discontinued.

In the burial-grounds of the Roman Catholic chapels of St. Chad's York-street Cheetham, St. Patrick's Livesey-street, and St. Wilfred Bedford-street Hulme (with the same exceptions), only one body to be buried in each grave; in St. Chad's and St. Wilfred's, no burial to take place within twenty feet of any dwelling-house; and burials wholly to cease in St. Chad's and St. Patrick's from and after the first of March, one thousand eight hundred and fifty-five, and in St. Wilfred's from and after the first of March, one thousand eight hundred and fifty-six.

In Christ Church Burial-ground Every-street, Ancoats (with the same exceptions), only one body to be buried in each grave, and burials to be wholly discontinued from and after the first of March, one thousand eight hundred and fifty-six.

In Ardwick Cemetery (with the same exceptions), only one body to be buried in each grave.

In Rusholme-road Cemetery (with the same exceptions), burials to be wholly discontinued.

Now, therefore, Her Majesty in Council is pleased hereby to give notice of such representation, and to order that the same be taken into consideration by a Committee of the Lords of Her Majesty's Most Honourable Privy Council, on the twenty-ninth day of May next.

And Her Majesty is further pleased to direct that this Order be forthwith published in the London Gazette ; and that copies thereof be affixed on the doors of the churches or chapels of, or on some conspicuous places within, the parishes affected by such representation, one month before the said twenty-ninth day of May.

C. C. Greville.

I saw from out the earth peep forth,
The white and glistening bones,
With Jagged ends of coffin planks,
That e'en the worm disowns,
And once a smooth white skull rolled on,
Like a football on the stones

From City Graves
Published in Household Words
Charles Dickens

Appendix 3: The Burial of Suicides

Until the early 19th century, burial in consecrated ground, which effectively meant burial in *any* burial ground, was denied both to those who had committed suicide and to those who had been executed for felony.

It was a legal requirement that the corpses of suicides should be buried at a cross roads with a stake driven through their heart. This law as to the burial of suicides was ancient but was not repealed until 1823[1]. It continued to be practiced to the very end. John Mortland, who murdered Sir Warwick Bampfylde in 1823 and then killed himself was buried in this manner in St. John's Wood, London. It has been suggested that towards the end of the practice, the stake was symbolically driven into the ground at the side of the coffin rather than through the heart of the corpse.

Despite the repeal of the statute, the authorities still regarded suicide as a violation of the law and specified that burial should take place at between nine and twelve o'clock at night without the performance of Christian burial rites.

There is some evidence to show that a number of suicides were buried in Manchester in this manner. The favoured burial place appears to have been New Cross — the junction of Oldham Road and Great Ancoats Street. In the course of excavations at New Cross in 1846 to connect the premises of a Mr. Wolstencroft to the sewer, two coffins were discovered, the first at about three feet in depth and the second within seven feet of the first, but buried about five feet deeper. Both contained skeletons. The discovery caused great excitement locally and the police had to attend to keep order. A seventy year old local resident recalled that the burials had taken place some forty years previously and he identified the remains as those of a man and a woman. The man was, he said, Thomas Tysick of 4 St. Mary's Gate, who was reportedly '*crossed in love*' and committed suicide. He had been buried at midnight by the '*runners*' who kept order amongst a crowd of spectators[2]. The woman he could not name but identified as a servant who had poisoned herself and was buried at New Cross on 22 September 1808. He also recounted that a soldier who had committed suicide had been buried in the same place in 1821.

New Cross was not the only place where suicides were buried. In 1807 James Massey hanged himself in the New Bailey where he was held charged with committing an '*unnatural crime*'. His body was buried first on Kersal Moor but then exhumed and either dumped or buried in a ditch. From here it was again removed and was finally interred '*near the Salford weighing machine*'.

There is some difficulty in establishing the number and location of the burials of suicides and the names of those so buried. By their very nature, such burials are not recorded in church burial registers and one must look to historical accounts and references in contemporary newspapers for such information as is available.

Notes for Appendix 3

1   London Gazette, 12 July 1823. The Examiner of 27 July 1823 notes that the new rules permit the burial of the deceased in a churchyard but without Christian rites and only between the hours of 9pm and midnight.

2   Manchester Guardian, Wednesday 29 April 1846. Richard Wright Procter in his Memorials of Manchester Streets identifies the man as a bootcloser called Smith, who had taken his life in similar circumstances to those described. This version is also to be found in a report in the Manchester Courier and Lancashire General Advertiser of the same date.

Appendix 4: Body Snatching

When the subject of body snatching is mentioned, the names Burke and Hare immediately spring to mind. These prominent Irish resurrectionists have entered popular culture, though it is often overlooked that it was not body snatching which led to the execution of William Burke (William Hare escaped the gallows by turning King's evidence) but the fact that they obtained their stock-in-trade by murder. The focus on Burke and Hare has somewhat overshadowed the fact that the stealing of bodies from graveyards was a widespread and lucrative activity.

BACKGROUND TO THE TRADE

The demand for recently deceased corpses came from anatomy schools. The only legitimate source of corpses was the gallows. The bodies of hanged felons could be taken for dissection if the family was not sufficiently well-organised to secure removal of the body immediately after the hanging. This restricted source provided insufficient numbers of bodies, even when dissection was carried out by a lecturer in front of an audience of students. The adoption of what was known as the '*Paris method*', by which each student was given a body or body part to dissect, created a demand which was considerably in excess of the legitimate supply.

Anatomy schools increasingly turned to criminals, who were prepared to open graves and remove the bodies of the recently deceased. Few questions were asked provided the purchaser did not suspect that the subject had met an untimely end at the hands of the supplier, a practice which acquired the name 'Burking' after the trial and execution of William Burke. Practitioners of this dark trade were popularly referred to as 'resurrectionists'.

The motivation for the body snatchers was purely financial. Medical schools had an almost insatiable demand for bodies. A fresh corpse would command a price of around ten pounds, equivalent to the wages of an artisan for a month or two or of a live-in house servant for a year, so there was a good reward for those prepared to undertake this unsavoury work. Some body snatchers worked on an almost industrial scale, removing several bodies in one night's work. For those with good organisation and good medical contacts, the rewards could be considerable.

Body snatching was conducted with a degree of impunity. While the resurrectionists did as much as they could to avoid being caught, the penalties if they were apprehended provided little deterrent. The reason for this is that a dead body was not viewed as property and so stealing a body could not be considered a felony; it was simply a misdemeanour. What could be prosecuted as a felony was the theft of items such as burial shrouds or jewellery which had been buried with the deceased. Penalties for stealing such items could be severe and most resurrectionists were smart enough to ensure that they removed the body and no more.

MODUS OPERANDI

One attraction of body snatching was that little capital was required. The tools of the trade were no more than a wooden spade (which made less noise than a metal one), a crowbar to break open the coffin, a 'dark' lantern (which had a sliding panel to dim or shut off the light), a length of rope and a large sack.

Resurrectionists typically worked in teams of two or three men with one acting as look-out. As soon as they became aware of a fresh burial in a graveyard which seemed to provide little security, they would move in under cover of night and dig down to expose the coffin. In very crowded churchyards this might involve digging down as little as two to three feet. To speed up the process, they would only expose half of the coffin and by introducing the crowbar under the lid at the exposed end, break off the exposed part of the lid. The body could then be pulled from the coffin using the rope, stripped of its shroud and any personal items such as rings, quickly placed in the sack and spirited away. By the time the crime was discovered, probably the next morning, it was likely that the body had already been sold.

BODY SNATCHING IN MANCHESTER

Manchester was not immune from this grisly trade but there do not appear to have been any cases reported before the 1820s. Body snatching required a local anatomy school to purchase the bodies since transporting a body quickly over any great distance was not a viable option. Manchester's first school of anatomy was opened at Manchester Royal Infirmary in 1814 by Joseph Jordan and was followed ten years later by a private school of anatomy in Pine Street (from 1826 in Mount Street) which was opened by Thomas Turner. The earliest newspaper reports of body snatching in Manchester appear to date from around the time Turner opened his school and may reflect both increased demand and adoption of the Paris method described above.

Jordan was himself a self-confessed body snatcher. At a prize-giving ceremony at Chatham Street School of medicine in 1854 he looked back at past practices:

'You have heard of body snatching, but you have never been behind the scenes. The students in my time were obliged to steal bodies themselves, and I am not ashamed to say that I was one of the very parties. You were required to understand your profession, but you were utterly forbidden to dissect. You had no means of obtaining subjects, you were prosecuted if you robbed the churchyards. Here you were; the public and the legislators demanding of you a knowledge of your profession, and yet the law utterly prevented you from obtaining that knowledge.'[1]

Jordan was involved well beyond satisfying his personal needs when a student. He obtained bodies from resurrectionists on a large scale and supplied other medical schools, including the school run by Dr. Robert Knox in Edinburgh, who had purchased bodies from the notorious Burke and Hare. He had on one occasion been prosecuted and fined £20 for instigating the stealing of bodies. One anecdote relates that he had on one occasion had a narrow escape from detection '...when driving in a gig with a defunct companion dressed up as a living being.'[2]

A well documented incident took place in Manchester in 1828. Two notorious resurrectionists called Callaghan and Stewart were stopped by a night watchman called Ralph Paxton on Hunts Bank Bridge. Callaghan was carrying a large bundle wrapped in cloth on his shoulder. This was found to contain the remains of a body which had clearly been buried for some long time. At the subsequent magistrate's hearing, a man called Walmsley said that his father, 75 year old Thomas Walmsley, had been buried the previous Monday, 9 November, at the burial ground near Hunts Bank (Walkers Croft). Because of his concern that the body might be stolen, he had persuaded the sexton to remove the coffin of his brother, who had been buried about a year and a quarter earlier (possibly Joseph Walmsley, aged 22, buried on 3 September 1827) and bury his father's coffin underneath that of his brother before re-filling the grave. Walmsley was able to identify the body found on Callaghan as that of his brother from a distinctive mark on the forehead. The father's body does not seem to have been recovered. The two prisoners were tried at the Salford Sessions on 27 January 1828, convicted and sentenced to six months' imprisonment.[3] This was just two days before William Burke was hanged in Edinburgh.

Around this same time a man called James Smith appeared in court for stealing the property of a surgeon called Mr. Sinclair, of Hulme. The occasion of the theft was a visit by Smith to Sinclair's house for the purpose of selling him a body, an offer which Sinclair had refused. Smith is described as '*a noted resurrectionist*' in the account of his trial.[4]

At a vestry meeting in 1832 the church-wardens' accounts came under scrutiny and there was questioning of a charge by Henry Rutter, the sexton, for '*removing the safety tomb*'. The precise nature of this arrangement is not described but it was evidently a device to prevent access to the '*pit*' in which paupers were buried *en masse* during the time before it was covered with earth. The justification for this was that there had been '*numerous instances in which dead bodies had been stolen from the burial ground*'[5]. One of these incidents had taken place four years earlier when as a coffin was being lowered into the '*pit*' it struck and broke open another coffin which had been placed there about a week before and which had contained the body of a young Irish girl. The broken coffin was found to be empty; the body had been stolen.[6]

It could not always be assumed that those managing the graveyards did all that they could to prevent robberies. In the extreme, they could be part of the business. In 1827 John Eaton, the sexton of St. George's Chapel, was convicted of the theft of bodies from his own burial ground.

FOILING THE RESURRECTIONISTS

Graveyard security was an obvious requirement. The Collegiate Church churchwardens' accounts include vouchers for the payment of night watchmen for the parish burial ground[7]. Ralph Paxton, referred to earlier, was probably employed in this role. However, it was costly to employ a night watchman and many graveyards went unguarded. When the first private cemeteries were created, the management made much of high surrounding walls, strong gates and watchmen to send out a message to potential customers that bodies buried there would be safe from the resurrectionists.

In the absence of watchmen, the family might maintain a nightly vigil over the grave but this was likely to be impractical for families who all worked and who could not afford to miss out on sleep for

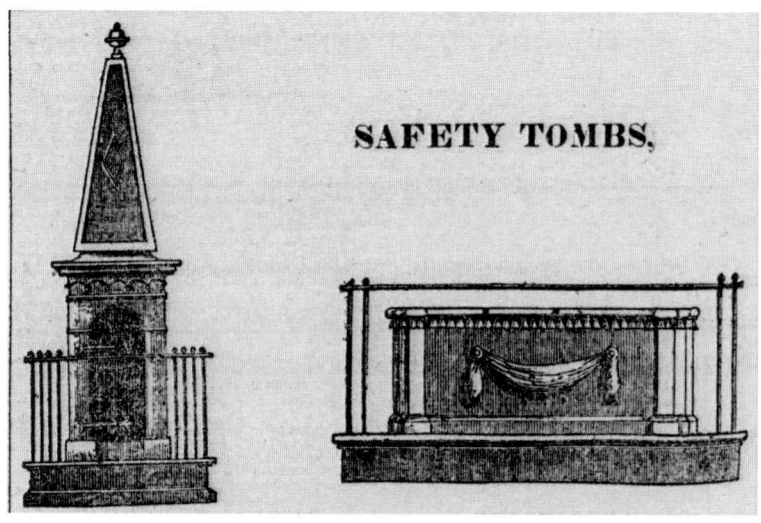

A variety of patent devices were available to those wishing to prevent the stealing of bodies. Safety tombs were offered by the Reverend James Scholefield.

several nights. One inexpensive expedient was for the family to keep the body of the deceased in the house for a couple of weeks after death, until decomposition was sufficiently advanced to make the body worthless to the anatomists. This was, of course, highly undesirable on health grounds and was consequently strongly discouraged.

A variety of mechanical devices were on offer, designed to make it difficult for the resurrectionists to steal a newly-buried body. Metal cages, sometimes called 'mortsafes', fixed over the grave, could prevent the grave being opened. It was only necessary to retain these in place for a couple of weeks since the anatomists would not purchase a seriously decayed body. There is limited evidence of how effective these devices might have been and it is possible that, just as with a burglar alarm today, the criminals simply found it required less effort to select an alternative target. The Reverend Scholefield of Every Street Chapel offered what he called a '*safety tomb*' and claimed that this had foiled three attempts to open graves in his burial ground. However, this may be no more than sales 'puff'.[8] Scholefield made his safety tombs available for a fee varying from one shilling and sixpence to protect the grave of a stillborn child to eight shillings for use to protect an adult grave.[9]

Another expedient sometimes adopted to frustrate the resurrectionists was the iron coffin. This fabricated sheet-iron coffin was fitted with a lid that locked into place with a number of spring-loaded catches which made it virtually impossible to remove. These coffins were not, however, always popular with graveyard proprietors since neither the coffin nor the body inside would decay quickly and this would limit the use of the grave for future burials[10]. Such safeguards as iron coffins and safety tombs were in any event almost certainly beyond the means of the ordinary working man.

THE END OF THE TRADE

Body snatching was largely eliminated, not by detection and prosecution, but by the Anatomy Act of 1832, which permitted the unclaimed bodies of paupers to be given over for dissection. The principal source of unclaimed pauper bodies was, of course, the workhouse and the sale of unclaimed bodies provided a source of additional income for these institutions. This provision added to the dread associated with entering the workhouse and also led to suggestions that the potential sale of a body gave the workhouse master little incentive to provide medical attention for seriously ill inmates.

The 1832 Act reduced the level of body snatching but did not bring it to an immediate end. Cases were still being reported as much as twenty years after the Act was passed.

The 1832 Act survived almost unchanged with little modification into the 20th century. In 2004 it was replaced by the Human Tissue Act which contained far more safeguards. In particular the informed consent of the deceased or their next of kin became mandatory.

Notes for Appendix 4

1   Some Manchester Doctors, Willis J. Elwood (Ed). Manchester Medical Society, 1984.

2   Manchester Courier, Wednesday 27 April 1904. (Taken from a biography of Jordan written by Dr. F. W. Jordan, possibly his grandson)

3   Manchester Courier & Lancashire General Advertiser, Saturday 31 January 1829.

4   Manchester Guardian 7 November 1829.

5   Manchester Courier & Lancashire General Advertiser, 2 June 1832.

6   Manchester Courier & Lancashire General Advertiser, 7 June 1828.

7   Churchwardens' Vouchers Mancath/1/3/1/1/16 22 May 1824-27 Jun 1825 (Voucher 35).

8   Manchester Courier & Lancashire General Advertiser, Saturday 7 March 1829. Scholefield's safety tomb included a bell, which rang if the device was attacked and a spring gun, which fired if the tomb was entered. Should the would-be resurrectionist enter the tomb it would close, locking him in until he could be released by someone familiar with the mechanism.

9   Manchester Medical Collection at John Rylands University Library, MMC/14/11/4. The prices for safety tombs are quoted on Scholefield's advertising 'flyer' dated circa 1830.

10 The Monthly Repository of 2 December 1820 carries a lengthy Consistory Court judgement in the case of John Gilbert vs the churchwardens of St. Andrew, Holborn, London. Gilbert had been prevented by the churchwardens from burying his late wife at St. Andrew's in an iron coffin, specifically to avoid the body being stolen. The churchwardens argued that the use of iron coffins, which would not decay, would lead to their burial ground rapidly filling to capacity. Sir W. Scott's ruling favoured the churchwardens but in the specific case of Mrs. Gilbert he recommended that the burial should be permitted.

Mary's Ghost

Thomas Hood (1827)

'Twas in the middle of the night,
To sleep young William tried,
When Mary's ghost came stealing in,
And stood at his bed-side.

O William dear! O William dear!
My rest eternal ceases;
Alas! my everlasting peace
Is broken into pieces.

I thought the last of all my cares
Would end with my last minute;
But tho' I went to my long home
I didn't stay long in it.

The body-snatchers they have come,
And made a snatch at me;
It's very hard them kind of men
Won't let a body be!

You thought that I was buried deep
Quite decent like and chary,
But from her grave in Mary-bone
They've come and boned your Mary.

The arm that used to take your arm
Is took to Dr. Vyse;
And both my legs are gone to walk
The hospital at Guy's.

I vow'd that you should have my hand,
But fate gives us denial;
You'll find it there, at Dr. Bell's
In spirits and a phial.

As for my feet, the little feet
You used to call so pretty,
There's one, I know, in Bedford Row,
The t'other's in the city.

I can't tell where my head is gone,
But Doctor Carpue can:
As for my trunk, it's all pack'd up
To go by Pickford's van.

I wished you'd go to Mr. P.
And save me such a ride;
I don't half like the outside place,
They've took for my inside.

Appendix 5: Summary of Burial Grounds

Burial Ground	Operative	No. of Burials	Notes
Collegiate Church	1578-1819	c77,000	Estimated from 1573 onwards
Apple Market	1766-1788	6,383	
Angel Meadow	1789-1815	c31,000	
Walkers Croft	1815-1848	c40,000	
St. Ann	1712-1854	6,335	
St. Mary Parsonage	1756-1871	5,623	
St. John, Deansgate	1769-1900	24,113	
St. James, George St.	1788-1854	2,932	
St. Michael, Angel Meadow	1789-1854	c3,800	
St. Peter, Mosley Street	1796-1866	213	
St. George, Oldham Road	1798-1854	1,249	of which 260 after adoption by CofE
St. Matthew, Campfield	1825-1854	39	
St. Andrew, Ancoats	1831-1855	1,080	
Quaker Burial Ground	1674-1847	631	Based on remains removed
Quaker Meeting House	1828-1855	c600	As per memorial plaque
Coldhouse Baptist Chapel	1770-1774	7	Based on newspaper report of 1874
Cross Street Chapel	1694-1854	609	1791-1839 only
Cannon Street Chapel	1762-1788	20	1786-1788 only
Grosvenor Street Chapel	1807-1854	n/k	No records survive
King Street Chapel, Salford	1800-1855	c30,000	
Christ Church, Every Street	1824-1867	c28,000	
Mosley St. Chapel	1787-1820	64	Based on remains removed
New Jerusalem Chapel	1793-1854	n/k	No records survive
Rochdale Road Chapel	1739-1822	88	Based on Owen's record of memorials
Gt. Bridgewater St. Chapel	1800-1854	2,417	
Smithy Door Chapel		-	Doubt as to whether a graveyard existed
St. Mary, Mulberry St.	1816-1837	c1,500	Some gaps in register - possibly more
St. Augustine, Granby Row	1820-1854	c10,000	Estimate. No records survive
St. Patrick, Livesey Street	1832-1858	c27,000	
Rusholme Road	1821-1933	68,241	
Manchester General Cemetery	1838-	96,059	Possibly 30,000 more in consecrated
Ardwick Cemetery	1838-1950	95,639	
Philips Park	1866-	c315,000	
Southern Cemetery	1879-	c350,000	
Manchester Crematorium	1892-	c250,000	

Totals are based on surviving burial registers unless stated otherwise.

Further Reading

Arnold, Catherine, Necropolis – London and its Dead, Pocket Books (2006)

Beach, Darren, London's Cemeteries, Metro (2011)

Brooks, Chris, Mortal Remains: The History and Present State of the Victorian and Edwardian Cemetery, Wheaton (1989)

Curl, James Stevens, The Victorian Celebration of Death, Sutton (2000)

Dobb, Reverend Arthur, Like a Mighty Tortoise (1978)

Edge, Geoffrey, A Guide to the Burial Grounds of Manchester & Salford, Manchester & Lancashire Family History Society (2011)

Holmes, Isabella M., The London Burial Grounds (1896)

Jupp, Peter c. and Gittings, Clare, Death In England, Manchester University Press (1999)

Kidd, Alan & Wyke, Terry, The Challenge of Cholera, Record Society of Lancashire & Cheshire (2010)

Lees, Hilary, English Churchyard Memorials, Tempus (2000)

Litten, Julian, The English Way of Death, Robert Hale (1991)

Makepeace, Chris, Manchester Crematorium 1890-1990, (1990)

May, Trevor, The Victorian Undertaker, Shire (1996)

Parsons Brian, Committed to the Cleansing Flame – The Development of Cremation in Nineteenth Century England, Spire (2005)

Rutherford, Sarah, The Victorian Cemetery, Shire (2008)

Scott, James J., Burial Acts 1852, 1853 and 1854, Knight & Co. (1855)

Scott, Ronnie, Death By Design: The True Story of the Glasgow Necropolis, Black and White (2005)

Stanford, Peter, How to Read a Graveyard, Bloomsbury (2013)

Stone, Elizabeth, God's Acre, John W. Parker (1858)

Wakeling, Alfred L. And Moon, Peter, Grave Concerns, Ellar (2002)

Walker, George Alfred, Gatherings from Grave Yards, Longman (1839) reprinted Kessinger (ND)

Warrender, Keith, Underground Manchester, Willow (2007)

Warrender Keith, Below Manchester, Willow (2009)

White, H.. Leslie, Monuments and their Inscriptions: A Practical Guide, Society of Genealogists(1987)

Index of Names

Acknowledgements

The assistance of the following is gratefully acknowledged: the staff of Greater Manchester County Record Office; the staff of Manchester Archives and Local Studies and in particular to Jane Parr for assistance with a number of the illustrations; Lawrence Gregory of Salford (RC) Diocesan Archive; David Rankin and Richard Davies of Network Rail; Laurence Hayes of SLR Consulting Ltd, Laura Lee of Future Metrolink and Richard and Liz Long of the Friends of Angel Meadow. Finally, but not least, thanks are due to my wife Judy, who patiently proof-read the manuscript and made invaluable suggestions to improve it.

The photographs which appear on pages 83, 111, 113, 114, 141, and 158 are reproduced courtesy of Manchester Libraries, Information and Archives, Manchester City Council. The photograph of Philips Park chapel, which appears on page 172 is reproduced by kind permission of Mike Berrell.

About the Author

John Marsden moved to the Manchester area in 1989 and has for many years since been active in the running of Manchester and Lancashire Family History Society. John has taken a particular interest in Manchester's history and in particular of the city's burial grounds. This book is the result of several years accumulated research.

Visit the Forgotten Fields Web Site

The Forgotten Fields web site can be found at:

www.forgotten-fields.co.uk

The author will be pleased to receive feedback about this book, to be notified of errors and to receive further information about the burial grounds featured. The web site includes a contact form.

It is planned to expand the web site to include further photographs of some of the burial grounds discussed and any information received subsequent to publication.

Printed by BoD™in Norderstedt, Germany